ADVANCE PRAISE FOR
TOUCHING GREATNESS

"Ted was a student at Fairfax High School in Los Angeles where I was his principal. I have admired what he has accomplished in his sports career. You will enjoy his journey as he has interviewed most everyone you wish you had. Reading this book will put you right there with him as he enjoys the company of these legends. It's a must read."

> —*Dr. Jim Tunney, author, speaker, NFL referee (1960-1991)*

"Ted Sobel's storytelling is but a glimpse of his wealth of experience with people and places and interviews he's done inside the ropes of any sports venue. His 'all-in' style creates more rich memories for everyone to enjoy."

> —*Amy Alcott, LPGA and World Golf Halls of Fame*

"Ted Sobel's stories are a delightful jaunt down memory lane and Secretariat and I are proud to be included! Enjoy this fun read all the way to the winner's circle."

> —*Ron Turcotte, Triple Crown winning thoroughbred jockey and member of seven racing Halls of Fame*

"Proud to be one of Ted's mentors and part of *Touching Greatness*. Our careers have been connected from Wisconsin to California with L.A. Kings and Badgers hockey, two Stanley Cup titles, and Packers football. I'm proud of his success in broadcasting and now as an author. This is a fun read for all sports fans."

> —*Bob Miller, L.A. Kings Hockey Hall of Fame broadcaster*

"To have had my broadcast work inspire Ted to become a hockey fan and then to pursue a sports broadcast career is the ultimate compliment I could receive. The feeling has to be similar to what an athlete feels when he or she scores the winner. Enjoy the read!"

> —*Ken "Jiggs" McDonald, Hockey Hall of Fame broadcaster*

"In the world of sportscasting, Ted Sobel is a Man of All Seasons, truly a Renaissance man. He has covered Super Bowls, World Series, all of the major golf championships (we worked together at the PGA Championship in L.A.), and NBA and NHL finals. He covered these noteworthy events with a stylish excellence that is rarely seen. His book relives some of his experiences with the same stylish excellence."

> —*Jack Whitaker, renowned 3x Emmy-winning Sports Broadcasting Hall of Famer*

TOUCHING GREATNESS

TED SOBEL

ISBN: 978-1-60679-543-9
Book layout: Cheery Sugabo
Cover design: Cheery Sugabo
Front cover photos (left to right): Tiger Woods—© Brian Rothmuller/Icon SMI via ZUMA Press; Aaron Rodgers—© John Fisher/CSM via ZUMA Wire); Wayne Gretzky—© Bildbyran via ZUMA Press; Don Henley, left, and Glenn Frey—© Jeff Siner/MCT/ZUMAPRESS.com; Vin Scully—© San Gabriel Valley Tribune via ZUMA Wire; Sandy Koufax—© Malcolm Emmons

Coaches Choice
P.O. Box 1828
Monterey, CA 93942
www.coacheschoice.com

DEDICATION

This book is dedicated to: my parents, Sherry and Bernie, who taught me how while always allowing me to be me; my grandparents, Fannie, Minnie, and Izzy, for their unconditional caring; my beautiful wife, Elisa, who inspires me to be better; Uncle Carl, who always encouraged bringing out my creative side; each of the song makers who's lyrics and tunes rhythmically rock my heart and soul; every loyal radio listener who didn't change the dial because I was on (no matter how tempted you were); anyone I've inspired with any of my words and passions; and all who've been a part of this long and winding journey—even the unknowing individuals who gave me more great stories to tell.

ACKNOWLEDGMENTS

It took almost three years to write all of this (around my Sports USA Network seasonal football broadcast duties and finishing during the COVID-19 pandemic), often being surprised by the dozens of emotionally reflective moments throughout the process. There were no ghost writers—I am the lone friendly ghost writer with a fortunate excellent memory to dig deep into my mind's vault, working off of only several old scribbled handwritten pages of notes and the constant emptying out of each search engine's tank, while never once having to go to a fossilized *Encyclopedia Britannica*.

So special thank you's are in order to that no longer newfangled thing called the internet, along with my occasionally smart phone, boxes of old audio cassettes (and even an ancient floppy disk) to fully make this book a reality complete with detailed historic accuracy. And to the many actual humans for their endless contributions to my life's favorite stories and the making of these pages including (in no particular order):

Dr. Jim Tunney, Dr. James Peterson, David & Paul Gold, Paul Olden, Richard & Glenn Sobel, Gary Strobl, Mark Langill, Elaine & Elgin Baylor, Alison Baylor Clayton, Jerry West, Wayne Gretzky, Ron Turcotte, Gary Player, Amy Alcott, Barbara Nicklaus, Fuzzy Zoeller, Bart Starr, Jr., Leigh Ann Nelson, Aaron Rodgers, Eli Manning, Bob Miller, Bill Dwyer, Graeme Agars, Larry Kahn, Eli Gold, Ralph Lawler, Dennis Murphy, Jeanie Buss, Chuck Blore, Bob Eubanks, Steve Futterman, Jonathan Foreman, Maria Cooper Janis, Elke Sommer, James Darren, Geoffrey Horne, Jim Mitchum, Julie Newmar, Dan Tana, Art Podell, Robby Krieger, Gene Carr, Ted Dawson, Len Weiner, Dick Stockton, Brady Riggs, Eddie Merrins, Terry Wilcox, Bob Kramer, Rod Laver, Jay Paris, Gene Buccieri, Steve Brener, Toby Zwikel, Mike Willman, Sacha Terrill, Bela Lugosi, Jr., Lynne Lugosi Sparks, Doug Plank, Keith Erickson, Ken Gurnick, Al Downing, Carl Erskine, Jim Denny, Tom Paciorek, Bobby Valentine, Tommy John, Peter O'Malley, Brent Shyer, Cookie & Victor Rojas, Cap Raeder, Allan Globensky, Paul Stewart, Jocko Cayer, Brian Patafie, Jon Wetterlow, Keijo Liimatainen, Jim Nocerino, Pat Duffy, Andy Ludlum, Crys Quimby, Scott Gorbitz, Ed Pyle, Chris Roberts, Joe Cala, Rod Van Hook, Randy Kerdoon, Bret Lewis, David DeMont, Jack White, Mark Howe, Gann Matsuda, Joel Bergman, Steve Thrap, John Robinson, Billy Kilmer, Alan Tannenbaum, Ann Cohen Aboulafia, Nancy Evans, Michael Yamaki, Mike Hope, Rex Fontenot, Jill Sleight, Brian Golden, Lyle Spencer, Henry Glenn, Ron Marmalefsky, Mike Garai, Dr. Robert London, Dr. Steven Silvers, Joe Block, Carl Mendelson, Michael Sondheimer, Joyce Sharman, John Patrick, Steve Tebb, Tom Klimasz, Steve Springer, all of my HOF endorsers, the many pro and college media and sports information departments, my godson Daniel Goodkin-Gold, and Dr. David Kuris (for bringing me into this world safely and for inspiring my mother enough to be named after your father).

To my mentors: broadcasters Chick Hearn, Vin Scully, 'Jiggs' McDonald, Steve Bailey, and Dave (The Hullabalooer) Hull and coaches John Cunniff, 'Badger' Bob Johnson, John Van Boxmeer, Tex Winter, and Bill Mulligan.

In addition, a big thank you to my many photog friends over the decades for their contributions here and beyond, including Paul Lester, Avery Helm, Kevin Reece, Jon SooHoo, Henry Diltz, Shelly Castellano, Jayne Kamin-Oncea, Mark Terrill, Juan Ocampo, Art Foxall, Wen Roberts, Burt Harris, Jerry Long, Mario Villegas, Martin Leon, Paul Olden, and the late Steve Grayson.

I am also grateful to Terry Sanders, President of American Film Foundation, for contributing with permission to use material from the complete transcript of his and co-producer/director Freida Lee Mock's 1981 TV documentary, 'Carl Foreman—Word Into Image: Portraits of American Screenwriters.'

Finally, in honor of those we've lost during the past three years while I was fondly writing about or just forevermore keeping them in my mind and heart, with most expressing their enthusiasm to read how their stories fit so nicely into my life and this book. There will always be an ocean-sized empty feeling for never being able to share these pages as hoped for with all of you: Elgin Baylor, Bart Starr, Ron Fairly, Dave Hull, Jack Whitaker, Tommy Hawkins, Kirk Douglas, Don Newcombe, Dick Enberg, Tex Winter, Bill Buckner, Frank Robinson, Tommy Lasorda, Norm Sherry, Lou Riggs, Phil McKeon, Reb Foster, Mitch Chortkoff, Roger Stein, Penny Chenery, Pat Bowlen, Julia Ruth Stevens, Peter Fonda, Scott St. James, Leonard 'Red' Kelly, Bill Withers, Jim Hardy, Tom Dempsey, Dan Jenkins, Richard Goldstein and the eternally inexpressible sudden loss of Kobe Bean Bryant. Thank heavens, words never die! RIP.

FOREWORD

The adage "no cheering in the press box" applies to journalists covering a particular sport on assignment. The one island of neutrality—or at least a space of quiet indifference—is supposed to be that limited work space within a stadium or arena.

As a former *Pasadena Star-News* sportswriter who later joined the front office of the Los Angeles Dodgers, it's impossible—at least for me—to keep my emotions in a bubble. I might pull off a pokerface in public or give a "historian's" perspective without a trace of bias. But my sports odometer has plenty of mileage from the highs and lows of watching the ultimate reality shows. The amazement of Kirk Gibson's 1988 World Series pinch-hit home run sailing into the right field pavilion is always balanced with replays of the Yankees' Reggie Jackson blasting three home runs in Game 6 of the 1977 Fall Classic, which crushed my youthful hopes for a Dodger championship.

Anyone who can still recite the most obscure sports details from their childhood can't help but feel the thrill and anticipation of any major sporting event possibly being decided by one swing of the bat or a jump shot at the buzzer. Overtime at the Super Bowl? A fifth set at Wimbledon?

I first met Ted Sobel in the press box at Dodger Stadium in 1987, so it was a chance to match a face with a voice of the radio reports that were already part of my daily routine. The first impression of Ted became a lasting one—a friendly person and dedicated professional who obviously loved his job. What I didn't see was the set of sports encyclopedias (pre-internet era) crammed between his ears, giving him the ability to discuss any subject with ease.

But Ted wasn't interested in filibusters or press-box debates. Like a master chef, he mixed history with humanity in search of telling a story and reaching beyond the statistical world of boxscores and percentages. He also lived in the moment, not trapped in the past and waxing nostalgia about "the way it used to be." Ted could make any athlete/interviewee feel at ease in a conversation, never knowing his second question until he had listened to the other person's first answer. Conversely, he could stand his ground and politely conduct business during tough times in a clubhouse or other less-than-rosy situation.

Now, Ted has turned the tables on himself and stepped into the spotlight as the interview subject. Throughout this fascinating journey, two themes emerge: enthusiasm and perspective. Ted's story is actually a celebration of life. Ted reminds me of Jimmy Stewart's George Bailey movie character. The difference, though, is that at a young age, Ted already knew it was going to be wonderful.

A stranger reading these stories might wonder how these scenarios could possibly be true. But who else but Ted could take a steam bath and crack jokes with a fugitive, meet members of the Rat Pack, and rub shoulders with Hollywood and musical icons, all the while determined to blaze a career in sports. Even if you're not a sports fan, Ted's stories will inspire and also make you hungry with memories and menus from iconic Southern California eateries. His family history includes the lessons he learned from his ancestors emigrating to the United States and watching his Uncle's prolific career as a screenwriter threatened by the post-World War II political environment that caused upheaval within the entertainment industry.

Although there are tales of casinos, a Friars Club "card room" with prying eyes and a bittersweet bet on a Thanksgiving Day college football game, I can't imagine Ted sitting down at a card table with a "poker face," because he wears his emotions on his sleeve. If the life of "Little Teddy Ballgame"—a nickname acquired from a memorable trip to the Sears sporting goods department—was performed in a ballpark, the score would be something like 15-13 in the top of the sixth inning (relax Ted; I'm not referring to Little League—the big leaguers play at least nine innings). The play-by-play sheet—something aspiring broadcasters covet along with pregame stat packs—would include tape-measure home runs, benches-clearing brawls, rain delays, and the hidden-ball trick. And as an ode to his favorite pitcher, we should add to the list a hit batsman called back to home plate by the umpire, because he didn't get out of the way of the pitch.

One of my favorite stories from Ted's childhood revolves around a fateful fly ball during a World Series game at Dodger Stadium. Somehow, a long drive from home plate to right field hovers in the air long enough for a kid to hold his breath with anticipation, and then generations later as an adult, ask his long retired favorite player to describe that same ball heading in his direction. Spoiler alert: the sunglasses malfunction, and the ball hits the glove. Whether the player makes the catch will be revealed.

In the meantime, sit back and enjoy, as Ted's passionate stories are a reminder to those in the grandstands that sports (and humanity) shouldn't revolve around just winning and losing—it's how you watch the game. And if you treat life like my friend Ted, you're already a winner.

Mark Langill
Team Historian, Los Angeles Dodgers

CONTENTS

INTRODUCTION

Photo by Paul Olden

Do you like stories? I got your stories RIGHT HERE! From the world of sports, music, entertainment, and just my crazy life—really something for everyone. It doesn't matter where you are from or how you were raised, who on this planet who's ever taken a breath wouldn't want to be a witness to greatness in whatever category you could imagine? And not just as a spectator, but actually participating in such significant occasions.

One of my prime earliest recollections was getting to meet THE 'Teddy Ballgame' in the same Hollywood Sears store that I would later work in (that story of watching Secretariat win the Kentucky Derby in the TV department there to come in a later text). I'll never forget the smell of fresh buttered popcorn being made in the candy section as we hustled through the store towards the sporting goods department. Baseball great Ted Williams was making an appearance to promote his brand as an avid sportsman (with his name seemingly on everything for sale), and my father took me to see the recently retired 19-time All-Star, only to learn that he was on his way out as we approached his assigned location.

It began with great disappointment as the lanky statuesque soon to be HOFer had just gotten up from his chair and was heading towards the exit. We drove all the way there, and I don't get to meet this all-time legend? THE 'Splendid Splinter' who had not so long ago cemented his immortality in my mind, when belting a home run in his final at bat, while owning one of the greatest swings in the history of the game?

Fortunately my father spoke out, causing 'The Thumper' (who else has so many damn great nicknames?) to turn around. "Mr. Williams, we just arrived and my son Teddy was really hoping to meet you." And Ted Williams stopped, looked way down at this eight-year old Little Leaguer and smiled, "Teddy it's very nice meeting you. ANOTHER Teddy Ballgame." He shook my hand and then quickly walked away into his day, while crowning one of my earlier voyages into truly touching greatness. If Mr. Williams only knew what those 10 seconds meant to me at the time and how that made me want to get to know the elite of any field ever since?

Or like the time a few short years later, having a random quick meet-and-greet with then L.A. Mayor Sam Yorty, who was known nationally due to his several appearances on The Tonight Show, when Johnny Carson would joke about him always being out of town. I was with my friend Dave on a trip to his doctor's office and while leaving the appointment, the elevator door opened, and there was Yorty standing there surrounded by a few others. I'll never forget looking up at him and saying, "Hello Mr. Mayor, what are you doing in town?" He belted out in laughter, while Dave couldn't believe how ballsy I was to joke that way with Mayor Sam. Just my personality and how I've approached life for as far back as I can remember, and I guess setting the tone for what was ahead.

Now, I can't help but think if I was told then that six decades later I'd be writing a book about my many experiences in the midst of so much greatness (which includes tons of my personal and/or professional life interactions with over 750 Hall of Famers from all sports and many other prominent folk), I'm sure that little Teddy Sobel would have said "I can't wait to read about how I got to be a participant with such people and events." I only hope you'll feel as enthused as you continue to consume these throwback stories from an easier and more innocent time, all the way up to our society's current evolution. And I'm eager for this to be like my Grandma Fannie's heavenly chicken matzo ball soup for your pandemic-ridden souls, with plenty more to nosh on here.

For those individuals who love to watch sports, it's not only our ultimate unifier and real life distractor, but is also our daily reality show full of drama and excitement (never knowing the final score) that can rarely be matched by other pastimes. And I felt that bug as a small boy, while always wanting to be a part of landmark events. To this day, I have an empty feeling when I'm not there to cover it.

What makes my sportscasting career somewhat unique from others was getting to cover everything in sports compared to a beat writer, whose assignment is to report on just one team. My circumstances gave me golden opportunities to be a part of so many historic happenings and special moments. And while most in my business just talk about events, I've often lived them. Not surprisingly, forever friends have often said to me, "Ted, you have personal stories about EVERYONE, as well as over decades of involvement with many of the greatest games, stars, rivalries, and they should all be in a book someday." And add to that the many unique story lines surrounding my family's sometimes bizarre existence? Well, HERE IT IS!

Yes the final score is always important in whatever we do, but the human emotions of an athlete in competition is what does it for me, which is what I've attempted to dig out when conducting my interviews. Getting to learn the inside stories from the people themselves is one of the best parts of the job. To learn how they tick when swinging a bat, golf club, tennis racquet, or hockey stick? Or what gives a person inspiration to write a song, a movie, or to play an instrument?

I am also proud to emphasize that there are no exaggerations or cock-and-bull stories in this book as I've tried to explain everything with complete accuracy. I consider myself a journalist—sadly a word that has begun to fade from our society, a scenario which we need to reverse ASAP. Facts and not distorted statements are truths that do mean EVERYTHING, specifically in the news business. And you should know of the great integrity in the news rooms that I worked in—almost 23 years at the iconic KFWB bookended by over three periodic decades with KNX, and at L.A.'s first full-time all-sports station KMPC from its birth. These were among the most respected radio stations in our country, and now like old times, I even break a few more stories in these pages just for your hopefully burning-with-curiosity reading pleasure.

After broadcasting more than 40,000 sports updates on radio (and I'm getting a dizzying headache just thinking about it), this book features my own compilation of Ted Sobel's greatest hits and personal timeline play-by-play of many historical times and places, with heaps of inside stuff that I've been fortunate (or not so much) to have lived through and/or covered professionally. As such, being a pack rat has finally paid off. All of those endless audio recordings from cassettes to digital have allowed me to share the many fitting comments from the greats and not so great, while trying to make it an enjoyable read whether you're into that subject or not.

One fun topic for discussion that often comes up on social media is, how many lucky fans have actually had the chance to meet their favorite player or celebrity? Well, if you've ever seen the Woody Allen film 'Zelig,' or Tom Hanks playing the part of 'Forrest Gump,' or know of the elusive 'Where's Waldo,' you'll probably notice that I've been an unusual combination of those characters in these pages. So often finding myself in historic circumstances, while sometimes wondering how the hell I ever got there? Even living the movie 'Slap Shot' in real time and space and just knowing that Paul Newman would've loved reading about that. AHH, how the observation that 'life is timing' is so true!

I've also been most fortunate to have experienced some special eras gone by in Southern California and Las Vegas from the late 1950s on, growing up in the surroundings of Culver City (the home of MGM studios and so many stories from that theatrically historic neighborhood). In the process, I got to live my dream of being around history-makers from fantastic to fickle: Hollywood's Rat Pack to the Fifth Beatles, to Koufax and Drysdale, to Baylor and West, to The Eagles and The Beach Boys, to Nixon and Trump, to Arnie and Jack, to Gordie and Gretzky, to Secretariat and Zenyatta, to Sampras and Agassi, to Kobe and Shaq, to Tiger and Phil, to Mickey and Yogi, and it's still ain't over til it's truly over!

Most of the individuals discussed in this tome are in the sports world, since that has been my beat, but others were in entertainment, music, and political fields that nicely fell into the crevices of my life. You'll get a word's-eye view (thank you Chick Hearn) of my very personal behind-the-scenes stories from the many all-time great performances I've covered including the N.Y. Giants Super Bowl upset win over the previously perfect Patriots, the Dodgers and Angels World Series, the Lakers championships, Rose Bowls, Kobe Bryant's final game, Tiger Woods' dogleg road to his last two major titles, the Serena Slam at Wimbledon, American Pharoah's Triple Crown win at the Belmont, a World Cup soccer tragedy, and Arthur Ashe's last competitive victory, to the process of breaking impactful sports news stories.

And in these multi-volumes, I'll paint some of the personally meaningful historic events of my lifetime back into vivid living color, with reproduced play-by-play from the JFK and RFK assassinations, my own 'Miracle on Ice' connection, working the gut-wrenching Magic Johnson HIV retirement announcement, Arnold Palmer's last day at the Masters, Nolan Ryan and

Clayton Kershaw no-hitters, hanging with John Wooden at his Pauley Pavilion floor-naming dedication night, being on the inside of Mike Tyson's return from prison fight, and the L.A. Kings finally winning the Stanley Cup—two in three years, and so much more! And don't miss my father's cherished times in the presence of Babe Ruth. Call it coincidence, or fate, or just pure luck, it's been too inspiring and fun to not want to share it all with you.

My stories also feature added informative notes to help you understand the history behind these happenings and those involved. Look for the many 'FUN FACTS' and 'DID YOU KNOWS?' throughout, which can surely be eye openers—or at least smile starters with the intended purpose of sharing my passion and feelings of what I experienced at the time, while enlightening readers via some spirited sidebars.

So many places, newsmakers, and newsbreakers from a time gone by, a time that should never be forgotten, along with tributes full of youthful treasured memories to my biggest sports idols, like Hall of Famers Don Drysdale, Elgin Baylor, and Bart Starr, among others! And even how the mob somehow affected the Sobel family, as we just tried to mind our own damn business.

I was extremely lucky to live in an era when radio was king in L.A., while subsequently being inspired to make this a career by maybe our greatest D.J. Dave Hull, AKA 'The Hullabalooer,' and local sportscasting legends Vin Scully and Chick Hearn. They all showed me the importance of research when calling a game or simply knowing your subject for any and all on-air work. And I took that to heart, while writing these pages, realizing that many of you won't know of some of the special names from an earlier time and place who had such impact on our lives. After several hundred hours of excavating through research, however, you will now. Providing more of their background is my way of preserving often forgotten history and great anecdotes that shouldn't wind up forever lost as just another fallen leaf off of a tree.

Of course, a parent's influence is always a massive part of our life's equation and mine were no different. My mother Sherry Foreman Sobel's early USO big band singing and piano playing led to the musical culture in our house, while my father Bernard was a child of the 1920s in New York City, a town that can easily eat you up. But Dad was more like the shark than the bait. He would never allow anyone to treat him like their dessert, and he tried to live his life as the one who was in control and NOT as a follower, all the while doing so with dignity. It was important for him to pass that same attitude on to his kids, to give us all a better opportunity to succeed in everything we do.

And there's my late uncle Carl Foreman who was world-renowned for his Academy Award winning screenwriting (seven Oscar nominations overall), and I'll never forget him telling me more than once to 'talk less and listen more.' Well, I've tried to do that, and now I'm in his immense shadow, writing my own stories which includes how Carl was a huge inspiration in my life, even when he was living in exile as a victim of the Hollywood blacklisting period. My intimate chapter on Carl (in Volume #3) is a thoroughly researched tribute to his work as a pioneer filmmaker, whose scripts were often meant to open the public's eyes to the injustices of the common man and fighting for all human rights via such classics as: High Noon, The Guns of Navarone, Champion, and his long overdue Oscar, after dishonorably receiving no screen credit for The Bridge on the River Kwai.

I'm far from alone in my beliefs of the man, just ask the iconic statesman Sir Winston Churchill who sought out Carl to make the film Young Winston about his pre-war days. That whole saga is well-chronicled in the Volume 3 chapter called Born Free, which gives me the opportunity to display how I believe my mother's only brother should be remembered in our bigger book of history, with his real story detailed as I saw it and lived some of it, while reinforcing family pride.

I also feel it's important (with hundreds of famous folk mentioned) to stress that this book is not just a bunch of name-dropping, as ever since losing my baby teeth, I'm not easily impressed with anyone just because they are well-known (notwithstanding the appreciation of a person's great talents)—and even more specifically, after getting to know so many of them and seeing their human flaws first hand. I can easily understand what is meant by, "don't always try to meet the people you admire most as you'll likely be disappointed!"

But it's a lucky day when someone with a noteworthy degree of fame turns out to be how we'd hoped. Thankfully, I've found enough four leaf clovers to include in these stories. The feelings of my youth will never leave me, and I'm proud to record in this book, the many ways of living out some of my dreams with plenty of persistence-pays-off stories, which can hopefully inspire anyone reading this. Besides who else do you know of with tales like randomly meeting the iconic comic genius Stan Laurel late in his life, or getting cussed out by the best in McEnroe, Kobe, and the one and only Wilt Chamberlain, or getting Joltin' Joe DiMaggio's autograph in his underwear, just after Roberto Clemente signed my book on one of the most important days of his career.

In reality, superstars aren't always super people, and I'll show you all sides of that spectrum, along with plenty of lessons learned from interviewing individuals from all different arenas. As difficult it is to reach an elite level in any of life's work, however a person has achieved greatness should be admired if not at least appreciated. In this book, you'll read of my boyhood idols and what it meant to experience things with them into adulthood (when most individuals can only wonder what it might be like just to have shaken their hands).

Being at the right place at the right time has so often amazed me, and mine has been good and bad, like everyone. But when it comes to chance meetings with well-known figures, do I have some stories to tell, including running into Governor Arnold Schwarzenegger in a Beverly Hills alley, actor Gregory Peck in Hollywood, The Fugitive's David Janssen in the old Friars Club steam room, and finding Kobe Bryant to get me into his Olympic practice, as well as many many more. Touching Greatness, while embracing various periods of history is what this is about. So, take a trip with me, from L.A. through Hollywood to Vegas, to Wisconsin, to New England, to Augusta, to Wimbledon, to St. Andrews, Scotland, and well beyond!

And OH the moods that songs can put us in or take us out of? I even weave some of the tunes of my life throughout these pages to give a better sense of its affect on that time, while sharing a little taste of what it was like growing up in the 60s around the big movie studios and the Laurel Canyon music scene. Hitchhiking down the Sunset Strip, going from Tower Records to The Troubadour was a real gas in those days. And I'll take you along for some psychedelic era trips from when sitting next to Flo and Eddie, while watching my brother's band rehearsals in our living room as they tried to beat out The Doors as the house band at The Whisky. And attending an early Beach Boys sidewalk concert overlooking the parking lot of Culver City's first outdoor mall.

My nature has always been to explore my surroundings and get answers to questions about everything (I even bizarrely kissed a few bees in elementary school just to show they weren't out to hurt anyone—and my mouth is still actually intact), with a different kind of California Dreamin' than the musicians of that era—another basis for so many stories and a chance to create some of my own magic.

There's plenty to learn from those musicians who want to change the world through the words and messages in their music, or simply for the sounds that hit you to the core. For me, it's the silky smooth Diana Krall, the passionately inspiring Alicia Keys, the soulfully rich Louis Armstrong, and the incomparable voices of Linda Ronstadt and Bobby Darin. Add the perfect vocal chemistry of The Beach Boys, The Beatles, The Turtles, The Mamas & the Papas, Poco, CSNY, The Eagles, Simon & Garfunkel, and the Mills Brothers (look 'em up), and what a lifetime of harmony to be hanging around.

And Chapter 2 will take you back to the 60s in L.A. with a Triple Crown menu featuring pop-culture, screen gems, and memorable cuisine that will get your taste buds craving for an edible time capsule. Ever enjoy a fresh donut from Helms Bakery or taste an amazing scoop of Wil Wright's ice cream that even Marilyn Monroe couldn't pass up? It's all there for your deja vu dining pleasures.

All of these pages, in one form or another, are a tribute to my parents who if they were around today, would be smiling so hard that their jaws would hurt with pride. Similar to when towards the end of each of their lives—40 years apart, they got to witness historic firsts that seemed unthinkable for so long. My father getting to see the first man walk on the moon and my mother relishing in the electing of our first Black president. Joyful tears for both told me all I needed to know on what those momentous events meant to them.

And you talk about timing? My dad was just a few months old when the Spanish flu hit (toddlers were then in a very high risk group) and now just over a century later, it figures that his son finishes writing this book during the coronavirus pandemic. And although Dad would be laughing his rear end off at the thought of all of this, I think there's a lesson to be learned in this instance. Not only that my life has been too ridiculously strange to chronicle, but how this is a perfect reminder that if we don't appreciate all of the little things now— we NEVER will. Simply put, we're all lucky to be here and the issue is, what are we going to do with this time—over and above the few hours of some reading pleasure that this book will provide, of course!

In conclusion, most people have kids to pass on their family's legacies, but for me, these pages are my babies! And no matter what continues to happen in this crazy world of ours, I will never allow it to make me jaded or not optimistic. We can't always control our surroundings, but we damn well can control our inner thoughts and hence our feelings, which helped me to attain so many of these experiences. It really is always about the journey and the stories behind it, and describing the lifelong emotional roller coaster ride to get there is a pure joy, after starting out as THE greatest gas station attendant/window washer EVER!

So for the mega mega millions of you who have no idea who I am as you trustfully read this—OF COURSE YOU DON'T!, I guarantee a bunch of smiles and laughs once you begin digesting these stories—and then, you'll definitely know! Although this may all be of my life, like in music, I only hope that more than a few messages mean something to everyone—whatever they might be. We've all heard the question, 'Where were you when something historic happened?' Well you're about to get busy finding out my many answers to that query while truly touching greatness. Finally, don't dream just to wake up and forget about it. Chase those dreams until they become your own stories. Now, here are mine...

CHAPTER 1

MY BACKSTORY: FROM THE BIG-INNING

The first thing my father taught me before I was able to say "Momma" or "Dadda" was, "IT'S WHO YOU KNOW, KID!" Get to know everyone and anyone, and you'll be way ahead of the game to succeed on this planet! Touch greatness, and it just might inspire to achieve greater things. So, I took that to heart from as early as I can remember, introducing myself to those individuals whom I'd either like to know or may want to know at some point in this journey.

Dad stressed to me to do what it takes to succeed with dignity and class but to always PUT YOURSELF OUT THERE! And he was right. I'll never be able to thank him enough for that advice, which has allowed me to touch greatness in so many ways that most people could only dream of. Who wouldn't want to be around the best in their profession or among the best in anything?

You should know about my father, Bernard Sobel, who himself succeeded the hard way, which really set the tone for my own future. He likely wasn't the best in his field (although he worked his tail off at it), or maybe not THE best in any other walk of life. But he was THE best in doing everything—and I truly mean EVERYTHING—with integrity, honesty, and class. And I watched him like a hawk, as he taught me to always observe people EVERYWHERE. As a result, of course, he was always my main focus. Dad strongly stressed that we learn so much more from observing our surroundings than any book could ever teach us. Or to quote him, "If you never read a book, read people and you'll be the smartest on your block!" And again he was dead right!

My dad was just another human born in Brooklyn on October 27, 1917 (just months before the Spanish Flu pandemic), when newspaper headlines read that day 'American Troops Are Fighting in the Trenches'—in WW1 for the first time in France. Subsequently, my father was in daily life's trenches ever since. He also grew up in the Bronx, and I would love to joke with him about his heavy N.Y. accent. Personally, I found it hard to believe that he actually did live at Tree, Toydy Tree, Toydy Toyd street. (and yes—no kidding, apartment number Tree). He swore that was the total 'Trute,' which always made me laugh hysterically.

His childhood, however, was no laughing matter, living through the 1920s with an abusive father while constantly trying to protect his mother (my Grandma Minnie). Yes, I knew my life would not be the norm, when realizing that my Dad's parents were named Minnie and Maxie. Not pads, or dresses or skirts—but MY Grandparents. You couldn't make that up! So I guess it was in the cards that Dad would eventually become a dress manufacturer.

❏ THEY'VE ALL COME TO LOOK FOR AMERICA

Like so many people, my lineage began with immigrants fleeing poor situations to look for a better life in the U.S., and you'll soon learn of how perseverance runs through my veins. Both sides of my family go way back to the 'old country' in a time and place of great oppression and injustices. Interestingly, three of my grandparents were born and raised within 600 miles of the others. My Dad's father, Max, had to swipe a passport from a soldier to get out of Odessa, Russia (Odessa is a vital port city in Russia along the Northwestern coast of the Black Sea), because the Jews there were not allowed to leave the country due to a form of 'blacklisting' that unfortunately became a dirty word on both sides of my family, a circumstance which you'll later read about.

The anonymous name on that passport was later shortened to Sobel (thank you very much) and voila, there's our new Americanized name. (Please don't ask what our 'real' surname was—as I never knew for sure and what I did hear, was not so easily pronounceable). My name could have been Bolshevik, and I wonder if the name Ted Stalin or Marx would've worked on the radio? It worked just fine for Groucho!

❏ OUR OWN FAB FOUR (PLUS ONE) CAME OVER FROM LIVERPOOL

Meanwhile just 7-years old, Grandma Minnie left with her family (the Tannenbaums) from their native Austria (then called The Kingdom of Galicia and ruled by Austria-Hungary, which is now a part of Ukraine). They boarded the S.S. Carpathia in Liverpool on August 23, 1904 (36 years before the eldest Beatle Richard 'Ringo' Starkey was born there), along with her three siblings and my great grandmother Gitel (AKA Gussie, whose maiden name we believed to be Ellenbogen) and arrived at the Port of New York on September 1st. Arguably, this country would never be the same! To think that my grandmother came to the U.S. on the same ship that eight years later would become famous for rescuing 705 survivors off the Titanic only two hours after it was sunk. Now that's touching greatness from the starting gate!

DID YOU KNOW?

The S.S. Carpathia made her maiden voyage in 1903 from Liverpool to Boston, and the next year was mainly used to transport Austrian-Hungarian emigrants to New York, before being torpedoed and sunk off the southwest shores of Great Britain in July of 1918 by the Imperial German Navy submarine U-55. Fortunately, 218 of the 223 aboard the ship survived.

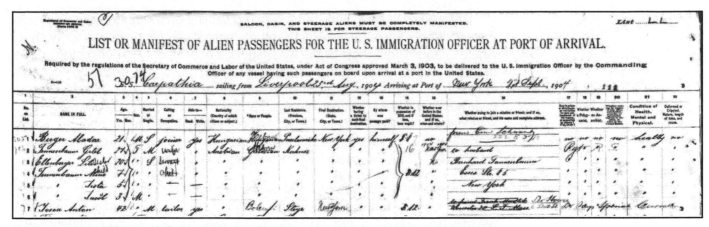

1904 Carpathia passenger manifest (Courtesy cousin Alan Tannenbaum)

FUN FACT

On that Thursday September 1, 1904 the eventual Sobel's newly adopted MLB team the Brooklyn Superbas (later known as the Dodgers) were shutout 3-0 by the Cubs near where my mother's side of the family would one day settle in Chicago.

❏ ONLY THE BEGINNING

My grandparents Fannie and Isadore Foreman

My mother's parents were both Russians from the Ukraine—Grandpa Isadore (Izzy) Foreman from Kerch (a seaport city in Crimea) and Grandma Fannie (Rozin) from Kiev. She spelled her name ending in both a Y and IE, which is what I'll do in her honor. Izzy was the leader of his 'gang' in fighting against the Czar of Russia, but left the country when the government was all out after him. Fannie was one of eight kids from a wealthy family in the diamond business. But that quickly ended when the Czar forced my great grandparents Mark and Ida Rozin to give up ALL of their precious stones (in other words, robbing them blind), causing the family to start over from scratch. There went my chances to become a wealthy 'rock' star!

MUST HAVE FUN FACT

In another perfect case of where DEFINITELY 'life is timing' Grandma Fannie went to a park on the beach with some guy, who while in the restroom, his friend (my Grandpa) asked her to a movie. She accepted and soon after they got married. Good move Grandpa Izzy— and a gigantic thanks for that decision to go for it, taking advantage of the greatest bathroom break in history—for my own existence!

Izzy studied to be a rabbi, but wound up settling on the north side of Chicago (several blocks from Wrigley Field) and partnered with Fanny in a drapery shop, where Grandma did most of the work, specializing not only in her custom-made drapes but also bedspreads, hats, etc. To see some of her beautiful work was truly like looking at classic art in which she also indulged. And Grandma was a fine musician, playing her favorite violin and the piano, which she swayed me to start learning to play the piano at the age of 5. Even now I remember her saying that she would pay for my lessons, if I promised to practice 'tinkling the ivories' EVERY DAY. (Basically, she talked me into it.)

I picked it up very quickly, and within the first several months, was playing songs by ear, which stunned my family. I would hear them say things like 'we think we may have a child prodigy here,' not surprisingly, my very young confidence was sky high. What they really had, however, was a kid who would rather eat Grandma's homemade potato latkes (pancakes), matzo ball soup, and grilled chicken and who wanted to play ball and not sit and practice for hours at the piano.

I easily gave it up for a bat and glove with Little League not far off. Of course years later, I would greatly regret not staying with it at all, wishing I could play and write songs at will (and now just only remembering "America the Beautiful" after all these years). I'm still available for parties to repeat A.T.B. for as many times as requested!

With Uncle Carl a few years before he was awarded his eternal Oscar

Young Bernie

In 1940, my mother Sherry Foreman (who also played the piano quite nicely) moved with her parents to L.A., right after graduating from Von Steuben High School in Chicago—just down the street from where her older brother Carl was an alum of Theodore Roosevelt High, before commencing an incredible career as a 7-time Academy Award nominee writer/producer including winning one posthumously for The Bridge on the River Kwai. He was a total inspiration to me that I'll greatly expound upon in my special tribute to him in a later volume. The extreme weather conditions and other factors in Chi-town were more than the Foremans could bare. As a result, they followed Carl to the land of palm trees and orange groves which suited their future Ted just fine.

❏ LESSONS WITH AN EMPIRE STATE OF MIND

Grandma Minnie had become a highly respected neighbor in Brooklyn with always open doors to her family and friends, one story that will live with me forever was Dad as just a kid at home one night, watching his drunken father come in late from wherever and totally abuse my grandmother AGAIN!

So, as Dad told me with conviction, he kicked Max out of the house and said to NOT come back until he was sober and ready to treat his mother with full respect. Well Max repeated this for an unknown amount of times until the LAST TIME. When at the very 'mature' age of 13, Dad threatened Grandpa Max (who I never met) that he better leave their home immediately. And Dad was far from kidding when seriously telling his father—'if you ever step in this place again, I will kill you'! He would do anything to protect his mother, ANYTHING!

This story was hard to hear my father tell with passion, while he held back some tears. Welcome to 1930 under President Herbert Hoover, with unemployment soaring but not for Wimbledon champs Bill Tilden and Helen Moody or Babe Ruth, whose $80,000 salary was his highest and the most for any MLB player for the next 19 years. A different time, a different world, but my father wouldn't let ANYBODY disrespect his mother not even at just 13 years of age, including even his father (who NEVER did step into their apartment again).

Dad said he only saw his father one more time the rest of his life, which was just fine with him. This was all ONLY about taking care of his family during the years of the depression and beyond, and NOTHING else mattered. Grandma Minnie was never able to talk about those days to me without crying some, but I would still love to see her so proud of her son and what he stood for. And what an amazing role model for us to have. After hearing this story, my perspective on life with a stronger paternal outlook would soon change for the better.

————————— ***FUN FACTS*** —————————

Grandma Minnie lived in Brooklyn for many years mostly at 18th Street and Kings Highway, less than four miles away from where little Sandy Koufax was born in Borough Park and 15 minutes away from Sandy's future baseball home of Ebbett's Field, which opened when Grandma was 16. Koufax later attended Lafayette High in nearby Bensonhurst (the mythical home of 'The Honeymooners' TV classics Ralph and Alice Kramden,) where he was a star basketball player who could dunk with ease and didn't make the baseball team until as a senior in the spring of 1953 (just months before I was born). Former Dodger owner Walter O'Malley once called Sandy 'the great Jewish hope,' perfect for his local demographics—and the rest was history. Sandy once told me of his fond memories of playing all sports in Brooklyn, right down the street from the Sobels many many moons ago.

❏ WIN, PLACE, OR SHOW ME THE $$$

Of course, without a father in the Sobel household and a mother who didn't have a career—who would bring in the money to survive during such a difficult time for our entire society? My father's life conundrum was being raised religiously (he also seriously considered becoming a rabbi), while having to deal with real everyday life—and make some moolah to support his family. Dad also had aspirations of being an electrical engineer but wound up in an alternative universe, manufacturing dresses after learning the clothing trade in the army (his task was to make soldier's uniforms, which had the advantage of not having to fight anyone in combat while wearing them).

As a young teenager, Dad had to work around his school hours (a scenario that was legal in those days) to provide for his family, which included just one younger sister. And my Aunt Bea also talked of how proud she was of my father for doing whatever it took. And I mean literally 'whatever it took.' Please remember that phrase as it will come up throughout these pages (and hopefully often in your life too). And again, I learned that from the horse's mouth.

Speaking of horses, that's another way that not much later Dad tried to enhance his bank account—as in going to the race track. Not quite the best financial advise someone could give (specifically to a kid), but my father loved the sport of kings and the rush of trying to beat the odds. Of course, there was always the NEXT race to make some hard-earned 'easy' cash if you didn't win the last one.

Fortunately, he taught me about that sport as a kid and oh how proud he would've been to see his son in the barn of triple crown winner American Pharoah many decades later or interviewing the greatest jockeys ever, like Bill Shoemaker, Laffit Pincay, or HOF trainers like Charlie Whittingham and Bob Baffert, etc., etc.! Much more on that later.

So, why do I feel so compelled to describe my father in such detail to you all? Because he helped shape me in so many ways, which I think are some of the great lessons which can be learned by all. And my passionate personality is similar to his, but we could also sometimes rub people the wrong way due to passion, or that 'whatever it takes' attitude. But what the hell is life without passion anyway? It's boredom, which is NOT FOR ME!

As rough as he sometimes appeared on the outside, Dad was a puppy dog at heart and was beloved by most who got to know him (another lesson learned—people too often judge others way too quickly). Maybe, the feelings he inspired were because he always made people laugh, not as a joke-teller, but just a very clever man—something I always tried to emulate.

I've never lived in New York, but some of that 'Big Apple' blood runs through me like the Hudson River. Likely why I was born with sports in my veins—or did my father simply share his love of games that would eventually become my life? My three siblings never took to it the way that I did, which made it an even more special bond with my father who when I was growing up, my friends parents would refer to him as a 'Damon Runyon character' (look that up if need be?).

Dad and his mother   *Me and Grandma Minnie*

❏ TOUCHING PLENTY OF GREATNESS

My proudly old-school dad was a sports nut who first played stickball in the streets and later attended more classic sporting events of which his future third son would be envious. Not only did Bernie Sobel work as a kid at Yankee Stadium during the Babe's and Lou's heyday, but also seeing games at Ebbets Field and the Polo Grounds, while attending so many events at 'The Mecca of basketball' Madison Square Garden. He was right there to watch the pre-NBA New York Knickerbockers and a number of huge college basketball games, while also making it to his share of N.Y. Americans and Rangers hockey games (later, often taking my uninterested mother as a non-sports person).

And oh how he loved when 'The World's Most Famous Arena' hosted some of the classic fights in boxing history. In fact, Dad was in that smoke-filled 'Old Garden' for some of the biggest—including a few of Sugar Ray Robinson's 21 main events fought there, for example, Sugar Ray's 10-round decision over Jake 'Raging Bull' LaMotta in 1942 and beating a shell of the legendary Henry Armstrong in '43.

——— **FUN FACT** ———

Like most experts believed, Dad said that Sugar Ray Robinson was the greatest pound-for-pound boxer he'd ever seen in person or on TV, which is good enough for me. And it was a kick for him to meet Sugar Ray at the Friars Club one day, and he took this picture (with a couple of fellow members) just for me.

Dad (right) with the great
Sugar Ray Robinson

Dad also witnessed the Joe Louis and Jersey Joe Walcott fight at MSG, as well as the Joe Louis vs. Billy Conn fight at Yankee Stadium in the first televised World Heavyweight Championship bout ever. Add names like Willie Pep and Barney Ross and simply put, many of the greatest boxers who ever lived fought with my father in the house, which is an awesome nostalgic memory on which to look back.

❏ LOVE AT FIRST SIGHT? NOT!

And then there's the Hollywood-like script of how my parents met…(a story enjoyed by all), and something I used to love asking them about. (I can hear them arguing now, concerning whose was THE MOST accurate account?) Both versions were great and made for Hollywood and I would laugh about Dad's persistence which would eventually give me a life on this planet. And the following is not from some old chick flick (although it could easily be one), but is the absolute truth on the first night my parents became a couple during just another moonlit evening in the mid 1940s at some popular nightclub in Manhattan. Ironically, Dad would often sing Perry Como's big hit from that year of 1946 'Prisoner of Love,' until I had to leave the room due to the monotony of the experience.

But it was my mother who was the 'real' singer in the family in the USO, with the big bands at the time, while working in the offices of MGM studios in Culver City, California, where ironically we would later live. She was scheduled to make her first of a hopeful many trips to Europe to sing for our troops with the USO but had to stop in New York City for a few days before heading abroad. Fortunately for Dad (and much later for us Sobel kids), she somehow got a gig singing at the same nightclub that just happened to be my father's regular favorite hangout... and he just happened to be there that night!

Mom's favorite head shot from the 1940s

So as my mother was singing away on stage with a band behind her, there was Dad sitting at his usual table all the way in the back of the room. And not really needing his extremely vivid far-sightedness, obviously close enough to know that he very much wanted to meet this beautiful singer from L.A. He told his friend the maitre d' to ask Shari Fare (Mom's stage name—they did that a lot in those days) after her first set, if she would join him for some friendly chatter at his table.

As Mom had explained it to me, she stood just off stage—as he pointed towards my father. Her reaction was HIM? NO WAY! Not that gangster-looking guy at the back table! Dad really was far from being a gangster, but I could easily see why her first impression. (Just look at these guys in this picture.) That was the style in those days, and it was New York City just after WWII. So the maitre d', whom I'll call Johnny (the name Dad always used to call most individuals who he didn't know—probably a New York thing at the time), went back to my father and told him the bad news. The beautiful singer had NO interest in meeting him. As in ZERO, NOT A CHANCE IN HELL! But Bernie Sobel wasn't about to give up so fast and he asked 'Johnny' to do a little sales job and tell my mother all about him, and that he's a really good guy, respected by all and blah blah blah (and to tell her only the 'TRUTE').

Dad (back right) with his dapperly dressed N.Y.C. club buddies

So, 'Johnny' waited until she finished her next set and gave it his best shot and told her a bit about Dad and how she would really like him. Mom said she was flattered, but that even if she was interested, she would only be in N.Y. for a very short time before flying to Europe. Accordingly, she flatly denied my father a chance to meet her. Dad told me how disappointed he was and asked Johnny if he could try just one more time. 'Johnny' subsequently replied, "you're on your own now Bernie, I gave it my best shot."

So that's the end of that story, right? Wrong! But wait, there's more... OBVIOUSLY, since I exist and have written these words. And toward the end of the show—Dad used that Sobel persistence and thought there was NO WAY he couldn't at least give it one last shot. Fortunately, he knew his way around the place and headed for the common NYC outside stairwell, from where he expected Mom to leave. And as she headed out, there was Dad waiting for her (in her own disbelief). He quickly introduced himself as the guy in the back of the room whom she had no interest in meeting. At that point, she could only laugh at (in a nice way) but declined him again.

As I always say, timing is everything, and this must have been the case again as he totally put on the charm in this very small window of opportunity and used his fantastic sense of humor to make her laugh again and again, as they walked down the stairs together. And then his last ditch effort, how nice it would be if she could just join him and a few friends at their favorite local all-night deli before calling it a night?

My Mother was suddenly intrigued enough by this guy who kept making her laugh—and begrudgingly said 'YES'! And as they both told me, they had a great time for the next few hours getting to know each other with stories that had them laughing throughout. Fortunately, they had such a great time that they hung out the next day and the next day after that...and guess who NEVER went to Europe with the USO? That's right! Mom never did get to visit Europe in her 92 years, but I got to go for her and sharing my several trips there was just fine for all! And every time I was there, I couldn't help but think that there would've never been a ME, if she had traveled abroad as planned. Thank you Bernie Sobel—your persistence worked out beautifully for all of your kids.

❑ OPERATOR, COULD YOU HELP ME PLACE THIS LONG DISTANCE CALL?

Theirs was hardly an easy courtship, given that they lived on different coasts. Since it was several decades before Skype was invented, Dad would fly Mom to New York whenever possible (not quite as simple a task just after WWII), but he would never come to L.A. He eventually proposed to my mother, and she accepted, but there was one HUGE problem. Mom's mother (my Grandma Fannie) said she had to meet this man who looked like a guy out of an old Edward G. Robinson movie first. She wasn't so sure that he would be someone to whom her only daughter should be married?

So, finally Dad flew to L.A., and it wasn't long until Grandma saw his same qualities that kept Mom in New York after that original fateful night. Grandma told me that he had her laughing and seeing that he wasn't anything like her first impressions through only pictures—again, a factor from which we can all learn. Less than two years later, my brother Glenn was born in Brooklyn, followed by Richard the next year, before the Sobels taught the Dodgers how to move to L.A., where my younger sister Janet and I were born and raised by our very far from perfect but always caring parents.

Mom raised us four kids after her previous life as a successful singer during the big band era—her final best gig being with Frankie Ortega (and for our troops at the old Hollywood USO). She also befriended one of the all-time great lyricists Sammy Cahn, whose parents were from the same area as her mother-in-law, in Galicia.

Mom at her favorite piano

Just another night of 'The Good Life' for the Ortega boys at the Grove

When working a NATPE convention back in my satellite TV days in the late 80s, I was walking through the hall and noticed a big sign in the corner that said Sammy Cahn. Subsequently, I wandered over. THAT Sammy Cahn? There was the man just sitting there looking bored. Of course, I had to introduce myself (to bore him even more) and to tell him how much my mother had mentioned him over the years. He quickly perked up and was extremely friendly (and witty), while telling me that he had remembered her from those many years gone by and to pass along his greetings in return. We shared a few stories and laughs and fortunately took this picture for me to take home to Mom, which caused her to smile all night long.

Sharing some 'High Hopes' with Sammy Cahn

Mom could still sing some in her 'more mature years,' but the voice was much raspier and not as smooth as the old '78' rpm albums on which I'd heard her. Of course, she would blame that on yelling at all of her kids. My obvious response to that, "Then STOP YELLING at us!" Well that never happened, but at least I tried! If only I still had her albums, but they were stolen along with all of our family memorabilia—an extremely sore subject with most of our childhood pictures and videos just tossed away by some moronic thief who took anything he could without knowing its value. Invaluable and never to be seen again, likely a reason why I've acquired so many pictures since.

FUN FACT

The 78 RPM album era lasted until mostly into the mid 1950s (while I waited for the 'Walkman' to be invented).

❏ L.A. PRE-DODGERS AND LAKERS

On July 14, 1953, Mom was watching I love Lucy on her little black and white TV with the top hit 'The Song From Moulin Rouge' by Percy Faith dominating the airwaves, when I caused her enough pains to head to Temple Hospital (significantly overlooking the area near where the future Dodger Stadium would be built) on Temple Street, where I was born some hours later as the third son of Sherry and Bernie Sobel. It's ironic that I always drove past this hospital on the Hollywood Freeway, when on my way to the Ravine, my eventual home away from home. Thanks to Walter O'Malley for moving his team from Brooklyn when and where he did. As a 5-year old kid who was just getting to know what baseball was all about, this scenario was beyond perfection. Again, timing is everything!

FUN FACT

Fortunately, six months after I was born, so were the first compatible (with black-and-white) color TV sets that went on sale for $1,000 (about $9,500 in today's inflated cash).

❏ START ME UP

It was a mostly uneventful first few years on this planet except for one very scary and almost tragic personal incident. My family had recently moved to their first home in the San Fernando Valley on a nice quiet street in Pacoima (surrounded by dairies and farms in those days), and I was just aimlessly advancing my new running skills around our backyard with my two older brothers nearby, when I suddenly ran directly into a stray wire sticking out from a fence. That rusty old wire got stuck in my left eyelid, and as my mother put it, she was in major emergency/panic mode, screaming in distress, while blood was flowing down my face.

*Me getting fit at age
two in Pacoima*

Thankfully, she was somehow able to delicately remove the wire without a more severe gash and rush me to the hospital, where the doctor then stitched me up back to almost normal. Mom would then forever tell me how lucky I was, given that wire was the closest millimeter away from major damage to my eye if not total blindness. I still have a nice scar to remember that wonderful day for as long as I'm around, something that my mother would never let me forget about anyway, thanks to almost scaring her to an early death. My father, meanwhile, said it was a 'toughen up' life lesson that would always be with me.

CHAPTER 2

THE CULVER YEARS—
A RETRO PLATTER OF
BALLPARKS, SCREENLAND
& COMFORT FOOD

❏ SO MUCH HISTORY FROM THE INNOCENT 60s IN SOCAL

After just a few early years in the valley, we were most fortunate that my parents made the decision to move to our Culver City house in 1958, with the great Bobby Darin's 'Mack the Knife" and Harry Belafonte's 'Day-O' soon blasting on our living room hi-fi all year long. Furthermore, a new local team called the L.A. Dodgers, with a young Vin Scully was constantly in my father's transistor radio. Blair Hills was a small, secluded, quiet, family community on the far eastern border of the city, alongside what we called the 'La Cienega freeway,' which buzzed just a few houses away from us. What an incredible neighborhood to grow up in and around a city that had everything and anything a kid could want. The following is a taste of a lucky SoCal childhood that I'll always cherish.

────────── *FUN FACTS* ──────────

Will Rogers, Jr. whose first house was in Culver City, when his legendary humorist father moved to L.A., performing in films at Hal Roach Studios, Will Jr. had once lived on a small ranch (AKA the Pitti Ranch) in my new quaint neighborhood of Blair Hills (directly behind our backyard wall) just several years before we had moved there. Our view had horses and typical farm animals, including beautiful peacocks from our patio during much of my years living there. Subsequently, we were told that during its heyday, this ranch was a popular spot for some big named stars to learn how to ride and rope for the numerous western movies made in our city, including Glenn Ford, Robert Taylor, Alan Ladd, and Zsa Zsa Gabor (although Zsa Zsa was hardly a cow girl). Horses were always a part of the Rogers family, and after selling this property, Will Jr. (once also our district's Congressman) was purported to be a frequent visitor to his old address in 1952 behind where our house was soon to be built, training for the film 'The Story of Will Rogers, playing his famous father in his first acting job. And it took me until too many decades later to learn from Will Sr.'s famous words, "Never miss a good chance to shut up!"

How I loved playing ball on our short street Vicstone Court (emulating my father's boyhood stickball days). Like most kids, I didn't mind dodging a few cars. But it wasn't until breaking a few windows with some over-zealous swings of the bat that brought enough neighbor complaints which had me then moving my games to the real ballpark just a couple of blocks up the hill. The new Blair Hills Park became my personal sports sanctuary for years, where I would spend many after-school hours playing ball until there was no more sunlight.

At almost anytime, I'd be there shooting 100 free throws and practicing my jump shots on the same rims where UCLA stars Sidney Wicks and Curtis Rowe came to dunk over our shorter heads, or hitting fungo fly balls to myself. Subsequently, playing a game of over-the-line or home run derby easily made my day complete. We also proudly enjoyed the best sports leagues for miles around with Culver City's six parks, participating like our lives depended on it—a bona fide juvenile sports heaven!

FUN FACT

To make a call then on our rotary phones, we had just one area code for all of L.A. County (213) and only used what was called exchange names until about 1963 (when our pre-Android number was UPton 0-1517).

❏ DOWNTOWN

While I was playing at the park, Dad was ALWAYS busy trying to provide for his family to give us the best lifestyle possible in our second home in L.A. Unfortunately, the situation also often meant that we were able to spend relatively little quality time spent with him. Getting into the clothing business downtown after learning how to make soldier's uniforms in the army, he even talked to me about one day possibly taking over his business (which he knew did NOT interest me at all).

On March 9, 1965, with The Temptations' 'My Girl' topping the charts and listening via my grandmother's new Chevy Impala radio and while the dynamic duo of Elgin Baylor and Jerry West each scored 37 points in the Lakers 123-114 win over the Baltimore Bullets, Dad incorporated his manufacturing business into an entity called Bernie Sobel of California. In time, his work became greatly respected in the industry.

Even as a little kid I was always so proud to see his name on the tags inside of his own created apparel (which were mostly dresses, suits, and blazers) at whatever store in any city. But it got really old to stop EVERYTIME we passed a storefront window with a dress on display to see if it had something Dad could relay back to his patternmaker or designers? And he wanted ME to do THIS for a career? No thanks!

A real kick was Dad often taking me with him on Saturdays to help in his plant by placing little blank white price tags inside of each piece of clothing's belt loop. Hundreds of them at a time, until I couldn't look at another one. But it really did make me feel important, prepping each piece for delivery to whatever store it was headed. Whenever I saw one hung up at major department stores, I always proudly said, "I put that price tag on it!" Not too bad for a pre-teen to boast about. But the best part of those Saturdays was getting to spend quality time with my father. I remember like it was yesterday how amazed I would be EVERY time we would walk those downtown streets—truly feeling touching greatness moments.

When watching the light turn green and while heading through a crosswalk, it was if I was with a big celebrity. Just a dress manufacturer? Yep! But at least half of the individuals walking toward us, would usually want to greet my father. "Hello Bernie." "Hi, Mr. Sobel." How could all of these people know him? If he had been walking anywhere else on this planet, they could care less. Then, the easy explanation, Dad would tell me that most of his colleagues were located there in 'the garment district.' One might be his belt maker, another made his buttons, and another zippers, etc. etc. While that was all true, it was also obvious how much each of these folk truly liked my father, which was a real eye-opener and made me one hugely proud young son, a feeling I wish for everyone.

To this day more than 50 years later, it's very gratifying every time I see one of his originals still being sold online, listed as a classic or vintage Bernie Sobel dress. A piece of clothing that stands the time of over a half century must be of some quality if people are still willing to pay their hard earned bucks for it—HE WOULD BE BEAMING!

This top-quality Bernie Sobel garment would sell for about $135 in 2021

❏ UNKNOWINGLY MAKING HISTORY

Bernie Sobel of California's factory was located on the top floor of the Harris Newmark building (right next door to the great Sam's Deli that endured at that spot for 40 years), a landmark location at 127 East Ninth Street that was once the tallest building in downtown L.A. (it's still a clothing mart). Dad's next gig was as co-owner of C&S Jobbers at the corner of Olympic and Santee streets—not just another store to sell other company's unsold clothing, but among the first of its kind. Dad would buy lots from major designers at a low price and sell at below wholesale to the public. SOUND FAMILIAR?

❏ THROWING STRIKES TO HIS OWN BAMBINO

As I could care less about the 'schmata' business as they call it, what really interested me was sports (and mostly baseball early on). Every time Dad talked about the game, I was all ears. Although he would only occasionally bring up his boyhood days playing stickball in the streets of Brooklyn and the Bronx, which I could only picture in my head, since I grew up in a totally different world. He said he was a damn good hard-nosed player in his day and could also pitch (sounded like some guy who wore #3 for the Yankees). But I could only take his word for it, given that it was a bit early for cellphone pics.

Finally, one day when about 9 or 10 years old on our slim Culver City backyard lawn, and with the sounds of Ray Charles and Peter, Paul, and Mary in the air, I got the chance to see my father right in front of my face do what I had heard him speak of in the past. As usual, I had my ball and glove with me playing catch with my brother (not so usual). Dad was just home from work and for some reason (completely out of character) in a playful mood after a long day. While watching me get animated about just playing catch, he began to boast about how he once had some pretty good stuff as a pitcher and that he could break off a mean curve ball.

So I asked him to show me how he did it, and vividly recall having to talk him into doing so. I was in shock as he rolled up his sleeves! I went into a catcher's crouch from about 60 feet away not knowing what to expect from the 40-50 pounds overweight and balding mid-40ish Bernard Sobel (still dressed in his business attire and wearing work shoes). After a couple of warm-up tosses, he began throwing me curves that were dropping off the table—BIG roundhouse curves.

Then, he'd fire one in Koufax-like. And then another one—and for strikes! My tiny hand inside my little glove stung like a bee. Those pitches were coming in like from someone who not only knew how to throw a baseball, but with some heat as well. And he was a lefthander like Sandy, but with his spindly legs below that round upper body, it was if I was catching Babe Ruth himself with even a similar motion (although in his black loafers).

The honest truth is that I never looked at Dad the same after that, and I wanted more, so much more! I wanted my father in his white dress shirt and wool business pants with dress shoes to play catch with me more often. Every day would be perfect, but just once in a great while would be fine too.

But as fate would have it, this was the one and only time we EVER did. A disappointment for sure, and something from which all Dads can learn, which is why I'm stressing this here. If your kid has ANY passion for whatever game or activity, play or share it with them and they will remember those moments forever. Just look at how I recall every second of our one and only less than 10-minute stint of just playing catch, which I will NEVER FORGET!

On occasion, Dad would watch me play in little league when always looking to make him proud. But this one special few minutes together at home stands above them all. Bernie Sobel was always my main inspiration, but from that moment on, I respected him in a whole new way. He really was an athlete like I wanted to be. Furthermore, somehow, I figured that I could do it too. And in some ways I could, but just not to the level to make it a career. So, as time went on I would have to settle for the idea of sports broadcasting. This is my story of how passion, conviction, and some talent came to fruition for me along a strange trip that's provided the inspiration to share so many of my special times with you all.

Visiting 'The House That Ruth Built'—photo by Paul Olden

❏ I GOT YOU 'BABE'

How could I not be enamored with baseball, with a father who as a youth, worked at Yankee Stadium selling peanuts and popcorn during the Ruth-Gehrig days. I can fully re-live in my mind Dad telling me when having his back turned to the field (while selling snacks to the fans), there was that one buzz that built up like NONE other, a scenario that could only happen when a major superstar was about to come to the plate.

Yes, when THE Babe Ruth began walking towards the batter's box, my father would stop working and just admire his greatness. Taking in what a person could only imagine was history being made almost daily. It was very personally gratifying to realize that about 30 years later, his son Teddy would be observing the same when joining him at the stadium to see a Sandy Koufax or a Willie Mays (the greatest all around player I've ever seen—until Ken Griffey, Jr. was at his best in Seattle and with Roberto Clemente right alongside).

Dad recalled that when 'The Babe' hit one out at Yankee Stadium, and raised his cap toward the grandstand when rounding the bases, "it was like every fan thought he was personally waving to them," including himself. It was an admiration that the game had never experienced. He was only around Ruth the man a few times with hordes of other kids, simply too busy trying to provide for his family to be your 'typical' teen hanging out after Yankee games to get autographs. But he said to be in Ruth's presence was no different than when UK residents grew up admiring royalty.

My father did say that he got 'Babe' to sign for him at least once and remembered his sincere smile toward all kids whenever hanging with them outside of the original 'House that Ruth built.' Unfortunately, those revered pieces of paper were somehow lost over the years. I never did get to see that immortal signature, which I bugged him about. I also wonder if any of those single-signed pages on eBay were a Bernie Sobel acquired original?

DID YOU KNOW?

Babe Ruth became beloved due to his greatness on the field while endearing the fans off of it. The 'Sultan of Swat' was the first athlete to make signing an autograph an art (similar to Arnold Palmer decades later), and during one time period, he even put quotation marks around his name "Babe." It will always be one of the treasured signatures to own as long as they can be preserved.

From Dad's original autograph book at age 12

My father only saved one autographed cut-sheet of paper from those early days, which happened to be signed by three of Babe's teammates in 1930 or '31—HOFer Earle Combs (the first of the Yankees great center fielders and the leadoff man for the '27 'Murderers Row' club), Jimmie Reese (proudly The Babe's roomy and team utility guy), and Lyn Lary (knocked in 107 runs in 1931—still the most ever by a Yankee shortstop).

The Jimmie Reese whom I knew was the elder popular SoCal-raised fungo hitter and conditioning coach for the California Angels who joined the club at the age of 71 (listed as their coach until age 93) and later had his Anaheim #50 uniform retired, while entering the Angels Hall of Fame. My favorite chat with Reese was sharing these stories about my dad, and he loved them. How cool is it to have your father get a roomy of Babe Ruth's autograph, and then chat with him about it several decades later? Actually, anything about 'The Babe' got Jimmie animated—although he was always about treating all people the way anyone would appreciate. Just a quality guy whose close friend, HOFer Nolan Ryan, named one of his sons after (Reese).

DID YOU KNOW?

The Angels honored the guy who many called 'the nicest man in baseball' fittingly before a Yankees game in 1989 with a "Jimmie Reese Day."

As a lefty himself Dad would describe to me his special appreciation for the two great Yankee stars who were also southpaws, while always giving cudos as well to Lou Gehrig. He loved his smooth swing and 'flawless' work at first base and the class that he faithfully exuded to the fans. My father would say that HE was the luckiest man on the face of the earth getting to regularly watch this all-time duo play the most popular game in the land. In reality, we could all learn from Gehrig's impeccable work ethic and courage when dealing with his awful disease with grace and dignity.

What an era to grow up in, as the 'Bronx Bombers' won six World Series during my father's formative years from ages 6-20. Their first was in 1923, when Ruth fittingly belted an opening day 3-run homer in a 4-1 N.Y. win to inaugurate the new Yankee Stadium in front of over 74,000 (by far their largest crowd of the season and at the time in baseball history). Rookie Gehrig rode the bench that day, while watching regular starter Wally Pipp cover first base. (Generations later, the world would learn to never get 'Wally Pipp'd'—something Dad would say "then just don't miss work!"). Actually, Pipp lost his job to a better younger player, but never let facts get in the way of a legendary story.

DID YOU KNOW?

Babe's opening day homer when my father was all of six years old caused sportswriter Fred Lieb to call the new stadium "The House That Ruth Built," a nickname that would live on until its demise for the 'new' Yankee Stadium to be built next to the old one. Ruth's second wife, Claire, said Babe talked about that home run more than all of his others and called it "The proudest moment of his life." A turning point in history for sure!

FUN FACTS

Lou Gehrig, AKA 'The Iron Horse' playing in his long standing record 2,130 consecutive games was voted by the baseball writers in 1969 as the the greatest first baseman of all time and was the leading vote-getter for MLB's All Century Team in 1999. As a philatelist myself, Lou being honored with his own 1989 U.S. postage stamp on the 50th anniversary of the end of his playing streak was a personal thrill.

DID YOU ALSO KNOW?

In those days, many schools didn't allow natural lefties to write with their left hands. My father was one student who was forced to learn with his right (which never felt comfortable to him). In fact, he was hit on his knuckles with a ruler if that order wasn't obeyed. How ridiculous society can be at times!

Because of my father's personal connection to Yankee Stadium, I've always felt a closeness to Ruth & Gehrig (despite neither hardly being Boy Scouts in reality). As a kid, I would try to find my father in the stands when watching an old clip of the stadium which, of course, was near impossible. So, the happy thoughts of it being in my blood would have to do. In fact, I can't tell you how many times I've seen my favorite movie 'Pride of the Yankees,' the story of Lou Gehrig.

❏ TAKE ME OUT TO THE BALLGAME

Any chance to "pull up a chair" in Vin Scully's booth was a total delight

My father taking me to stadiums and racetracks and watching it all together on TV got me hooked. I loved baseball as early as I can remember. I started by listening to the soothing tones of Vin Scully in my trusty transistor radio from the games at the not-so-old L.A. Memorial Coliseum in the late 1950s (once called the 'The Greatest Stadium in the World').

My mother reminded me that they first took me to the Coliseum on July 13, 1958 for my 5th birthday (and for my brother Richard who was born on the 12th). I don't remember much from that doubleheader against the Reds, but I later found out that in the opener, Don Newcombe had lost his second straight to the Dodgers, after they had earlier traded him to Cincinnati. Don was 1-9 on the season after that loss in which he gave up homers to Carl Furillo and Charlie Neal. L.A.'s team that day was an aging version of their Brooklyn days, with Junior Gilliam leading off followed by some guys named Reese, Snider, Furillo, and Hodges. But what the hell did I know? I was at some baseball game, and it was fun, with the Dodgers winning 3-0 over Newk and the Redlegs.

As a five-year old attending my first games, I guess it was only fitting that the youngest to ever play in the big leagues Joe Nuxhall started the second game for the Redlegs against the Dodgers. Fourteen years after pitching as still a 15-year old, Nuxhall gave up homers to Gilliam, Joe Pignatano, and Steve Bilko and our new hometeam won again, 3-2.

And a totally obscure fun fact to mention here: 21-year old Dodger starter Bob Giallombardo picked up his lone MLB win in that game. And as I later learned, the Brooklyn-born lefty was the star pitcher at Koufax's high school the year after Sandy graduated. Small world for the boys from Lafayette High!

❏ A NEW L.A. FAN IS BORN

Meanwhile, the first baseball game that I do recall attending was May 17, 1959 on a Sunday afternoon, with the Dodgers hosting the Milwaukee Braves. What a lineup card on both sides (I would learn more about it years later), as the Braves had sluggers like Henry Aaron (Scully called him Henry, so I did too), Eddie Matthews, Wes Covington, and Del Crandall with career 203-game winner

Lew Burdette on the mound. The Dodgers with a lineup that included Duke Snider, Gil Hodges, Don Zimmer, and Wally Moon (who was famous for his Scully-originated 'Moon Shots' over the short-porched left field screen). I'll never forget the smile on Mr. Moon's face when I got to tell him about that game during an appearance at Dodger Stadium...it was like he had just parked one more over that screen.

FUN FACT

Moon was told by his friend and ex-Cardinal teammate Stan Musial that when traded to play in L.A., he could use the big 42-foot high screen to his advantage as a batter who could hit to all fields. That encouragement changed his career and legacy with the Dodgers.

DID YOU KNOW?

Wally Moon not only hit a homer in his first big league at bat in St. Louis, but also beat out the likes of a young Henry Aaron for N.L. Rookie of the Year honors in 1954.

Even though I was still two months shy of my sixth birthday and hearing some stories about their days in Brooklyn, I already felt some sense of history watching Snider roam the huge right field and Hodges playing 3rd base that day (even my eventual favorite everyday player Ron Fairly pinch hit). But it was some tall right hander from Van Nuys, wearing #53 named Don Drysdale, who caught my eye the most. Even from our upper seat location, I remember thinking his look was different than the rest. His sidewinding motion was something I studied closely, later imitating while standing in front of a mirror so many times and perfecting how the Big D looked so fiercely at the batters. I wanted to be like Don Drysdale—despite my pint-sized body type.

Unfortunately, Drysdale gave up long home runs to Crandall and Aaron in that game (Charlie Neal and Don Demeter hit round trippers for the Dodgers), and the Braves sent over 49,000 home disappointed with an easy 8-3 win. But seeing these greats on the field in person for the first time got me wanting to play the game so much more. Just 10 weeks later, I got to celebrate my 6th birthday at a Dodgers-Cardinals game, with the home team winning handily over messers Musial, White, Boyer, and Flood 8-2. And guess who started that day? Drysdale!

This time the 'Big D' not only pitched a complete game seven-hitter for his 13th win of the season, but also belted his 4th homer into the left-center field

Dealing with Coliseum stars Maury Wills (left) and Tommy Davis over the decades has been a sheer pleasure— photo by Kevin Reece

stands, while going 2-4 with 3 rbi's and of course, he hit a batter. Wow, I loved this guy. He could do it all. And Fairly got two hits with an rbi, as did Snider and Wills. Neal went 3-5 with a solo blast and needless to say baseball was solidified in my life FOR GOOD!

I couldn't wait for my turn to play and finally got that chance in Little League while setting my piano lessons aside for good. But the key word in this instance was "little," as I was usually the smallest kid on any team. Not exactly what a coach or manager was looking for but again, whatever it took to first make the team...and then get some playing time. I never had little man's syndrome with any bitterness, like others I knew of. I only wanted a chance to play.

From Little League to American Legion to my thankfully one and only game of semi-pro ball (to be recalled later), I played the game with passion. Just the feel of that horsehide in my hand and playing catch was enough to make my day. From my earliest memory, I would always leave our neighborhood grade school at Linda Vista and walk right around the bend to Blair Hills Park just to play with any ball—a baseball, basketball, and sometimes football. We had some great home run derby games that really honed my skills— just play baby!

FUN BUT PAINFUL FACTS

I broke my nose playing in one of those home run derby games after a collision with my close buddy Dave Gold. He saw stars, while I saw the ball in my glove—with blood pouring out of my nose like a faucet. But I caught it! And then there was the time while in high school that I was playing at Poinsettia Park in L.A. and lost a battle with a huge metal light post. Playing left field I ran down a foul pop fly, hustling like chasing after a burglar, and just missed hitting that pole straight on (head first) and fortunately only clipping it with my knee. That was a very close call but again—I caught it! What else matters?

Maniacally playing center or left field, I got to roam the short outfield at Blair Hills Park (surrounded by a basketball court) and dive into a protected hillside made of ice plants as our outfield wall. That gave me something soft with which to collide when trying to catch every hit ball and steal hits away from my friends, which built up more courage to go after anything hit near me. Green ice plant stained clothes was my personal badge of honor as a kid, getting me ready to bang into real outfield walls.

With a decent arm for a slightly built teen, I begged for the bigger and faster guys to run on me...whom I could tell would look at me as an inferior athlete. But that was just fine, specifically when I threw them out at a base. No one should underestimate me on that field! At least that's how I felt at the time. Again, whatever it took...while just enjoying a playful childhood that evolved in my native town of L.A.

❏ WATCHING AND MEETING MY TV FAVES

As a very young guy, I loved watching television (even in only black and white), and the Southland had some perfect programming for us little tykes. Definitely one of my earliest favorites was 'Cartoon Express with Engineer Bill.' He called all of his audience 'engineers,' which made us feel important. My mother (and likely millions of others) regularly got their little ones to drink their milk with his "red light/green light" routine from what he called 'the roundhouse.'

Whenever Engineer Bill's train station light flashed green on the screen, it would be time to lift my glass to take a gulp and of course it was then time to stop whenever the red light came on, teaching us to never go on red. Furthermore, the staff announcer loved to mess with us by saying 'red light' a few times, instructing us to be patient and to wait for the green light signal. This made my mom's job a helluva lot easier, using a TV show to occasionally babysit me when I wasn't very motivated to drink my entire glass of milk. In addition, on occasion, when I actually finished my glass, it was a time to be praised. Not bad for a fake train engineer who would teach us kiddies good manners as a true authority figure outside of our own family.

In time, Engineer Bill became like family, similar to the smiley host of another kid's show called "Sheriff John's Lunch Brigade." 'Sheriff' John Rovick opened the show by singing 'Laugh and be happy and the world will laugh with you.' Pretty solid words that every kid of ANY age should try to live by. Me and the rest of the city wanted to have one of his personalized birthday presents, when he sang 'put another candle on my birthday cake.' If it was sung to you, YOU were the star of the day and all of L.A.

What a kick to meet Sheriff John one time as a kid (almost like meeting an uncle for the first time) and always appreciated him trying to help teach young kids good behavior and values. I understand that he really was a good guy in real life too (which is always refreshing to learn).

To me, however, there was nothing like religiously watching Popeye cartoons and then imitating his voice to anyone who would listen. How cool is it that decades later, actually getting to work at the same radio station (KNX) with our local Popeye show host Tom Hatten? He was a trained actor (he did a movie with Elvis called 'Easy Come, Easy Go') and hosted a live show called 'The Pier 5 Club,' later known as 'The Popeye Show,' while wearing his navy whites on KTLA Channel 5 for eight years. What Tom and our other childhood TV heroes of the day who entertained us daily meant can never be measured in importance!

A special Tom Hatten treasure

Those early TV game shows were the best, like 'Let's Make a Deal' with host Monty Hall. I later learned he was Canadian and a hockey fan, and it was a blast to meet him at the Inglewood Forum when he became a Kings fan and attended many games there in the early days of the Kings expansion franchise. Monty was a little more subdued in person but always pleasant to say hello to, whether we had guessed what was behind door #1 or not!

I was also inspired by many of the game show announcers as there was something special about their tone that I hoped to emulate someday. My earliest recall was a game show called 'Seven Keys' with Jack Narz (who was the brother of longtime popular TV host Tom Kennedy). I admired Mr. Narz' deep toned voice, which was like listening to a top opera star. His smooth enunciation just stuck in my mind, as those inner inspirations continued to grow.

❑ SUPER CLASSIC TV

My favorites of the golden age TV shows before age 10 were 'Superman,' 'Sea Hunt,' 'Combat!,' and 'The Rifleman.' Give me George Reeves as THE perfect and ONLY Superman and Clark Kent—no matter the movie or era? There could never be another actor who could come close to matching what he brought to those roles. Reeves WAS Superman, the rest were just wannabees—end of story!

What will always stick with me was when my mother said that Reeves had suffered a tragic death at the age of 45, when I was just six years old, and how stunned I was that Superman was actually dead. His mysterious reported death (by a suicidal gun shot) will likely never be solved and what a waste of a life—selfishly resulting in no more great new Superman episodes to enjoy.

DID YOU KNOW?

You can also find a young George Reeves in his first credited film role in the classic 'Gone With the Wind' (as Scarlett O'Hara's beau), but credited under the wrong casting name—check that out sometime!

And then there was 'Sea Hunt' and its star Lloyd Bridges. I was too young to realize that he had been in two of my uncle Carl Foreman's movies ('High Noon' and 'Home of the Brave') and that he too, was a victim of the 'Blacklist' period, and this was his comeback from that national debacle.

Decades later, I would very proudly get to meet Mr. Bridges when he was a season ticket holder at our pro tennis tournament at UCLA, finally getting the opportunity to shake his hand and introduce myself while receiving that classic smile. WOW, I used to love watching him play Mike Nelson, who as a former Navy frogman gave us weekly underwater adventures, regularly stopping villains in only the way that he could. It's always special to meet someone whom you admire, but when they're as friendly as Mr. Bridges was, it was even that much more gratifying.

I thought it was awesome when finding out that Bridges actually learned to scuba dive just for this part, which was so serious yet totally believable, and had many of us wanting to do the same. At the end of each episode, Mr. Bridges always stood out to me when as himself, delivering either a personal promo to watch the show next week or with some very believable message, often to be careful in the potentially dangerous waters when skin diving. The show lasted just four seasons on TV until I was eight years old. If you've not seen any of the 155 episodes, I highly recommend checking it out sometime to watch TV's greatest frogman ever!

Us more mature SoCal folk would be the only who remember that 'Sea Hunt' was filmed around the ocean waters at our long extinct 'Marineland of the Pacific,' only the 2nd public oceanarium when it opened in 1954 and one of our local tourist attractions located at the Palos Verdes peninsula, until it closed forever in 1987. To this day, the P.V. locals mourn the loss of this special site, but fortunately now have a beautiful 5-star resort in its place. I guess that's progress?

And then there was the ridiculously zany slapstick comedy of the Soupy Sales Show. It was an unusual kid's show that was really written for adults with 'co-star' puppet characters White Fang, Black Tooth, Pookie, and friends doing and saying things that only grown-ups could truly get. He became so cult-like that the likes of Frank Sinatra, Sammy Davis, and Joey Bishop would make pie-in-the-face appearances. Sales was an hilarious radio guy turned TV performer who always provided belly-laughs. Subsequently, when I got to meet Soupy once at a local appearance, it was like meeting comedy royalty. On the way out I got a picture, but would've preferred a pie in the schnoz, while doing the Soupy Shuffle! Never forget this TV pioneer's sage advice, "Be true to your teeth, so they won't be false to you."

From the Sobel collection, giveaway at Soupy's personal appearance

❏ NOT JUST ANOTHER DAM DAY!

On what should've been just another Saturday morning on December 14, 1963, while 'Louie Louie' by the Kingsmen could be heard seemingly every minute on your car radio, my mother got ready to play in her regular bowling league at nearby Rodeo Bowl. Just after finishing their games, she was informed that no one could leave the building, with word of the now infamous Baldwin Hills dam disaster taking place at that moment.

Mom and others had to be helicoptered from the roof to safety as we watched on KTLA-TV, with cars being sent down river-like water surges just down the block from us at Rodeo Road and La Cienega. It didn't take us long to realize that this was about to cause some seriously destructive flooding in the area, with a leak in the reservoir getting worse by the minute. It was only a few short blocks away—just west from where my Grandma Fannie lived. We were extremely fortunate that it was just out of harm's way when the entire area was informed with barely enough time to safely evacuate.

DID YOU KNOW?

This was the first time in TV history that aerial pictures of any disaster were broadcast live (while also shown nationally), It was four hours after the original leak that the dam totally gave way for over another hour of major flooding until it was dry. This was millions of gallons of water up to 30 feet high flowing down the steep streets of Baldwin Hills (about two football fields away from my neighborhood, just on the other side of La Cienega). It was later reported to be 380 million gallons of water crashing down those streets in just 77 minutes.

We had to wait a few hours until knowing for sure that my mother was safe, as her car along with many many others were either severely damaged or sent through the streets (along with large appliances and furniture) literally like toys. A downhill run of mud of about a mile long was formed by all the flooding. All in all, it was fortunate that only five people lost their lives along with the major damage or total loss to about 250 homes and apartments (64 completely washed away). This was in a 4-square mile area affecting 9,000 homes below the reservoir that was officially declared a disaster area on that fateful afternoon, an event that will stay with me forever.

❏ TESTING THE MUDDY WATERS

Of course, being just 10 years old I was as curious as a pack of cats to see what it was like up close and couldn't wait to make my 5-minute walk down the hill to find out. We were warned by our parents about the dangers, with police-controlled restrictions and curfews that some areas were literally like quicksand, and if we had stepped into some of the deeper fresh mud (which wasn't always obvious), that we would likely sink into it without a chance to get away. Because there were many reports of scavengers and looters in the area, we were simply told to stay away, with around 5,000 tons of mud and debris lasting on some streets for up to four months. It was a few weeks until we felt that it was safe enough to get anywhere near that area, which meant speaking to Grandma on the phone more than visiting her place for awhile.

Some days later, I finally walked down towards our favorite local coffee shop Pepy's (at the southwest corner of La Cienega and Rodeo Rd.) and experienced the totally devastated area just northeast of our house. I remember a time sticking one foot in the still moist mud, and it was stuck like a suction cup. Finally prying it out, I thought how cool it was to come home with some very muddy shoes from this infamous disaster. My mother though wasn't laughing when needing to clean those shoes, which got me yelled at Beaver Cleaver-style for just another stupid life lesson learned. On the other hand, I did see some devastation that I could hardly believe was so close to our everyday lives and dealt with it for the following several months and even years.

In those days for most in Southern California, it was the norm to turn on Channel 5 to watch the legendary L.A. newsman Stan Chambers, who was as nice a man as he was an elite reporter. Of course, like the so many other important local news events that he covered, Chambers was the guy we watched reporting on this dam disaster, and I vividly recall going outside and running to the top of our hill so that we could see the famous KTLA telecopter hovering above La Cienega Boulevard in Baldwin Hills just a few blocks away.

FUN FACT

Stan Chambers worked at KTLA for an amazing 62 years, and I had the honor of attending his retirement dinner celebration. It meant a lot just getting to shake his hand that night and to say thanks for an unbelievable career—truly unmatched by anyone!

On a side note, me and a close friend since kindergarten, Carl Mendelson, had been collecting bottle caps from soda machines that were at gas stations, inside stores, or wherever we could find them. This dam disaster was pretty much the end of our collecting days, with too much mud everywhere to wander around as we previously did, and no longer worth the effort. An occurrence that Carl's parents would rejoice over! What a dirty, but fun hobby!

Every kid needs a friend like Carl (who became a highly acclaimed Professor of Geology for 37 years at Beloit College), and I'll always be grateful to him for exposing me to some of his other interests, including stamp collecting which I would do for many years to come. I have always

Bottle caps from heaven were ones with sports stars pictures inside

recommended it as an incredible learning tool for anyone to get to know more about our country and the rest of the world. Unfortunately, the post office is no longer quite needed as in those days. As a result, collecting stamps will soon become as extinct as any of the dinosaurs printed on them!

Although there were no tyrannosauruses in Blair Hills (that I knew of), there were plenty of old relics within driving distance that I'd like to share, giving you a better picture of what our city was all about from the early 1960s. Mom would tell me that her favorite thing about L.A., besides the obvious always better weather than Chicago, was the first time she drove over the mountains towards the valley (now the 405 freeway), with the strong sweet odor of orange blossoms in the air.

Yes, the San Fernando Valley used to be the land of orange groves— EVERYWHERE! When living in the valley, we were surrounded by farms that produced much of our milk (specifically the best chocolate milk EVER at the Jessup Dairy in Pacoima) and other dairy products. Experiencing having the milk man deliver those (very fresh) products on a daily basis and then putting out the empties in steel bottle carriers on the front porch for pick up was fun for a kid. Yes, farmland in L.A. is mostly just a memory now. Frankly, if we don't watch it, so will be more of our film making!

❏ DAYS OF WINE AND ROSES

When moving to Culver City (AKA 'The Heart of Screenland' since 1936), we were surrounded by the world of filmdom. Our town could be regularly seen on some of the early TV shows and in many movies, something that always seemed so personal to me. It wouldn't be unusual in the 60s-70s to see them filming shows like Batman, CHiPS, or Starsky & Hutch on our streets—in their own pre-pandemic lockdown (always told to watch from afar and to stay out of their shots).

They used to film the classic TV series 'The Untouchables' down the hill from Blair Hills close by at its Culver-based Desilu studios. The show's star Robert Stack (AKA Elliot Ness) could be seen just down the street at the iconic Tracton's Restaurant on La Cienega at Rodeo Road, along with the likes of Frank Sinatra (with N.Y. Steak Sinatra on its menu), Bob Hope, Charlton Heston, Ann-Margret, Rock Hudson, FBI Director J. Edgar Hoover, and even the occasional visit from former first lady Eleanor Roosevelt, just to name a very few (who probably loved their amazing Green Goddess salad dressing as much as I did). It was a very old school classic steakhouse that opened in 1956, which served a fantastic prime rib, while labeling themselves as 'exceptional cuisine,' a moniker that was very much the truth.

What made this spot special for the Sobels was it being just five minutes away from our house and my father would take us to this thoroughbred racing museum-like setting on special occasions. As usual, Dad knew the owner 'Red' Tracton (likely through their horse racing connections), another east coast transplant who had settled in L.A. Red subsequently became a restaurateur, because as he once said, "I needed a place to gamble out of, so I opened a joint. The damn thing turned out to be successful, and I've had this pain in the rump ever since!" It was a hangout for some 'mob-types' and according to Red's daughter, Tracy, actual real mobsters, on occasion, as well as individuals who loved to frequent the racetrack (like my dad).

There were beautifully framed pictures from all of our local tracks displayed all throughout Tracton's, of which I couldn't get enough. Bill Shoemaker, Charlie Whittingham, and almost anybody who was anyone in racing could be seen on their walls and often sitting at the tables. This was THE classy hangout after the races, specifically when Hollywood Park was open. It still exists, appropriately, directly across the street from Del Mar race track. And it is still run by Tracy Tracton, who told me she has her own book full of stories to tell us all someday—no doubt!

———— *FUN FACT* ————

The Dodgers once stopped in at Tracton's on their way back from the airport after a road trip. Reportedly, they consumed 62 pounds of prime rib and 24 lbs. of steak, with Big Frank Howard taking individual honors at the plate, putting away four pounds of prime rib all by his lonesome.

❏ A CULVER RETROSPECTIVE

Culver City was L.A.'s much larger neighborhood version of TV's Mayberry (and the actual filming location of the original Andy Griffith Show). Just down the road were two classic old theaters where I attended many movies, some filmed just around the corner. The Meralta opened in 1922 and closed in the early 1980s, and the Culver opened in 1946 and was renamed the Kirk Douglas Theatre in 2004. Just show up in time for the Disney or Woody Woodpecker cartoons, and you were all set for the movie of your choice.

I would ride my bike another block past them to MGM Studios (which were bordered by Washington Street, Culver Blvd., and Overland Ave.) and look through and above the tall green fences, hoping to catch a glimpse of anything that I had previously seen on the big screen as in props or buildings, etc. On occasion, I tried sneaking onto their backlots to get closer to film history. A few times, I actually pulled it off! Seeing the big ship from "Mutiny on the Bounty," starring Marlon Brando, and so many other amazing props (including picking up and throwing their giant fake boulders) made it worth the effort.

Wondering if Mom's old entrance to work was like 'Singin' in the Rain'?

We once got a school-related tour of the MGM backlots, the only time I was ever 'legally' inside of their fantasy land (seperate from the few times I snuck under, through, or over their fences). I very much remember watching the 1963 mythological adventure film 'Jason and the Argonauts' at the theater and then some time later seeing its best-known props rusting on the lot from afar and thinking how cool that was. If only we had true access to getting inside (which was like seeking out the Golden Fleece, just as in the movie).

KING KONG FUN FACT

In the 1976 remake, the over 40-foot tall giant mechanical gorilla could be seen above the Lot 2 wall on Overland and Washington when used in the movie for his escaped captivity scenes. As such, it was damn scary to drive by him at night.

My mother had once worked in the offices at those same historic MGM studios in its heyday, not long after moving to L.A. in the 1940s. They would then boast of having "more stars than there are in the heavens" and making such classics there as 'Gone With the Wind' (not a single scene was shot in the state of Georgia—ALL were in Culver City), 'The Wizard of Oz,' 'Singin' in the Rain,' 'Ben Hur,' and 'Tarzan of the Jungle.'

Mom talked about walking those unknown-to-the general-public hallowed halls and eating in the commissary, alongside the likes of Judy Garland, Mickey Rooney, Lucille Ball, Gene Kelly, June Allyson, Clark Gable, Van Johnson, William Powell, Rosalind Russell, Robert Taylor, Shirley Temple, Spencer Tracy, Lana Turner, Esther Williams, and many others. It was also good to hear that most of these names were very nice to her, despite their dissimilar status. (I wish I could remember those who weren't, for your reading pleasure).

I also heard stories about the great five-time Olympic Gold Medal winning swimmer Johnny Weissmuller filming some of his original Tarzan movies there, while doing his own swinging on the vines (which were ropes), because he had once been a YMCA champion on the rings. In addition, from a very few sight lines on its adjoining streets (along Jefferson Blvd., east of Overland), we could see a huge billboard sky backdrop painted blue with white puffy clouds along with some of the tree locations on Lot 3 where Tarzan did his jungle scenes, which I would try to recognize when watching those old flicks. If only we had cellphones in those days for some classic drive-by pictures. I always thought that Weissmuller was the best and most believable of the Tarzans, and I loved seeking out his history in Culver City.

LOCAL FUN FACT

The community of Tarzana in the San Fernando Valley was named after the Tarzan novels, which were written by author Edgar Rice Burroughs who had moved to the area in 1919 at his newly named Tarzana Ranch. Be thankful Tarzanians, you could be living in Weissmullerville or Janestown.

—— CULVER FUN FACT ——

As a big fan of T.V.'s 'Combat,' I wondered if the neighbors ever got used to hearing the machine guns going off when they filmed that show on Lot 3 (the largest of the open air backlots in the city) with some of my other favorites like the Twilight Zone, The Man From U.N.C.L.E., and My Favorite Martian that were all shot on Culver's greatest backlots.

As a proud member of U.N.C.L.E., I'm still waiting to get the call

Unfortunately, a huge (still mysterious) fire on a rainy March day in 1968 (not related to us moving away five months later) destroyed three significant exterior street scene sets, with some familiar New York and Paris backdrops used in such MGM films as 'Easter Parade,' 'An American in Paris,' and my prized 'The Man From U.N.C.L.E.' A year later, millionaire Kirk Kerkorian bought MGM and began dismantling the storied studio. He sold the land on some of the surrounding studios and used the money to build his hotel chain—the MGM Grand Hotels.

It was a sad day for many of us who appreciated its storied history, when the roaring MGM Lion sign came down in 1986, ending an era that will never be forgotten in Culver City which housed other popular studios during my youth, including what is now called Culver Studios. All of the old backlots with standing sets are now residential developments without a trace of its storied past—except for names of streets.

Those studios made such iconic films as the original King Kong, Citizen Cane, and E.T. When I was a kid there, it was still called Desilu, previously operated by Desi Arnaz and his wife, Lucille Ball. I had always hoped to see either of them when riding my bike past the place, but never did. RKO's "40 Acres" backlots were locations for a number of top TV shows, like Hogan's Heroes, Star Trek, Mission Impossible, Bonanza, My Three Sons, The Real McCoys, Gomer Pyle U.S.M.C., and Mayberry R.F.D. Most enjoyable to me was learning that the fictitious town of Mayberry were actually the same streets of Atlanta constructed for 'Gone With the Wind.' And the same site for the streets of Metropolis in the original 'Adventures of Superman' TV shows, meaning that my fave George Reeves often roamed those grounds along with the hillsides near my house around Culver City, making this a much smaller world than most would ever realize.

—— DID YOU KNOW? ——

The Batman TV show also used the Desilu backlots as its main studio. For some unknown reason, however, it was never listed on its credits. The one classic scene I recall was when Batman and Robin are shown standing on the old Desilu water tower, which we would see anytime driving in the neighborhood. HOLY SOUPED-UP 1955 LINCOLN FUTURA BATMOBILE, BATMAN!

The third major studio in the neighborhood was the Hal Roach Studios. They often stayed close by to film street scenes which were not only fun to look back at, but also to try and find specific locations when wandering around the neighborhood. Culver City will forever be known for serving as a backdrop for so many movies and TV series. And in its early days, downtown was particularly prominent in the Laurel and Hardy and Our Gang Comedies for Hal Roach (and later some Twilight Zone TV productions on the grounds of the old Roach studios). So much history for a kid to grow up around, and I tried to take advantage of it all. We should never forget that many old films whose tagline read "Made in Hollywood," were actually truly "Made in Culver City."

❏ STOP AND SMELL THE FRESH BAKERY

I'm craving warm donuts just thinking of one of our best field trips EVER when my Linda Vista elementary school class visited the one and only Helms Bakery when I was in 3rd or 4th grade. I can remember like it was NOW, just how that fresh baked bread smelled inside of their plant on Venice Blvd. The ultimate was inhaling the fresh scent of baked goods inside of their delivery trucks which we regularly bought our freshly-made breads and the best glazed donuts on the planet from in front of our house. Did I say FRESH? On the way out, they gave us a mini loaf of bread and little a cardboard Helms truck. Priceless!

FUN FACTS

Helms started in 1930 and became the official baker of the '32 L.A. Olympic games, Helms remained popular with many Olympians for years to come. Actually, the '32 Olympic Village was located in Baldwin Hills just a few short miles from the bakery, where the Helms logo was actually sporting the old Olympic symbol on it, which would be worth a ridiculous amount of 'bread$$' these days.

DID YOU KNOW?

When Neil Armstrong walked on the moon, NASA made sure his crew's first lunar meal were sandwiches made with Helms bread. I told you that bakery was 'out of this world' good!

I can smell the baked freshness again just looking at this truck!

It was always a highlight in our day when the Helmsman drove up in their yellow and blue trucks blowing his whistle, signifying that it was time for me to get a dollar or two from my parents so I could buy our share of baked carbs. Add that to the daily milk man and you suddenly had a freshly delivered breakfast. Good luck finding that anytime soon or EVER again! Just something from a more innocent era that's now long gone.

❏ THANK YOU FOR BEING A (KID'S BEST) FRIEND

Speaking of fresh, there was nothing like visiting THE Farmer's Market on Fairfax, now an historic landmark, which has enjoyed success since its opening in 1934. Most visit the market for its eclectic foods. We were no different except for one day in 1958, when my mother said to me, "How would you like another sister?" She meant a furry one, as in a dog. They had a great pet shop adjacent to the iconic big Farmer's Market clock and after checking out all of our options, we brought home the ultimate diamond in the 'ruff,' a silver toy French poodle puppy that only my mother could name 'Fifi.'

For the next 16 years, Fifi was the love of our lives and many of our neighbors, as well as the canine Queen of the family. As you can see here, she knew how to pose like a show-off (although with a true sense of humbleness). The smartest dog and the greatest companion EVER. Fifi has to be mentioned, given that anytime you looked into those huge brown eyes and petted her cotton-like fur, that was truly Touching Greatness! She was the 'Toto' in our real-life Kansas-type neighborhood, but just never made it to the big screen.

Fifi proudly followed in the paw steps of Culver City's top dog 'Toto'

❏ OUR OWN 'HAPPIEST PLACES ON EARTH'

Since baseball was my thing, playing Little League at Ron Smith Field meant everything after taking batting practice at 'Bat-A-Homer' on Jefferson, where we got ten machine pitches for 25 cents.

Among our most memorable well-known special party spots in Culver City was the long standing Culver Ice Arena on Sepulveda, where I attempted to skate mostly during birthday parties. Later, I learned how to really skate for my hockey broadcasting days. The time and extra effort put into that was totally worth it. I didn't want to be one of those who 'never' played the game, so I would have much more than a clue when things happened on the ice.

My years in Culver's Little League were a grand slam!

Culver was also the L.A. Kings practice site for over 20 years, including the Gretzky era, when those of us who covered the team, would spend dozens of hours around this special club. Among my fondest times at

Guess who's the only guy on his knees?

the rink was getting to speak with Wayne's dad Walter, who told enough personal stories to get his own Culver City-produced flick! After 52 years in business, it was put on ice forever when its doors closed for the last time in 2014. Such a waste!

Then there was the old Rollerdrome on Washington, where Tellefson Park is now located, with its famed roller skating wooden floor (the largest west of the Mississippi), pre-World War II special Hammond organ, and with its never to be forgotten 'skate slowly at all times' sign—yeah, good luck with that trying to avoid the reckless crazies! I remember waiting for the 'men only' call to get on that floor, trying just to stay upright going around and around. The 'Drome' was another spot for the stars to get away and skate to their heart's content. Seen there at parties were the likes of James Cagney, Ginger Rogers, Bette Davis, Cesar Romero, and many more. It was sadly demolished in 1971 after being open since the '20s—a definite city landmark.

FUN FACT

The Rollerdrome was featured in films like 'The Stripper' in 1963, with Joanne Woodward; ' Idol of the Crowds' (1937), with John Wayne playing a pro hockey player; and the first season of the TV classic 'The Fugitive.' That March 1964 episode was called 'Taps for a Dead War,' with lead character Dr. Richard Kimble briefly working at the rink as one of his usual short-lived jobs. Check it out online sometime.

❏ DISNEY, WHO?

Not far away was good ol' Kiddieland at Beverly Park, near the corner of Beverly Blvd. and La Cienega (exactly where the Beverly Center is now). It was created by an individual named Dave Bradley in 1945, surrounded by what was once a Standard Oil drilling site. It was also next to Beverly Ponyland, where I loved to ride the Shetland and Welsh ponies around their triple dirt track ring, while donning a cowboy hat. I thought about being a jockey because of it—but never realistically. Although, it is a kick to think that decades later, I'd be professionally connecting with many of racing's all-timers!

Kiddieland became a local landmark during the 50s and 60s, with over 30,000 people crowding this about 200x200 foot park on occasion, on very busy weekends. Bradley was involved in everything at his playground, including maintaining it all, which included its kid-sized roller coaster, ferris wheel, boat, and train and helicopter rides. He was also the voice of the big blue hippopotamus that talked to us kids at the scary Haunted Castle, which was not my favorite.

There were ducks and geese waddling around while I had a few of my earliest birthday parties there, with my grandparents on hand at the huge picnic tables and benches (and it had one of my favorite cotton candies ever). It was also where I got to enjoy personal firsts, driving my own little miniature car (which I was too small to do at the Disneyland autopia), along with riding those little shetland ponies at next door's Ponyland—my favorite was named 'Princess.'

Kiddieland was truly a first of its kind, and it attracted many families with small kids, including Hollywood types who lived nearby (this was on the border of Beverly Hills). Seldom would more than a few days go by without seeing elite celebrities like Carol Burnett, Errol Flynn, Lana Turner, Charlie Chaplin, Judy Garland, Roy Rogers, Glenn Ford, and another gentleman that you may've heard of—Walt Disney.

Walter Elias Disney lived in Beverly Hills at the time and was a frequent visitor to Kiddieland and loved to take his two daughters to this early amusement park. (I wonder how many times Disney walked across the way to the Tail O' the Pup for those classic hot dogs?) Walt studied the children's activities and every detail of the operation from its rides' que lines to the food operations. Bradley's philosophy was to keep his park immaculate, safe, and comfortable for all. Sound familiar?

_____ VERY FUN FACT _____

You probably didn't know that Kiddieland was one of the big inspirations for Mr. Disney to create his own amusement park, not coincidentally called Disneyland and styled "The Kiddieland for Adults.' Bradley was asked to be a member of the consulting team when Disneyland was still on the drawing board in 1950. He was the person who convinced Walt to build Main Street at a reduced scale, along with other prominent concepts at its Anaheim theme park.

As the years went on and Bradley's type of small park was quickly becoming obsolete, along with the increased area rent, etc., he closed Kiddieland in 1974. Four years later, Ponyland then closed for good to make way for the monstrosity known as the Beverly Center. In the process, there went the neighborhood! Bradley did continue to help in the creation of celebrated rides and attractions like Disneyland's Space Mountain, Opryland in Nashville, and others that had become industry standards, which continue to operate to this day. A most impressive legacy—all due to his formative years on our Westside!

❏ JUST A PROUD OL' L.A. FOODIE

Driving down L.A.'s memory lane is making me hungry! I was so lucky to spend my formative years in Culver City, right between downtown L.A. and the Pacific Ocean and so close to La Cienega's 'Restaurant Row' in its greatest era with the opportunity of eating at old classics like Ollie Hammond's Steakhouse, Stear's for Steaks, Tail O' the Cock, Miceli's Pizza House, The Captain's Table, Alan Hale's Lobster Barrel (yes, the Skipper on Gilligan's Island was the owner and often present in his restaurant), and the original Lawry's The Prime Rib (still going strong)...that was some street for top of the line food.

❏ THERE REALLY IS A RESTAURANT HEAVEN

This section is my chance to shout out to my old local favorite spots that should never be forgotten in SoCal lore and I must begin with Sinatra's and the preferred Chinese haunt of numerous celebrities. Ah Fong's in Beverly Hills was owned by actor and avid golfer Benson Fong, who served the best Cantonese dish I've ever had and never to be found since. It was called Beef Soo Chow and don't just take my word for it. Ernest Borgnine and health guru Jack LaLanne couldn't get enough of that specialty dish comprised of stir-fried slices of filet mignon. Throw in their best ever chicken in a bag (paper), and someone needs to clone that old place.

The Brown Derby restaurants whose heydays were during the 'Golden Age of Hollywood' (the original was on Wilshire with the big brown hat) was taken over in 1934 by a gentleman named Robert H. Cobb, whom the Cobb salad was named after. It was where the Shirley Temple drink originated. Miss Temple once admitted that she "hated the drink, too sweet!"—go figure! The Derby was a very popular place for decades, frequented by folks like Groucho Marx, Jack Benny, Katharine Hepburn, and Howard Hughes, and even my dad. In fact, one of its locations was originally owned by Cecil B DeMille…an amazing history for sure!

Chasen's on Beverly Boulevard was another iconic spot for its most famous regulars, including W.C. Fields, Jimmy Stewart, Gregory Peck, Rod Steiger, Buddy Ebsen, Jimmy Cagney, Pat O'Brien, Frank Capra, Orson Welles, and Ronald Reagan, who proposed to actress Nancy Davis there in 1952. Former President Reagan's friend Frank Sinatra often used the more secluded back room for his functions. And no one loved their chili and garlic bread more than Elizabeth Taylor, who had it shipped to Rome when she was filming Cleopatra there. Look up that recipe online sometime, and you'll forever thank me.

Finally, the Hollywood-based Dino's Lodge on Sunset Boulevard, which opened in 1958, was briefly co-owned by Dean Martin (with his own likeness staring at you from above the entrance), and it was used in the show intro for the private eye TV series '77 Sunset Strip.' Just another celebrity hangout that fizzled out early on.

❏ PARSLEY, SAGE, ROSEMARY, AND TOMMY

Everybody's favorite Italian spot downtown was Little Joe's on North Broadway. It was a hangout for baseball fans and a lot of ballplayers who had just finished their game at Dodger Stadium. Legendary manager Tommy Lasorda also held frequent news conferences as a regular there, while having his usual favorites Italian sausage and linguini delivered to his clubhouse office for postgame meals, even while we'd be standing there interviewing him (if we all didn't smell garlic in the room—something was drastically wrong!). And legend has it that Little Joe's was often a watering hole for the great W. C. Fields, who was 'supposed to be' drying out in our area during his heaviest drinking years.

The Luau Restaurant on North Rodeo Drive in Beverly Hills was another fun place to eat. It was decorated with tikis everywhere, with an actual lagoon in the dining room and a different type of Polynesian menu. They opened their doors around the day that I was born, and finally closed them 25 years later. Not far away was Trader Vic's, another tiki laden spot for families, and virtually any familiar show biz face could be seen there at any time. They both had special dishes that are not often on menus anymore. Although those days are long gone now, my taste buds have a very long memory!

❏ A MORE FILLING TASTE OF L.A.

Nickodell on Melrose (at the corner of Melrose and Gower and literally sharing a wall with Paramount/RKO/Desilu Studios, next to the old KHJ Radio during their heydays) has a special place in my heart that will come up in a future volume. Mom liked taking me to the Bullock's Wilshire Tea Room, where I loved their desserts including an amazing coconut cream pie. They closed in 1993 after 64 years in business, but I can taste that scrumptious pie by just closing my eyes.

❏ AT THE HOP

Dolores and Tiny Naylor's were two great carhop drive-ins, where most customers loved their awesome burgers with a BBQ sauce and salads, as well as Dolores' hot fudge sundaes, which were to die for. The old Ontra and Clifton's had the best variety of quality cafeteria-style meals you could ever find. It was also a great dining spot for kids. Some of my favorite fast-food joints included Pioneer Chicken (specifically the Elgin Baylor-owned location on Olympic near Fairfax) and The All American Burger on the Westside, where they regularly cooked up my favorite hickory burger.

Craving ribs? There was always Kelbo's on Pico with their world famous habit-forming Hawaiian spareribs, which really weren't very Hawaiian, except for the piece of pineapple on every plate. In addition, the long forgotten (but not by my taste buds) The Rib Joint in Inglewood on La Brea was a popular Sobel stop in the 60s for the best ribs of that era, attracting some actual celebrities who didn't mind making pigs of themselves in their Gucci shoes on its sawdust floors.

❏ HUNGRY EYES

So many of Culver City's greatest tastes are gone, but not forgotten...the highly popular Ships coffee shops gave customers a 1950s atmosphere, with a toaster at every table and a chicken pot pie to always remember. Their motto was 'never closes,' until they truly did for good in '96 (for years, its Culver Center location was right across the street from the great Surprise Store).

Watching movies and eating cardboard-like pizza from the back of our station wagon at Culver's Studio Drive-In Theater next to the now long gone Bob's Big Boy (another SoCal original) was always like a mini-vacation for the Sobel family, as was the within walking distance Swedish Inn Smorgasbord and its all-you-can-eat menu, including great Swedish pancakes.

I can also still smell the Kings Tropical Inn on Washington Boulevard just east of La Cienega, with a big white dome at the top of the building that always reminded me of the Taj Mahal. It was like being on vacation on some island, surrounded by large gorgeous parrots in the tropical jungle-like lobby and with sky high palm trees everywhere. The

huge dining room served the best 'World Famous' fried chicken dishes in town, with warm honey butter on each table. It later became a Culver City Historical Landmark, until its demise due to the 1994 Northridge earthquake. At that point, you had to settle for the much cheaper fast food, but still just a tasty phone call away 'Don't Cook Tonight, call Chicken Delight'!

❏ WOULDN'T IT BE NICE

Ah, if only to go back to our Culver City Little League banquet at the original Joe Petrelli's steakhouse, where a side of spaghetti with their awesome red bolognese sauce was a perfect combo. Fosters 'Old Fashion' Freeze on Washington Blvd., California's original soft-serve ice cream was the first place I knew of to get a chocolate dipped cone (the only problem was to finish it before its contents melted all over you). It was a place where teens would love to show off their cars with their burgers, fries, and malts—whether they were impressing anyone or not!

Ponderosa steak house, unrelated to the chain with the same name, with wagon wheels as part of its huge wooden roof had all-you-can-eat family dining, specializing in a carving station with outstanding prime rib. They unfortunately went into extinction when realizing that us hungry folk were taking advantage of their big servings, which soon shrunk along with their patronage.

The list of mouthwatering eateries in our area was relatively large. For example, Sterns 'Famous' Barbecue was started by a transplanted Texan who made slow-cooked meats and their amazing baked beans and BBQ sauce; Archie's Submarine sandwiches were most popular well before those big chains showed up; Al Penny's and its ridiculously long 75-page menu, making for a most difficult dining decision; and A&W root beer drive-in stands, where for an extra dime, it was a must to take home a chilled mug!

❏ I 'GIT' AROUND

A garage band called the The Beach Boys from nearby Hawthorne were also very much into the A&W and Fosters Freeze early craze, writing the memorable song 'Fun, Fun, Fun,' with the line "driving thru the hamburger stand now." The band first heard themselves on the radio (KFWB) at their nearby Fosters. The song 'Chug-a-Lug' on their first album 'Surfin' Safari' was also inspired by a great root beer stand, when they would cruise the A&W. In reality, if you never tried their root beer float in those days, you just hadn't lived! Even former Beach Boy Glen Campbell recorded some local A&W radio jingles.

I had my own awesome experience to see this legendary band before they got real big, when my brother Glenn met a guy named David at the beach in 1963 and was invited to watch his guys play at the Grand Opening of Culver City's brand new shopping center Studio Village on Jefferson Blvd. As a 9-year old I tagged along on the back of his Honda 50 to see this new group, which had one single climbing the charts called 'Surfin' USA.' With occasional curious shoppers wandering by the nearby record store, The Beach Boys played this outdoor concert/jam session on a little round concrete stage just off the parking lot at the center court sidewalk, just a few feet away from us. As such, I don't recall much more than 50-60 people wandering by at any time, while we were just ba-ba-ba-bobbing our heads to this classic new surf sound.

Glenn pointed out our host David Marks who was a guitar playing original band member (although not on their first single 'Surfin') and neighborhood friend of the Wilsons of Hawthorne. They had a new sound with uniquely fantastic vocal harmonies. I remember closely watching Dennis the drummer, as he was totally into it in front of his parents, along with lead singer and frontman Mike Love doing his thing, dancing around while belting out the high notes with cousins Carl and Brian.

I later learned that Chubby Checker who popularized 'The Twist' was also hanging around that day. Five decades later, before The Beach Boys sang the National Anthem at Dodger Stadium, I got to ask singer Mike Love if he remembered this event, but he understandably did not, stating, "We played too many of those one-time-only gigs in those days, but we certainly spent our share of time in Culver City." What a way to see one of the all-time bands not long after their debut album came out, before they sold over 100 million more records—during the earliest days of the newly evolving SoCal music culture.

The early Beach Boys courtesy Jerry Long Photography

Chatting with Mike Love at Chavez Ravine

────── ***FUN FACT*** ──────

Coming full circle 13 years later, I attended The Beach Boys 1976 Fourth of July weekend Bicentennial concert (co-headlining with America and Santana) in front of a sardine-packed Anaheim Stadium crowd when the long reclusive Brian Wilson played his first full concert with his original band members in six years as sort of a sad prop behind the piano. This was followed by the greatest fireworks show I've ever seen.

❏ STRAWBERRY FIELDS FOREVER

Now that you're really thirsty after those delicious root beer mentions, there was always Orange Julius (another L.A. original), which was a must as a kid to lick off that sweet orange or strawberry frothy mustache to its last drop. Combine that taste with Culver's early-mid 60s eating hangout Airport Village at the corner of Centinela and Sepulveda (later uprooted for the 405 Fwy), with its unusual, for the time, international food court near where the old Culver City and Hughes airports were located (Howard Hughes and his rich and famous friends regularly flew out of those airstrips, and folks like Clark Gable, James Stewart, and Henry Fonda learned to fly there).

This was also across the way from the old Fox Hills Country Club that hosted the 1954 L.A. Open golf tournament and the '53 comedy teams exhibition charity match between the winners Hope & Crosby and Martin & Lewis—no more golf, or go-kart track or Red Riding Stables there now. Just the Fox Hills Mall, which is hardly an upgrade?

FUN FACT

During their heyday in the 60s, L.A. natives and surf music pioneers Jan and Dean (of Uni High) performed their hit songs at a few Culver High senior proms at Fox Hills CC, as well as at the current L.A. Open site Riviera CC in the Palisades.

DID YOU KNOW?

Lakers owner Dr. Jerry Buss owned a luxurious apartment building in Fox Hills/Culver City where he put up many of his players, including Magic Johnson when he first moved to L.A. And even 'little' Johnny Egan (as Chick called him) was a tennant in a Blair Hills apartment building, giving our neighborhood a slightly higher profile.

❑ HAMBURGER HEAVEN

Our Airport Village, with its large dirt and gravel parking lot full of potholes, was the site of the first Sizzler restaurant in 1957. The original Tito's Tacos were created there, Zeno's savory pizza was served, and my favorite Hamburger Handout—a direct knock-off of an early McDonald's and home of the 19-cent small but tasty burgers (with those $0.10 specials on Tuesdays), which were better than Mickey D's. Furthermore, a red star on your receipt meant a free burger—like winning a mini lotto. I recall separate lines of up to 50 people and more, when affordable food options were much too few, waiting to place their orders (each made fresh) which might include some outstanding jumbo 15-cent malts. By 1962, however, Hamburger Handout was gone.

FUN FACTS

The Hamburger Handout story didn't end there for their owner who wound up working with some guy in an all-white suit named Colonel Harland Sanders, opening more than 200 Kentucky Fried Chicken outlets on the West Coast and then later built up the Sizzler Restaurant chain...not too bad starting with those less than 20-cent burgers.

Aaah, more burgers! Woody's Smorgasburger in Culver City and other locations had the best char-grilled hamburgers outside of your own backyard BBQ—give me the multi-pattied Matterhorn and a trip to the sundae bar and I'd be happy for days. Hamburger Hamlet, an old reliable with a killer onion soup fondue and overpriced but good burgers, regularly kept my parents happy. In addition, maybe *the best burgers in downtown L.A's history* were served at a little stand called Red's, a short walk from my father's office on 9th street. The burgers came with THE best tasting grilled onions on the planet, making Red's a cult-like spot for locals.

Fortunately old reliables exist to this day, like Tito's Tacos (it's all about the crunchy hard-shells and special red salsa recipe) which is still serving amazing Mexican fast food in Culver City. You can still smell Dinah's fried chicken, while driving to or from LAX on Sepulveda since 1959 and The Apple Pan's old school burgers and delicious pies diner are a throwback to its Pico Blvd. location that now looks totally of place—but it still works for anybody's munchies.

❏ THAT'S AMORE

Certainly, more L.A. food and entertainment history spots that are no longer with us can be mentioned by those of you who lived and tasted it. Few, however, could live up to one of my favorites eateries and earliest jobs that also paid for some of my gas money. When the moon hits the sky like a big pizza pie, that's Damiano's! A truly ultimate New York Italian-style cuisine in all of L.A. was Damiano Mr. Pizza on Robertson, with to-die-for dishes, like homemade minestrone, veal parmigiana, real New York Pizza, and as good a red sauce as ever made locally. I worked there one high school summer with my friend and future Sports USA boss Larry Kahn delivering pizzas of course—crappy tips but amazing (and very occasional) free slices for its drivers. The oil poured off of it like the bottom of most of my early cars, but it was Italiano heaven on earth.

FUN FACT

Our boss and owner Damiano Albanese became pretty well known in our parts, seeing him on TV shows with Regis Philbin and others. He would cook his famed pasta, calzone, and other classic dishes with perfect red sauces, which everyone would rave about. Truth be known, it doesn't take much to get me smelling those garlic laden meals just thinking about them.

Other nearby 'unforgettables' that even the great Nat King Cole would've loved were: Anna's Italian on Pico in West L.A. serving amazing pizza, lasagna, and minestrone soup; La Barbera's Pizza on Wilshire in W.L.A., with one of THE most popular pies in our city's history—although don't tell that to lovers of Jacopo's of Beverly Hills since 1970. Just down the block on Beverly Drive, RJ's for Ribs was always packed. I can still taste their baby back ribs with that sticky and tangy rattlesnake sauce followed by the mile high chocolate cake for dessert before a take-home leftover was wrapped up like a foil swan.

Victoria Station at Pico and Sepulveda was a California original classic railroad-themed stop with their specialty a juicy prime rib. Virgilio's offered superb Italian cuisine on Venice Blvd. at La Cienega, particularly their entree of pollo alla (chicken) Vesuvio (mushrooms, garlic, onions, white wine, potato)—a perfect dish, accompanied by incredible crunchy garlic toast in the ultimate local romantic Italian setting. The memory of it has my mouth watering for just one more fork full.

❏ IN A PICKLE

Delectably in a pickle at the classic old New York Carnegie Deli—photo by Paul Olden

Then there was Junior's Deli on Westwood Boulevard, where I would see Mel Brooks almost every morning for a few years at his back table, surrounded by his posse of friends who were of course, laughing constantly. Not the best deli by far, but a prime location that somehow became a magnet for well-known folk. It was very common to see the likes of Robert DeNiro, Jean Claude Van Damme, and Richard Dreyfuss there, despite an owner who was once a customer of mine and extremely difficult to deal with. On the other hand, he lasted a hell of a lot longer than I did in that business.

The actual deli greats of my childhood, many of which are still prospering, are Nate 'n Al's in Beverly Hills since 1945 and Canter's on Fairfax since 1931. Dad would wake me up most Sunday mornings to go to one of them for fresh cut lox, whitefish, chopped liver, bagels and whipped cream cheese. This was our ritual for years. I still make the best lox, eggs, and onions dish straight from my father's own from-the-heart recipe and for dessert a piece of my mother's (via Grandma Fannie) chocolate chip cake, and you're set for the day!

FUN FACT

Recently departed longtime broadcaster and Dodger fan Larry King had been a regular for years at Nate N' Al's. At one time he ate there seven days a week. It wasn't difficult to greet him there while he was scarfing down a hot pastrami on rye. It would be a great prop bet with King vs. Brooks on who attended their favorite deli the most?

❏ EAT YOUR HEART OUT (THEN MAY I BORROW YOUR CREDIT CARD?)

Another job had me in the sales and delivery of first aid supplies to businesses, including some of the classic high-end Beverly Hills/Westside restaurants of the time. You may've heard of L'Ermitage, L'Orangerie, or The Bistro on Canon

Drive a very popular spot where one of the nicest celebrities, Jack Lemmon, used to be a regular. My list of customers also included Scandia on Sunset, the previously mentioned Chasen's (President and Nancy Reagan's fave), Santo Pietro's (T.V.'s Vanna White was married to the owner), Ginger Man—co-owned by actor Carroll O'Connor, and Stellini's on Pico—for 16 years a local hangout for sports figures and well-to-do fans.

Owner Joe Stellini a former maitre d' at the revered Luau in Beverly Hills brought some of that polynesian style to his menu, along with some of his very well-known friends, like O.J. and Nicole Simpson (which is for a whole other book). Legendary Wolfgang Puck, the Austrian-born SoCal transplant who founded the well-known restaurant Spago, recently stated that L.A. has the best food in America and the most diverse restaurants which I won't dispute.

❑ WE ALL SCREAM FOR ICE CREAM

I can hear Chico Marx now, "GET YOUR TOOTSIE-FROOTSIE!" Our best ice cream parlors were absolute hangouts for the rich and famous (as well as us contrary Sobel types). The list of beloved shops included Farrell's and my personal fave Wil Wright's on Beverly Drive, where many legendary names in Hollywood went to get their extreme cholesterol fill including Sinatra and his 'Rat Pack' buddies as regulars, along with Elizabeth Taylor and Richard Burton, Bing Crosby, Ingrid Bergman, and numerous others.

Marilyn Monroe's favorite stop on her way home from drama class was for a classic Wil Wright's hot fudge sundae, one year before I was born. She never did return my texts! Photo by Andre de Dienes—courtesy Peter Sneyder.

How great was Wil Wright's you might ask? Well one story that can be shared occurred when Howard Hughes had someone take him a pint of their ice cream, when he was hospitalized after his infamous plane crash. Good 'ol eccentric Howard became addicted to it and from then on, absolutely had to have his regular fix of Wil Wright's—with its exceptionally rich (and most unhealthy) heavy cream remaining on his taste palette all-night! Perhaps, he also liked those little almond flavored macaroons that came with every order. Personally, I could live without them. My own personal fix was the combination scoops of vanilla bean and peppermint stick—and oh how I'm dying for just one more scoop!

❑ L.A.'S FIRST SPORTS BAR

On occasion, on our way to Hollywood Park, Dad would show me what was considered to be L.A.'s original sportsbar/restaurant which was owned by Ernie and brother Nick Serfas, called 'House of Serfas' restaurant and motel on the hill at La Brea and Stocker. As a hangout for professional athletes from the mid 50s to the mid-60s, it was very normal to see regulars from the Dodgers,

Rams, and Angels there, including Don Drysdale, Ron Perranoski, Lamar Lundy, Jon Arnett, and pro wrestler Gorgeous George, as well as numerous athletes from visiting teams.

FUN FACT

A few Rams players stayed at the Serfas motel near the start of one season until team G.M. Pete Rozelle (later the NFL Commish) made a stink about it being a gambler's type hangout. As a result, they were all found apartments for the season instead. It was a time and place that saw most gamblers as 'types' that you shouldn't invite home to meet mom.

❏ HOCKEY NIGHT IN CULVER CITY (FIVE MINUTES FOR HIGH SPEEDING)

Around 1970, when I was learning to play hockey during late-night pick-up games at the Culver ice rink (the future Kings training site), I was driving home in my grandmother's 1965 White Chevy Impala (my first car that I inherited from her), which was a bit faster than the musically famed little old lady from Pasadena—Go Granny Go! The transmission was going downhill (much faster than the car) and I could only drive in low gear. It sounded like a tank going down the street at any speed over 30 miles per hour.

One night, after a game well past midnight, I was driving up Sepulveda Blvd. at Washington, when suddenly six cop cars converged on ME from every angle. I was surrounded like a bank robber on the run. They pulled me over. What the hell was this all about? I knew I was going a bit over the speed limit but SIX cars?

I never did find out from the police officer who questioned me, although he did begin to waive his colleagues away, after realizing that I was hardly the guy he was looking for, after showing him my hockey equipment bag on Grandma's plastic covered back seats. I vividly recall opening my wallet and while showing my license, naively pulling out a picture of Elgin Baylor and said to the officer, "do I look like a bad person to you? Furthermore, if you can get this car to drive (in low gear) as fast you say I was going, you can have it!" Whether he was a Lakers fan or not, the cop let me off without a ticket, and I drove all the way home about 20 miles an hour, while thinking how lucky I was—but still wondering, what the hell just happened?

❏ BEATLE-MANIA BEGINS ON A REALLY BIG SHOE

Only weeks after the JFK assassination, the word spread that some hot new rock group from Liverpool, England (wherever that was?) would make its U.S. debut on the popular Sunday night weekly variety program 'The Ed Sullivan Show,' which ran on television for 23 years. We had heard of this new trendy foursome, with their mop-top haircuts, several weeks earlier from a story on the 'CBS Evening News with Walter Cronkite,' followed by the airing of their song

"I Want To Hold Your Hand" just after Christmas. Soon, there were mentions on radio that 'The Beatles Are Coming!' But who were these guys? My mother asked, "what kind of a name is that? After a bug?" I saw clips on the news of their arrival in NYC, and the anticipation really built.

Then finally on February 9th, my entire family sat in front of our TV, as a fraction of the over 73 million others watching the Fab Four come out and play in two segments, beginning with the song 'All My Loving.' It was another defining societal moment. We all laughed as the girls uncontrollably screamed their lungs out, while the guys were covering their shrilled-out eardrums, immediately stamping this as not your typical group.

The next day in school that's all everybody talked about. Who was your favorite Beatle and why? Was it time to grow our hair longer? Although looking back at how not so long they truly were, the scenario feels ridiculous now. My mother warned us not to be influenced by these new mod visitors from the UK. It was the start of a whole new movement in this country, which certainly affected the Sobels as much as any others.

❏ I'M A MAN, YES I AM (BUT A NAUSEOUS ONE)

When a Jewish boy turns 13, he is traditionally initiated with a bar mitzvah ceremony to become a man (to be accountable for his actions), but mine was not of your everyday variety. In truth, it was almost traumatic, as I had what they correctly called a dual bar mitzvah, in which another hopeful soon-to-be an adult got to perform his ceremony simultaneously with mine. So, while I was singing in Hebrew the Haftarah (the most integral part of the services) in the synagogue at Temple Mogen David in West L.A. and just hitting the highest notes of this entire ultimate moment, I could hear the 'other' guy sitting maybe 25 feet behind me, and it wasn't pleasant.

Simply put, as I was becoming a man, he was literally becoming nauseous. Yes, he was actually throwing up...COME ON NOW! Imagine during the most important moments of one's life in front of family and friends, we all hear this dude (whom I really didn't know) loudly and grossly tossing his cookies directly behind me with the scent of used breakfast suddenly in the air. This could happen to ONLY ME.

The reaction from the congregation watching this will never be forgotten by me. It was like one of those cheap B movie horror flick promos, when the audience gasps and puts their hands to their mouths. Why me? Why the hell didn't he put his hands to his mouth? Stupid question to ask, Ted—it's timing, just deal with another not-so-pleasant lesson in life!

I stopped, looked at the Rabbi and he stared back at me shrugging his shoulders (like Michael Jordan in the finals), as they quickly called over this nice gentleman who was the Temple's janitor, and as quietly as possible, he began cleaning up the floor on his knees. The Rabbi then pointed to the small podium which held my many pages of bar mitzvah copy, saying "go ahead, everything's ok." Yeah, maybe for him it was!

So, while I'm back to singing away and prepping to be a man in front of my stunned, yet still smiling, parents (and some of my giggling friends), the man continues sanitizing with a big towel and strong cleaning fluid right behind me. I found out afterwards that my bar mitzvah 'partner' was so nervous that he couldn't help but toss his breakfast in front of everyone—FORTUNATELY, not because I didn't hit those high notes well enough. Thank goodness!

CHAPTER 3

LIFE'S A MUSICAL TRIP!

My elder brother, Glenn, was into motorcycles and music and was always playing the bongos on table tops (or just the tops of his thighs) a rhythm that I fortunately inherited some of. He eventually put his money where his hands wanted to be, by buying a great set of drums to play at home. Even with the door closed, it sounded like guns were going off in his room, but it was just him pounding away with those drumsticks (despite occasional complaints from the neighbors).

The best to come from that was then as a Culver High School student, joining a band called 'The S-Squires,' which was later changed to a more hipper name at the time 'The Trips.' They would practice in the garages of some of the group members and friends until my dad built a beautiful new add-on den, which was big enough to have the band (and Glenn's drumset) regularly house their jam sessions.

I would often watch them set up their equipment, thinking and hoping that one day they were going to make it big. They really had a great unique sound, rapidly evolving as a group with much of Culver City and nearby neighborhoods quickly catching on—definitely THE top band of the area for about a two-year span. Unfortunately, they'd made a deal with a local business manager who had some questionable dealings, while the youthful guys also made some poor decisions, screwing themselves from what could have been a nice successful run—not unlike too many bands from any era.

Glenn thrumming his drums

❏ GROOVY MAN

The Trips, however, did play some interesting gigs for a few short years including once opening for comedian George Carlin at a New Year's Eve charity show at a hospital in Culver City. Because the audience was mostly there for the charity and to drink, they didn't pay much attention to Carlin's act, and he eventually said 'FUCK THIS!' and just walked out during his act. Glenn happened to follow Carlin outside and found him to be a very nice guy, as they spoke for about 20 minutes, mostly about how crappy it was spending New Year's Eve this way. A total wasted night for George, but not so for the band who got to do their thing and make a few bucks at it.

The Trips at their grooviest

The Trips once missed an audition at a Sunset Strip club called It's Boss (a popular hangout for The Byrds), because they randomly ran into the amazing James Brown and his Famous Flames next door in the Hotel Continental lobby. The band stood out because they were wearing their Nehru jackets (the big style of the time made popular by the Prime Minister of India), something that caught the eye of Brown. That chat with greatness (the ultimate distraction) couldn't be passed up for this once-in-a-lifetime chance to hang with the originator of funk and his band members. And The Trips never did audition that night.

T-TIMERS *of Culver City*
OPEN DANCE
GARY LEWIS and THE PLAYBOYS
(This Diamond Ring)
ALSO THE ESQUIRES
CULVER CITY VETERANS MEMORIAL AUDITORIUM
OVERLAND AND CULVER BLVD.
FRIDAY, FEBRUARY 19, 1965
Donation $1.50 per person   7:30 p.m. to Midnight

The misspelled S-Squires was the favored home team that night

Glenn's band was so popular locally that they were asked to be the first to ever play at the now newly renovated 55-year old Robert Frost Auditorium adjacent to Culver High in 1964. And they once opened for Gary Lewis and the Playboys just up the street at the Culver City Veteran's Memorial Auditorium in February, 1965. Each act played three sets for an outrageously steep $1.50 a ticket (the year after Elvis and Ann-Margret acted up on that same stage in 'Viva Las Vegas'). The Trips last song of their set turned out to be an exact duplicate of the much more well known Playboys' opening tune. And guess who got booed by the full house, while the hometown band got the last laugh with local bragging rights! Lewis was not so friendly with the guys from Culver City...as maybe a little envy set in?

❏ THE SOUND OF SILENCE

During the British Invasion in early 1966, the hottest tight band in L.A., with a kick-ass rock 'n' roll sound from El Paso—the Bobby Fuller Four, scored a brand new Top 10 hit called 'I Fought the Law' (and the law won), turning them into teen idols almost overnight alongside the Beatles and Stones. I loved that song along with so many others who would hear it regularly on the radio (written by the friend of another gone-too-soon Texan, Buddy Holly, and originally released by The Crickets in 1960). After performing it on the L.A.-based TV shows 'Hullabaloo' and 'Shivaree,' they played at the new Frost Auditorium in the spring, with The Trips as their opening act. My brother took me along for what turned out to be a great concert, with a screaming audience, particularly when the original BFFs played their new hit.

Just after the concert, Glenn went backstage to speak with the band's drummer and came back with his broken drumstick (which I still have). These guys were truly headed for greatness, until just a few short months later in July, Bobby Fuller was mysteriously found dead in Hollywood at the age of only 23. In reality, we'll likely never know what truly happened to end what could've been a group for the ages, but now just mostly forgotten? Not quite. Even after just six months of stardom, the Bobby Fuller Four were inducted into the Grammy Hall of Fame in 2015. I just knew they showed greatness from the start!

─────────── **FUN FACT** ───────────

The Frost Auditorium was a great new all-purpose venue in the 60s, holding concerts performed by The 'CHICAGO' Transit Authority, Three Dog Night, The Seeds, and of course, the Electric Prunes. The space age-looking Frost was also seen in the Woody Allen flick 'Sleeper.'

❏ PARANOIA RAN DEEP

The strangest place The Trips ever played was at a maximum security prison for minors, which was somehow set up by a friend of my father's from the Friars Club. For whatever reason, they actually played The Animals new hit "We Got To Get Out of This Place"... (if it's the last thing we ever do?), and it almost caused a riot, LITERALLY! Everyone in the room was reacting to the words and then screaming them out together "We got to get out of this place" on a night that they allowed the girls and guys in the same room at the same time? BAD TIMING, don't you think? The band members had to be hustled through mechanical security double doors (similar to a bank vault) to safely get the hell out of there. Sounds like a goofy Beatles music video on MTV, but it's all true!

With Johnny Rivers 'Secret Agent Man' climbing the charts, The Trips also got to play on two local TV shows in March/April of 1966—'9th Street West,' with host Sam Riddle, and 'Top 40,' with guest host Bobby Rydell. And after the first show which they were promoting their new record, the guys headed to East Hollywood for a surprise late night gig in front of a packed house that included their friends from The Turtles for a perfect ending to their ultimate magical musical day. The Trips also often played at the old 'Pandora's Box' nightclub/coffeehouse on the corner of Sunset and Crescent Heights, with who knows who in the crowd, including the likes of Sonny & Cher, Frank Zappa, and Jack Nicholson all reportedly on the premises during one historic night.

The Trips just happened to be playing at Pandora's Box on the same night as the infamous November 1966 Sunset Strip curfew riots (AKA the 'hippie riots') and protests began right outside of those walls with too many arrests including actor Peter Fonda—just three years after winning a Golden Globe Award for most promising newcomer for his role in my uncle Carl's film 'The Victors.'

Stephen Stills immediately wrote the Buffalo Springfield classic 'For What It's Worth" in response to that night and recorded it a few weeks later. Stills first performed the song at Pandora's Box, which was owned by 'Shindig' TV host and then KFWB radio D.J. Jimmy O'Neill, the first voice heard on famed KRLA, when it changed to a Top 40 station in 1959. There was also a movie made about that night called 'Riot on Sunset Strip,' with a couple of Dodgers Jim Lefebvre and Al (The Bull) Ferrara getting their acting groove on. This was quite a gig for The Trips who joined some other very popular bands who you may've heard of playing that same stage...like the Beach Boys, The Byrds, and yes, Sonny & Cher.

❏ KNOCKIN' ON HEAVEN'S DOORS

THE LOVE CONSPIRACY COMMUNE PRESENTS
THE
DOORS
★ ★ APPEARING LIVE! ★ ★
WHISKY-A-GO-GO
8901 SUNSET BOULEVARD · TELEPHONE 652-4202
12-16TH FEBRUARY 1967
TICKETS $2.00

Still known as the S-Squires, they got a VERY SPECIAL gig at the famed 'Whisky-A-Go-Go' on the Strip as a fill-in 'house band' one weekend night. Glenn said they really thought they had a chance to be a regular there until later being told that some other new local group 'The Doors' (who also played that night—among their earliest stints at the Whisky) was the club's preferred choice. Take a guess which band ended up in the Rock and Roll Hall of Fame and which one didn't? Just another 'battle of the bands' in the 60s.

The S-Squires/Trips lead guitarist/vocalist and my brother's Culver high school friend Jim Nocerino filled me in on his recall of that night at the Whisky sometime in 1966, "We didn't know who The Doors were, and it was just obvious that NOBODY there knew them. The way the club was talking to us, it was their first time in there. Then, it was explained that they had a new house band coming in that they couldn't tell us much about...and it turned out to be The Doors. We had to go backstage after our set, because a few of us were just 17 (underage to be with the patrons). I think it was Jim Morrison who told us that they had a record coming out in six months and back then, it was magical, and you heard that a lot. On the other hand, you don't know if they're gonna make it or not? And then 'Light My Fire' comes and, WOW!" Not an exact accurate timeline, but you must know that this was all by Jim's memory.

——— *DID YOU KNOW?* ———

The four members of The Doors all met when attending UCLA and three of the band's studio albums: 'The Doors' (with their huge hit "Light My Fire" in 1967 written by group guitarist Robby Krieger), L.A. Woman, and Strange Days were all featured in Rolling Stone's 500 greatest albums of all time.

Enjoying some golf with Robby at Riviera CC

——— *FUN FACTS* ———

The Whisky (maybe the most famous club in rock history) was also inducted into the Rock'n Roll HOF in 2006. Johnny Rivers and his band were the first to play live music there in 1964 and were regulars two years before The Doors took over as its house band. Other new artists practicing their wares there at the time were Jimi Hendrix, The Byrds, Janis Joplin, and Otis Redding. Smokey Robinson and the Miracles recorded the song "Going to a Go-Go" in honor of the Whisky, and it being the first of the L.A. clubs to fully integrate their acts. I loved to walk past the club's marquee on an almost daily basis to see who was playing there next?

—— *Q&A WITH THE DOORS ROBBY KRIEGER* ——

I recently asked Krieger to contribute to this section to suit my curiosity on a few things, and he was awesome in doing so while first wondering if he recalled my brother's band at all? Not surprisingly, he didn't.

> *TS: Do you remember anything about the first time you played the Whisky? And did you guys also play The Trip and/or my high school Fairfax?*
>
> *RK: The first Whisky gig was with 'Them,' Van Morrison's band which was great! We all played 'Gloria' together the last night. Van Morrison and Jim Morrison singing together! We did play The Trip but never Fairfax; we played Beverly Hills High and Birmingham in the valley.*
>
> *TS: Your favorite recollection of the 60s Laurel Canyon days?*
>
> *RK: Laurel Canyon was the best! All the rockers lived there at the time. Mamas and the Papas, Frank Zappa, Carole King, The Doors of course, and Neil Young all lived near us.*
>
> *TS: Did you expect 'Light My Fire' to be a special hit after finishing writing it?*

Watching Robby and Alice Cooper jam at the LPGA'S KNC Pro-Am party in Rancho Mirage—photo by Paul Lester

RK: We knew immediately that it would be big, because every time we played it at the Whisky or anywhere, people would go nuts!

TS: What was the inspiration from Laurel Canyon for writing your song 'Love Street'?

RK: Jim's girl friend Pam lived right near the country store in Laurel Canyon, I came up with the music and Jim put the words to it.

TS: Did you ever play the 12-string guitar and on what album? And were The Byrds an inspiration for doing so?

RK: I loved The Byrds, and I used the 12-string on 'Love Her Madly.'

The Trips never did get to produce any albums, but they did have one '45' single, released in 1966 which got played on some local stations. The 'A' side was called "At Least She's Happy" (it can be found online), and according to Nocerino, it entered KFWB's Top 40 for six weeks, selling over 50,000 copies in California. The group's lead singer Chris Maynard (who went on to a nice solo career) also wrote the 'B' side "There Was A Girl." Nocerino gleefully recalled the first time he heard it on the radio, "I was one of the few 16-year olds with a car then. I was driving through Culver City, with the seats full of friends and with my AM radio blasting, and IT CAME ON. Everyone was hanging out of the car screaming and yelling...it was like THE BIGGEST THRILL OF MY LIFE!" And of course, he heard it on my future station KFWB.

Jim also laughed when reliving hanging in his local Culver City record shop (one of the few where this record was actually available—poor record distribution also helped to kill the band), hoping to see somebody come in to buy or at least inquire about their new '45. He swears that his eyes opened from here to eternity when singer Art Garfunkel once walked in, asked for, and bought their single.

And it's fun to see this record still occasionally being sold on Ebay...I guess for those interested in collecting obscure but the clean sounds of its era.

❏ GUITAR MAN

Word on the street was growing about the potential of The Trips, and we started getting more interested locals filling up the den at our house to watch them perform their songs with my favorite being from one of L.A.'s earliest big folk-rockers 'The Byrds' 1965 hit "I'll Feel A Whole Lot Better." It featured the great new sound of a 12-string Rickenbacker guitar played by the late Tom Ferguson and made uniquely famous by R&R HOFer Roger McGuinn (a big inspirational sound to The Trips).

That same incredible 12-string guitar ('The Ric') sound can also be heard on some of my personal all-time faves, like 'More Than A Feeling' (Boston), 'Over The HIlls And Far Away' and 'Stairway to Heaven' (Led Zeppelin), 'A Ticket To Ride' (Beatles), 'Early Morning Rain' (Gordon Lightfoot), 'Give A Little Bit' (Supertramp), and 'Hotel California' (Eagles), with Don Felder playing the lead acoustic 12-stringer after originally composing the melody at his home.

I had the pleasure of meeting Felder a few times at the LPGA Kraft Nabisco Championship Pro-Am parties where he played his all-time classic 'Hotel California' and was boldly open to talk about some of his well chronicled legal issues on how he got the short end of the financial stick in the group and why he was no longer an Eagle. Don admitted to me that with all of the friction caused by too many intense power-struggling greats in the same room, causing growing resentments and feeling treated like a 'second-class citizen,' it seemed like the biggest band in the land was always ready to break up—which they did in 1980. Subsequently, Felder was dumped for good during the band's comeback tour in 2001, and the rest is history. Just the two of us discussing his guitar expertise, how he loves playing in general, and his co-writing of the lead song from the best selling album of the 20th century, was a true touching greatness experience for me.

Felder playing a great rendition of Hotel California at our 2013 KNC Pro-Am party

❏ NOT JUST ANOTHER TEQUILA SUNRISE

The writers of Hotel California's lyrics were the genius duo of Don Henley and the late Glenn Frey, who became a great Lakers and Kings fan (he was born in Detroit—AKA 'Hockeytown') and whom I would often see at games over the

Glenn wearing Gene's #12 with original Eagles member Bernie Leadon, backstage Anaheim Stadium Sept. 1975—photo courtesy of Henry Diltz

years. I once chatted with Glenn at the same Forum where I'd seen his Eagles on their original Hotel California tour (among my top concerts EVER) and asked about the rumor that his hit 'New Kid In Town' was a tribute to L.A. Kings mid-1970s speedy forward Gene Carr (who became a very close friend of his, even sometimes wearing Carr's #12 jersey on stage)?

He only smiled but never revealed that answer, leaving me wanting to know more. Always looking for the REAL STORY for posterity purposes and my own curiosity, I went in search of the now 69-year old Carr, who opened up and kindly gave me some previously unrevealed insight on that and some other Eagles hits. Gene, whom the band called 'Hockey Hollywood' and was part of the deepest NHL draft class ever in 1971 (picked 4th overall by St. Louis), began by admitting to me all about Glenn's intentions and the rumored origins of 'New Kid in Town,' "He NEVER told ANYBODY EVER about that story. NOT EVER!" I then replied, Not even co-writers J.D. Souther and Don Henley? GC: "NOBODY!"

Gene said after Frey had died, more stories came out on the internet about his own connection to the song, and so I wondered who he told if anyone? "NOPE. I NEVER SAID IT. It came from somebody else, and I don't know why? People asked me, and I said, 'What are you talking about?' But I never said anything. I don't know where that came from. All I knew was that I KNEW IT. Glenn never said a word; I never said a word. It was a thing that we just didn't talk about." How cool is that, for Gene to feel comfortable enough to tell me something that he's never spoken of in public?

Carr continued to give me what I (and many others) have been wondering for decades, "I was basically the inspiration" And although the lyrics have nothing to do with hockey, Gene said he was the inspiration for the title and some of its lyrics, "It's like hey, Everybody loves you—so don't let us down, ya know?" Carr was supposed to score 30 goals and not 15 every year, and that's how that evolved in Glenn Frey's creative head.

Then, out of nowhere, Geno just smoothly dropped into our conversation, "And I was with Glenn when he wrote 'Tequila Sunrise.' He couldn't think of how to finish the song, and I was at his house one night and we went out with Bob Seger. They were close friends, both being from Detroit. For those who may not know, Glenn played with the Bob Seger band before he came to L.A., when he was starting the Eagles.

We were at his house (Frey's) in Hollywood, after leaving Lucy's Adobe, Glenn's favorite spot where we went all the time. And after that we went to his place. It was summertime about 3 or 4 in the morning. And Glenn brought out a bottle of tequila, like we didn't have enough? Of course, we were young, we were 25 years old, and it was summer. We had a couple of hits, and then all of a sudden, Glenn says, 'let's have one more.' And we went out on his backyard and the sun's coming up. At that point, Glenn looked at the sunrise, and he looks at me and looks at the shooters—and says "HOLY CRAP. THAT'S THE NAME, TEQUILA SUNRISE!" I love that story almost as much as I love that song.

Close buds Gene and Glenn in the early days— photo courtesy Gene Carr

I asked if that was a commonly known story? Gene replied, "You know what, I never knew what was commonly known about Glenn. He didn't say a hell of a lot about that stuff. All I know is he had a girlfriend there in the 70s who made him ZILLIONS of dollars. Because every song was about her issues, like Lyin' Eyes and she goes to the cheatin' side of town and everything he was writing was about all the issues he had with her. He used to say, THANK GOD FOR HER, she made me millions of dollars."

Gene also spoke of the unusual way he met Frey. "When I was traded from the Rangers to the Kings, there was a big article in the paper, and because I had long hair, one of the questions towards the end was 'who's your favorite group?' Well, I said, I really like this group called The Eagles. True story. When I first came to L.A., I loved The Eagles, and, of course, Glenn, being a big hockey fan knew I was traded and read the article and went, "HOLY CHRIST. HE LOVES OUR BAND!" So about a week or so later I was going into the Forum to a game and saw this big brown box and it says, 'Gene Carr c/o L.A. Kings. In the top left, all it says was Eagles, Sunset Boulevard."

He continued on a roll, as I'm really getting into this story. "And I looked at it and I go, 'What the hell do the Philadelphia Eagles want with me? And I opened it up it was all the Eagles albums, I was thinking of football. There was a note with a telephone number that said, 'Hey Geno, if you love my music as much as I love watching you play hockey, then we've got to meet. That's how that went."

I then asked "did you ever go to the Troubadour with Glenn?" After a quick chuckle, Gene's reply was, "You know where we used to start out? At Dan Tana's (restaurant), then we'd go to the Rainbow Cafe, one of the CRAZIEST PLACES I've ever been in my life, and then we'd go to the Troubadour. We'd be hanging with Ronstadt and Jackson Browne and all these guys." What an era to be around the right people, in the right town, at the right time.

Carr was also the first and only pro athlete managed by Irving Azoff, who was, of course, also the Eagles manager and he mentioned another great related story. "I hung out with musicians more than I did hockey players because of my close friendship with Glenn. When Irving negotiated my contract with (Kings owner) Jack Kent Cooke, he went in personally to see Mr. Cooke in his office, and the negotiations went like this. Irving said to JKC, I need you to sign a new contract with Gene Carr, three years and an option—just what he needs to make. And JKC said, 'Well I don't think so.' And Irving looks at Jack and says, 'Jack, you either sign him to that contract OR THE EAGLES WILL NEVER PLAY AT YOUR FORUM EVER AGAIN! It was over, and Irving signed it himself personally."

Gene also said he missed out on a wonderful real Hollywood experience, "I was gonna be in 'Slap Shot,' but we were in the playoffs at the time, and it didn't work out." Carr has so many great stories from his up and down career, on and off the ice, and hanging with his music buddies that I hope to get him on a podcast sometime to discuss it all. Meanwhile Frey who was such a fun down to earth guy who loved golf and was totally into sports recently left us far too soon, just when it seemed his band might be ready to extend their successes for who knew how long? If you look closely enough, you'll see Glenn on some old Lakers Showtime videos—sitting in his up-close season seat next to actress Dyan Cannon, bringing back some fantastic memories. These guys really took it to the limits, living it up in the 70s.

❏ TURTLES IN OUR HOUSE

So, here were The Trips regularly practicing in our beautiful new den. At least a few times, my brother Richard invited a couple of nearby Westchester High School grads (AKA two guys from Westchester) Howard Kaylan (before he had changed his name from the more ethnic sounding Kaplan) and Mark Volman (the class clown who couldn't play any instruments but a tambourine—but what a voice!) and both sitting next to the 11-12 year old me on our old leather couch. They were the lead singers in a popular local group then called The Crossfires. Although you probably know Kaylan and Volman more as the founders of 'The Turtles' and eventually 'Flo and Eddie.'

FUN FACT

Yes, THAT Howard not only became the lead singer of so many hit singles including "Happy Together" named in 1999 by BMI as one of the top 50 songs of the 20th century (although originally arranged by him as a joke), but his Turtles were also the first rock group to perform at the White House at the invitation of President Nixon's 16-year old daughter in 1969.

Flo and Eddie just as they looked when sitting on our couch—photo courtesy of Henry Diltz

Of course EVERYBODY has known of The Turtles since (with their upside-down bass drum logo). My brother Richard loved telling me how he had just randomly been driving down the street one night in Redondo Beach, when he heard some amazing music coming from the house band at a teenage club called 'The Revelaire' (the song at the time was 'You've Lost That Lovin' Feelin' sounding just as good as the Righteous Brothers hit single of 1964).

It felt like an absolute MUST to go inside for Richard and to check these guys out, discovering this incredible rhythm and blues sound, which came from a surf band with saxophones that got him to recently describe to me his passionate thoughts at the time. "I had NEVER, EVER, EVER heard live a sound as good as them" referring to the eventual HOF lead singers. A helluva good ear, as these guys later in life were asked to be background singers for other greats like Bruce Springsteen, Blondie, Duran Duran, and The Ramones.

It was only a year or so later, when I heard this new hit record of the Bob Dylan song 'It Ain't me Babe' on the radio from a group called The Turtles. Of course, my brothers then filled me in that 'The Crossfires' had become The Turtles, and the rest is history. Their new folk-rock sound seemed to come out of nowhere, as Richard explained to me, "it was such a different type of music (for the time) that it didn't make any sense." I tried to get a comment from Howard on this, but he wrote to me on Facebook "No brain cells left. Don't remember the 60s at all. Sorry." (Well, fortunately I do) Unfortunately, he didn't want to respond for whatever reason—but at least I tried.

FUN FACT

A totally unknown factoid is The Trips bass player Danny Obst (a Blair Hills neighbor and friend of my brothers) also played some with the Crossfires/Turtles, thanks to Richard's connection, but never latched on as their regular.

DID YOU KNOW?

Howard Kaylan had become close friends with one of my previously mentioned faves Soupy Sales until the end of his life. And Soupy who also was a music aficionado, occasionally played Turtles songs during some of his gags. Who knew?

I was really beginning to appreciate music even more then specifically, when it was played live in my own house. This had me starting to buy '45' singles at a little store down the hill from Blair Hills. I still have that collection to this day, including The Turtles, The Beatles, The Rolling Stones, and some other classics from the mid-60s. As for Glenn, somehow he wandered over to the country western side, and now has his own Las Vegas-based home museum for the country dance bar 'Gilleys' and has been seen on the popular TV show 'Pawn Stars.'

Just when The Trips manager had them lined up to play the music-based daily TV variety show 'Where The Action Is' (a Dick Clark spin-off of his American Bandstand that catapulted the career of house band Paul Revere and the Raiders and lead singer Mark Lindsay), all of their hopes and dreams came crashing down due to some internal business issues. At that point, it was back to the real world!

❏ TALKING L.A. RADIO/MUSIC HISTORY

I had a wonderful chat in 2019 with former KRLA D.J. and later program director Rebel Foster who had hired Dave (The Hullabalooer) Hull—my radio inspiration, Casey Kasem, and 'Emporer' Bob Hudson at the station. He informed me of

Foster (left) and Hull during their KRLA days. Photo courtesy Jerry Long Photography

his strong involvement in the music scene during this iconic era in L.A. Reb just happened to be the co-owner and originator of The Revelaire Club, where he kept the The Crossfires as his house band before becoming their manager. Reb Foster Associates also proudly managed Three Dog Night (he formed the group) and Steppenwolf.

Reb had a special affinity for The Turtles as his management group's first band, he's also the guy who came up with their name. So, I asked, 'Why the TURTLES?" His reply, "I don't know, they kind of reminded me of turtles, they were two fat boys: AND VERY VERY TALENTED!…which certainly outweighed anything else." Not trying to be punny, I don't think?

DID YOU KNOW?

Foster's Revelaire Club was so big for a few years that they brought in such name performers as The Righteous Brothers, The Beach Boys, Jackie DeShannon, Sonny & Cher, an unknown Buffalo Springfield, and many others. Reb also proudly told me that he helped Johnny Rivers pick 'Memphis' as his first hit single.

Foster had The Turtles sign a deal with the new White Whale records. In 1965, their first release was 'It Ain't Me Babe,' and their first record was a hit. Reb said he found the group's biggest hit (and top selling single of '67) 'Happy Together' at all places 'The Whisky.' He heard it played for the first time there, as just a demo record by a group called 'The Magicians.' He thought, "God, that's a hit song!" He got the publisher's ok to give it to his band, and the rest was history. This man obviously knew his music, and there's more from Reb Foster later (including his special connection to the Beatles).

CHAPTER 4

HOLLYWOOD BOUND— HERE'S LOOKING AT YOU, KID!

❏ CH-CH-CH-CH-CHANGES AREN'T ALWAYS EASY

Dealing with life's twists and turns are never easy but certainly always some lessons learned and at this time in the 60s, my brain was all over the place and simply 'gnarly'! My parents were contemplating upgrading our house and living status, and my days in Blair Hills were coming to an end. My father had somehow managed (and I'll never know how) to move us from the only neighborhood I really ever knew (which some had nicknamed 'Kosher Canyon,' due to the amount of Jewish families in the area) to a more upscale neighborhood called Doheny Estates high atop the hills above Sunset Blvd. and Doheny Drive just northeast of Beverly Hills. We were never more than a middle class family, but Dad would always 'find a way' to make it seem as if we were more well off.

The summer of '68 was a total bummer, as my whole existence was greatly affected by moving away from my lifelong friends and surroundings. Like Stevie Wonder's 'For Once in My Life,' it was time to make the most important decision imaginable. Pass a driver's ed course at Culver High before heading down the road to a new school. But in what universe during this supposed Age of Aquarius?

Already feeling homesick for Culver, I first turned down Hollywood High, from where Carol Burnett, James Garner, Judy Garland, Lana Turner, Ricky Nelson and my mother's look-alike Ruta Lee all graduated. The truth was that I likely wouldn't have wanted to attend any school after having my life all mapped out to play ball (baseball and basketball) at Culver, where they knew me and I had solid expectations—although hardly as some elite athlete.

Trying to look at it from 'Both Sides Now' as per Judy Collins, I grudgingly chose Fairfax as my new school. Subsequently, I had to grin and bear it for the next three years and hope to achieve my goals of playing any of my favorite team sports which would be 'outta sight'...can you dig it?

Always practicing my swing

❏ BREAK ON THROUGH TO THE OTHER SIDE

Another of life's most difficult lessons was now upon me, dealing head-on with my all-important baseball tryout day for a man they called Coach Stone, who again didn't know me from Adam—which I was afraid might be my eventual downfall (specifically with this unimpressive body type). I asked a lot of questions beforehand, trying to learn about my competition and what kind of team they previously had fielded? I heard that they could use another good outfielder, which was all I needed to know. I was ready to show them that I would be their guy.

The tryout only consisted of several fly balls hit to each of us (which was too simple), as well as having us throw to whatever base they designated. All in all, it went as well as I could hope for. Nothing out of the ordinary and truly easy stuff to show them my abilities, but it also didn't really give me much of a chance to do what I did best. Cover the outfield like a tarp. Run down balls in the alleys and hit the cutoff man. On the other hand, I had to live with what this coach wanted to see from us.

I closely watched my competition in the field and knew that I could play with any of them. I only saw just a handful of pitches to swing at and did ok...although very much knowing that I would never overly impress anyone who didn't know me. I was a slap hitter with warning track power—simply my reality. But again, I did everything asked of me and then was told we would have to wait a few days until getting word on who would make the team? I felt this wasn't quite enough to impress, so I tried to convince myself to stay positive.

❏ LESSONS LEARNED ON STRIKE THREE

The anticipation was truly overwhelming, as the new kid who if I didn't get picked, didn't know what I would do? This WAS my life. This WAS my passion. I wanted to play ball in high school and nothing meant more to me. The day finally came when Coach Stone read the names who were to be on his team. They were all names of guys who of course I didn't know...I anxiously listened, and then he was suddenly finished, and my name was NEVER called. THIS COULDN'T BE IT?

I was totally devastated and in disbelief—although not really surprised, just simply in denial! I went home disgusted, and although knowing the answer, I asked my parents that night if there was any way I could transfer to another school? NOT A DAMN CHANCE, so what next? I had to play ball, but I had no team. I was miserable for my entire first year at Fairfax, although at least I made the 'C' basketball team which was something to take my mind off of the reality of not playing baseball.

But that still wasn't enough. I insisted on a meeting with Coach Stone to hear from him why he didn't pick me for the team and what he needed to see from me? I barely got a few brief moments with him, when it became obvious that he could care less about my feelings. He showed me zero compassion and no hope with an answer like, 'that's my decision and you'll have to live it.'

I emotionally lost it and told him to his face that he had made a big mistake, while ruining my dreams. It was the first time I had told an adult authority figure where he could stick his decision! Which was an immature gaffe, costing me any future chance of ever even thinking of making the team. Given that it was pretty obvious, knowing that the next three years I likely would not be playing any organized ball, I certainly didn't look forward to seeing this coach around campus. But I would get some minor revenge later, learning a valuable lesson that while tough times don't last, tough people do.

If only these two guys could've been around to speak on my behalf

❏ WHITE MEN CAN'T JUMP, BUT SOME CAN SHOOT!

I did get the opportunity to play for longtime Fairfax basketball Coach Marty Biegel and newcomer Robin Paulsen, both of whom I liked personally. But neither gave me much playing time with my patented unorthodox 'rain-maker' jump shot (borrowed from UCLA's Lynn Shackelford), a high arching attempt to clear much taller defenders in my face. But that wasn't enough to ever make it to the J.V. level, which was also another disappointment with Culver's team always a strong 'what if' in my mind.

I can still feel the splinters in my butt, recalling 'riding the pine' during most games. Somehow, however, I was still awarded my senior season "B" team's 'Most Inspirational Player' honor, whatever that meant? Furthermore, it was given to me during another banquet at the Forum hosted by ex-Laker and future friend Tom Hawkins. The most gratifying thing that came of my relationships with Biegel and Paulsen happened many years later, when I was able to share with them some of my professional successes. They were truly proud, which meant a lot to me.

sobel, ted
"b" basketball

It's ok to be smallest guy on any team, specifically when they let you stand in the middle with the ball (1970)

In 1990, Coach Biegel was inducted into the SoCal Jewish Sports Hall of Fame. Some years later, legendary UCLA coach John Wooden told the L.A. Times this about him, when establishing a winning tradition at Fairfax during a time of strong racial tensions (despite no City championships), "Give him credit, he knew you don't win games just with talent. You have to bring people together." Marty Biegel was also a reserve NBA referee who blew his whistle while the likes of Baylor, West, Russell, and Cousy were on the floor at the Sports Arena.

FUN FACTS

Our 1969-70 season-ending basketball team awards banquet at the Forum Club had principal Jim Tunney give introductory remarks with a guest speaker by the name of Coach Wooden. How many schools do you know that would get 'The Wizard of Westwood' to speak at their banquet—or to have a head coach who was an NBA ref? That was pretty cool stuff for any kid!

❏ LISTEN TO THE MUSIC (AND THE JOKES)

Fairfax High was also known for their yearly free student concerts, as our principal Jim Tunney recently informed me that I had missed out on some fantastic earlier performances (via unpaid performers) by Herb Albert and his Tijuana Brass, Sergio Mendez and Brazil '66, The Byrds, comedy by Allan Sherman and Bill Cosby, and The 5th Dimension, during our 'Age of Aquarius' period. We also enjoyed a number of nationally well-known bands playing on campus, including the Grassroots, Spanky and Our Gang, and one of my all-time favorite groups Poco. Unfortunately, my class came in a year or so too late to see Buffalo Springfield in our auditorium. Only near Hollywood? Probably, and even though most of these groups did play their own high school circuit, Fairfax led the league in quality musical roster-depth. Such huge names for any school concert, which certainly led to more that a few great memories.

FUN FACT

The Carpenters were Plan B, if Poco didn't work out, but nobody had ever heard of the sister and brother band YET. This was just before their first hit hit album Ticket To Ride was released (possibly recommended by Fairfax's Herb Alpert before signing them to his A&M label?).

❏ LIVING 'SPORTS CHALLENGE'

All of the aforementioned was thanks to our principal, who led us for most of my three years at Fairfax. Now Dr. Jim Tunney, who then at 34 was believed to be the youngest high school principal in L.A. School District history at the time of his hiring, also just happened to be the same guy whom I regularly saw on TV many Sundays and now for decades has been known as the 'Dean of NFL Referees' when wearing his familiar #32. Mr. Tunney was very open and personable (far from the expected task-master principal type), extremely liked by most and just an easy person to approach. On occasion, when Jim shared some of his moments on the NFL gridiron with those of us students who would ask, that group would crowd around in a hurry.

My fondest memory was when Jim spread the word that he'd been contacted by the producers of this new TV game show 'Sports Challenge,' likely due to our close proximity to Hollywood and its production home at the Gene Autry-owned KTLA/ Golden West studios (two decades before my working there at KMPC). They were looking for six sports-minded students who could sit in the chairs of some of the scheduled athletic greats for their run-through rehearsals before the debut taping of its first few shows. A sports-minded student? There was NO WAY I could be passed up for this opportunity!

Visiting with my principal five decades later, and Jim is who opened the door to getting my stories published

After fortunately getting chosen, I was asked to sit in the seat later to be occupied by Yankees outfielder/1B Tommy Henrich (AKA 'Old Reliable'), as we took on a Brooklyn Dodgers trio represented by the other selected Fairfax students. I preferred being in Don Drysdale's seat but did what I was told. We answered some of the trivia questions as best we could, while the show's producers worked on using their historic video clips and getting the timing and lighting issues resolved, before the real stars would tape the first shows a few days later.

My ticket to watching greatness

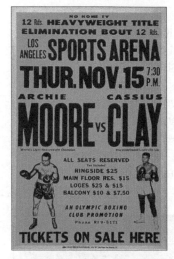

As he'd predicted when I was just nine years old, Clay (Ali) got his 4th round knockout of Archie, who lost that sports challenge in my future broadcast home.

My HOF boxers autograph page from that day

— DID YOU KNOW? —

Tommy Henrich hit the first walk-off homer in World Series history with a lead-off shot against Don Newcombe to beat Brooklyn 1-0 in the 1949 series opener. Yet his most famous at-bat may've been when striking out to seemingly end Game 4 of the '41 World Series—but Dodger catcher Mickey Owen dropped the third strike with Henrich safely racing to first, before his Yankees rallied for four runs and a 7-4 win for a 3-1 series advantage.

It was also quite exciting to get to meet for the very first time show host Dick Enberg, along with his studio announcer Johnny Gilbert (who's STILL working on 'Jeopardy!') and producer Gerry Gross, as they got ready to do a show that would last for the next nine years. Little did I know, until many years later, that ironically my future friends and colleagues Jim Pells and Bob Borgen had also worked on that rehearsal show, and they didn't even go to my high school.

❏ DAYDREAM BELIEVER

After our rehearsal shows, we then got an invite to its debut taping on December 23, 1970. Singing 'Bridge Over Troubled Water' on my way to the Hollywood studio, what a thrill it was to see this amazing opening day lineup in person, which included two of my boyhood idols: the Dodger team of Drysdale, Duke Snider, and Don Newcombe that took on 'my' team of Henrich and a couple of guys named Mantle and DiMaggio. Subsequently, came the new Lakers trio of Elgin Baylor, Jerry West and Wilt Chamberlain, along with boxing greats Joe Louis, Sugar Ray Robinson, and Archie Moore. It was like a dream being around these all-time sports heroes, but it was a pinch me reality which I could easily get used to.

What happened after we got to watch these legends tape their first shows is what is still most vivid. We were then given a special invite backstage and got to shake hands with a few of them (mostly the boxers), while getting their autographs and enjoying some special small talk. They were all very nice and gentlemanly, and I was really excited to meet Joe Louis and shake the hand that had sent so many others hard to the canvas. We later met again, when he was a greeter at Caesars in Las Vegas. Sugar Ray, who was called by most pugilism experts the greatest pound for pound fighter ever, gave me that big smile while signing my book which I'll never forget. Mr. Moore spoke as if we were old friends and wished me a Merry Christmas.

───────────── **DID YOU KNOW?** ─────────────

Archie Moore one of the great punchers in boxing history, with the all-time record of 141-ish knockouts, is presumed to be the only active fighter to span the eras of Louis, Marciano, and Ali (whom he later trained, along with George Foreman).

I just wanted to hang with these guys forevermore...but it was time to get back to the real world, after waiting in the parking lot, hoping to see the other Hall of Famers as they left the grounds. Jerry West was the lone holdover, before settling for the memory of these few hours as the rest of the greats had already vanished into the day. It was if we had spent a full afternoon in a sports Hall of Fame with the actual athletes there to greet us. This scenario really wet my appetite to touch true greatness even more!

❏ SCHOOL'S OUT (FOREVER!)

I wrapped up my three years at Fairfax with graduation ceremonies to be held at storied Pauley Pavilion on the UCLA campus. But after much thought, I told my parents that I wasn't interested in attending and that I wanted my last day on campus to end high schooling as soon as possible and be somewhere else that made me happy that night. When they gave me the ok, I of course chose going to a ballgame instead for plenty of pomp without circumstance (or cap and gown).

The story I've been told that others always laugh at goes like this...as the well over 1,000 names were announced alphabetically at the graduation, they finally got to the S's and some goofball named Ted Sobel. Since I was not in attendance, there was a brief pause after my name was called, before someone yelled out "HE'S AT THE DODGER GAME!"

I heard that provided some huge laughs for the small percentage on hand who knew who the hell I was. So, on a night that ended my very disappointing high school era, I was very happy to be at my favorite place on earth, knowing that I'd never have to step onto that campus again. Like the 1971 Ten Years After classic 'I'd Love to Change The World' '...but I don't know what to do,' it was onto the next phase, with the great Alvin Lee's lead guitar solo constantly blasting away in my brain.

❏ BE TRUE TO YOUR SCHOOL

Like many individuals in life, it took some years until I learned to appreciate some of my days in high school and have since been proud of our fantastic list of quality Fairfax alumni who preceded and attended after me. Among those Lions notables are actors & entertainment folk like David Arquette, Mickey Rooney, Demi Moore, Ricardo Montalban, David Janssen, Timothy Hutton,

With Jim Hardy, who sadly passed away during the writing of this book as the oldest living USC and Rams player at age 96

Mila Kunis, comedian Allan Sherman, Darla Hood of the Little Rascals, TV producer Quinn Martin, and M*A*S*H creator Larry Gelbart; Sports/politics figures like Mike Epstein World Series champion with Oakland, NFL quarterback Jim Hardy, Az-Zahir Hakim Super Bowl champion with the Rams, Sean Higgins NBA and NCAA champion at Michigan, Jack Kemp pro quarterback, two-time AFL champion/league MVP and U.S. Presidential candidate, Chris Mills NBA first-round pick, Larry and Norm Sherry World Series champs with the Dodgers (Larry was W.S. MVP), Roger Stein racehorse trainer, L.A. Assemblyman Zev Yaroslavsky, Anaheim Ducks owner and Broadcom co-founder Henry Samueli, and my friend since school Larry Kahn CEO/Founder Sports USA Media.

Fairfax has also become known as the rock and roll school, with such notable alums as Herb Alpert (who donates to more than 350 music related causes annually and has subsidized Fairfax's music department), producer Lou Adler, Leiber and Stoller lyricist Jerry Leiber, singer/songwriter Warren Zevon, record producer Phil Spector, 'Slash' (AKA Saul Hudson) and Steven Adler of Guns and Roses; opera singer Jerome Hines; singer/songwriter P.F. Sloan; the founding members of The Red Hot Chili Peppers Michael 'Flea' Balzary, Anthony Kiedis, Jack Irons (also member of Pearl Jam), and Hillel Slovak; guitarist Tracii Guns, founding member of Guns N' Roses and founder of L.A. Guns; Rami Jaffee of 'The Wallflowers'; and last but not least Tito and Jackie Jackson of the Jackson 5.

FUN FACT

The Jackson 5 had three number one hits, while Tito (the guitar playing brother) and Jackie attended Fairfax. I sat next to both in art class (Jermaine Jackson may have also briefly attended our school). But they were rarely there during the time of the group's quick rise to stardom, immediately after appearing on the Ed Sullivan Show in 1969, when they soon enrolled in private school. It was an inside class joke when our teacher took roll call that OF COURSE, our two suddenly famous musical classmates were absent AGAIN. With Tito using smart bribery attempts at offering the teacher records to get out of doing assignments. Nice try anyway. I could hear them in my head singing "I'll Be There." Hardly! If only we all could get to perform in a concert that's more important than our art class!

❑ HEART OF GOLD

A special shout out to now 86 years young Herb Alpert who has a heart a thousand times larger than his bank account as a wonderful philanthropist, giving back to our society like few others and to my two schools. Probably best known for his musical triumphs with the group Herb Alpert & the Tijuana Brass, he is the only artist to achieve the #1 spot on the Billboard 100 as both a vocalist as well as an instrumentalist.

He and his wife singer Lani Hall do a lot of charity work through the Herb Alpert Foundation, which supports many causes dedicated to education and the arts. Most important and personal to me was the 2016 LACC Department of Music's $10.1 million grant from The Herb Alpert Foundation as the largest-ever private donation to a California community college, which was after a $500 thousand dollar-grant given three years earlier.

The gift to create the LACC Herb Alpert Music Center now provides free tuition for all qualified music majors interested in any of their programs, which is a rare and almost unheard of opportunity at the community college level. What makes this even more special is that Herb never attended LACC (his musician brother David did), but he still wanted kids without the necessary funds to be able to pursue their passions as he did. Alpert currently sits at No. 7 on the list of the top Billboard 200 album artists of all time, but he's No. 1 in many families' hearts and always greatly appreciated by this reporter.

❏ FROM SILENT FILMS TO MUSIC

Alpert and his friend/associate Jerry Moss started with $200 in 1962. Four years later, they bought the old Charlie Chaplin Studios (which Chaplin built himself in 1917) in the heart of Hollywood on La Brea Avenue to create the hugely successful A&M Records. I remember my parents driving us past this spot over the years and pointing out that it was Chaplin's old place. Every independent film he had ever produced was made at that studio.

Decades later, shows such as the original George Reeves 'Adventures of Superman' series, Perry Mason, and the Red Skelton Show were made there. In 1958, it became known as Skelton Studios, before CBS sold it eight years later to Alpert and Moss who made it the memorable home of A&M Records. In 1969, it was designated as a Los Angeles Historic-Cultural Monument. Its prominence continues, as most recently, it was the home for Jim Henson's Muppets AKA the Jim Henson Studios.

I've also been most fortunate to have had some wonderful dealings with Alpert's long-time business partner Jerry Moss, whom I've interviewed several times as the owner of the great thoroughbred Zenyatta. Jerry is a wonderfully humble guy who got to live out his dreams through his music business and then later with his horses for a very special and complete life that only few ever realize. It was awesome to be in his surroundings, when celebrating in the winner's circle like a kid in a candy store.

In the winner's circle with Jerry Moss (far left) after his greatest win with Zenyatta and jockey Mike Smith in the 2009 Breeders Cup Classic

Herb would regularly play the Star Spangled Banner with his famed trumpet before Saturday morning baseball games at Fairfax during the 70s.

❏ LUCKY MAN

Of course, it's always a kick to meet successful co-alumni, and I was once lucky to speak with L.A. native and former Presidential candidate Jack Kemp, and he couldn't have been more pleasant and smiled with pride, when I told him that we were both Fairfax boys.

Kemp was an original member of the 1960 L.A. Chargers and one of a distinguished group of athletes from the Fairfax class of 1953 (my birth year), which includes Larry Sherry, pitching hero of the 1959 Dodgers World Series championship; Barry Latman, pitching ace of the Cleveland Indians; and Bob Bergdahl, a member of Coach Billy Barnes' football staff at UCLA. Bergdahl and Kemp were teammates in the Fairfax backfield, when Bob played tailback and Jack was a blocking back in an old modified single-wing system.

These autographs, obtained by a curiously fascinated teen, were a result of a very special 30 minutes of mingling with some of the greatest names in football history.

──── **FUN FACT** ────

When getting a few minutes with Kemp after a special charity affair, where I got to meet many all-time greats at the old Century Plaza Hotel back in the late 60s, I was also extremely fortunate to walk up to the most forgotten inventive genius of modern football Clark Shaughnessy. You'll have to look him up, but his greatest legacy was re-inventing the T-formation in the college game, as well as coaching Stanford's perfect 1940 season with a Rose Bowl title, and serving as a technical adviser for legendary Bear's head coach George Halas, aiding their 73-0 NFL Title win just days earlier.

DID YOU KNOW?

The origin of the forward pass dates back to a very few, including none other than Branch Rickey. Yes, the man who signed Jackie Robinson in Brooklyn and the father of the farm system in baseball. He was also one of the first to use the forward pass in a T-formation as a young coach in football—his actual favorite sport.

A College Football HOFer and somehow never voted into the Pro HOF, Shaughnessy is the guy who put the 'T' in gridiron TNT. Without question, it was fantastic to get to briefly chat with him. I even joked that it was nice to have used my initial in the name 'T-formation.' Among the other all-timers whom I was fortunate to meet that night were HOFers Marion Motley (one of two African-Americans to break the NFL color barrier in 1946, the other being Cleveland teammate Bill Willis); Cowboys great Roger Staubach; Baltimore's sure-handed receiver Raymond Berry; three-time NFL champion QB Bobby Layne; Bob Waterfield who

'Crazylegs' in his prime in L.A.—from Sobel collection

helped lead the Rams to their first NFL title in L.A.; Mel Hein Pro/College HOF center; Emlen Tunnell the first black to be inducted into the Pro HOF; and the great Rams receiver Elroy 'Crazylegs' Hirsch who early-on played in L.A. for the same Coach Shaughnessy, who also designed one of the first plastic helmets in NFL history for Elroy to wear after suffering a couple of major head injuries. So much greatness in one night for any kid to be in the huddle with!

FUN FACTS

When I got the hockey play-by-play gig at Wisconsin, Hirsch was his alma mater's athletic director and I had one opportunity to visit him in his office, surrounded by some classic pictures when he was wearing that Rams horn. We spoke some L.A. sports, Hollywood, and his prideful days as a Ram in their first (and still only) NFL Championship in SoCal, when he had his best season in 1951. The late great L.A. Times sportswriter Bob Oates (who covered 39 straight Super Bowls) once called 'Crazylegs' (a name he preferred over Elroy) "the greatest long-distance receiving threat of all-time" and that's including Jerry Rice. Oh and let's not forget his days as an actor in Hollywood and that one not very memorable role on the TV classic The Munsters, in the same episode with baseball's Leo Durocher.

When Jack Kemp was proudly the starter for the new 1960 AFL Chargers' only season at the L.A. Coliseum, they won their opening game for HOF head coach Sid Gillman and his HOF position coaches Al Davis and Chuck Noll over the Dallas Texans and their own future HOF head coach Hank Stram (whom I worked with, alongside Paul Olden in the CBS TV booth in Buffalo). Stram of course returned to the Coliseum with the K.C. Chiefs, where he lost Super Bowl I to the Packers. To think the Chargers came back to L.A. 57 years later, and what Kemp's opinion of that might've been?

— FUN STRAM FACT —

Working with Olden and Stram (right)

As a spotter behind Coach Stram, he was having some hearing problems; which caused me to be extra sure that he would watch my spotting board and not wait for me to tell him anything. Despite this 1992 NFL season opener being a blowout (Bills 40-Rams 7), Hank was very serious about his job but also a lot of fun to be around. I got in a few jabs about my Packers beating his Chiefs in SB-I. "They were just the better team," he admitted.

DID YOU KNOW?

The original AFL L.A. Chargers had a pre-season game at the Coliseum in August 1960, with an announced crowd of 27,000 (reportedly closer to 15,000 with many comps given out). Amazingly, they actually had fewer in the stands for their true season opener, with an announced crowd of only 17,724 on hand, with Hall of Famer Tom Harmon calling the action on radio.

CHAPTER 5

LAUREL CANYON DAZE

The power of music never meant more than when Laurel Canyon was one of rock's most storied neighborhoods and a whole new world to me. There was a beautiful scent of eucalyptus in the air, along with smells of some illegal plants too, as it seemed that everyone was smoking grass. But OH, the music in the air. It had already become a legendary musical paradise, where the best of the era had their careers launched...Crosby, Stills, Nash and Young first melded their voices into harmonic perfection there; Joni Mitchell and Jackson Browne took off from there; and Frank Zappa welcomed artists including Jimi Hendrix and Mick Jagger to parties at his infamous "Log Cabin" in 1968. Laurel Canyon was also the inspiration for The Doors' "Love Street, " CSNY's "Our House," " the Mamas and the Papas' "12:30 (Young Girls Are Coming to the Canyon), and an entire album by British blues legend John Mayall.

Hitchhiking past Laurel Canyon was a daily occurance for this guy— photo by Henry Diltz (in front of the Canyon Store)

So, what does all this have to do with me? Well, when turning 16, with my family moving just a mile and a half west of there, this mostly naive teen would often have to hitchhike and take long walks down Sunset or Santa Monica Blvd. to Doheny Drive to get home from school each day. Groovy man! Peace signs to everyone! This was a whole new counterculture that my virgin eyes were just learning about as a student in a newfangled school of reality. Did I need to conform to their ways? Or was it just another bummer?

'The Canyon' was also the perfect musical melting pot of artists from all over, Linda Ronstadt from Tucson, Glenn Frey from Detroit, Canadians Joni Mitchell and Neil Young, Texans Stephen Stills, J.D. Souther, and Don Henley. And then there was 'Teenybopper Ted' from Culver City, as just a most casual yet very curious observer. Now I was REALLY feeling stoked at the power of music!

DID YOU KNOW?

The Byrds bassist Chris Hillman wrote "So You Want To Be A Rock 'n' Roll Star" in his house up Laurel Canyon, just one of the many mega-hits written in the most melodic neighborhood in pop music history. It was The Byrds honing their sound at nearby Ciro's (now the Comedy Store) with their first single 'Mr. Tambourine Man' going to #1 in 1965 that was the catalyst for all of this neighborhood's progressive folk-rock success.

Just maybe if Jim ever got to speak with Mr. Koufax, 'The End' wouldn't have come so soon—from Sobel collection

From 1962 to the late 60s Sandy Koufax owned the long since departed nearby Tropicana Motor Hotel on Santa Monica Blvd. (AKA Route 66) just down the street from the Troubadour, where Jim Morrison and the Doors stayed during some of their Laurel Canyon 'dazed' days. Sandy's place was located right across the street from where The Doors Workshop Studio recorded Morrison's last album L.A. Woman. Doors' guitarist Robby Krieger told me "Jim wasn't much of a sports fan, and I doubt if he even knew that Koufax owned the motel"—and Robby added 'neither did I!'"

❏ LIKE A ROLLING STONE

I was wandering past the West Hollywood landmark Whisky A Go-Go on Sunset one night in the late 60s when there was suddenly a swarm of people scrambling around and I heard someone bark out, "THERE'S JAGGER!" Yes, it was Mick coming out of a fancy car and hustled into the club, as I continued on up the Strip. Far out man! Totally boss! This was just an example of who you might bump into around there in those days, a popular spot at which even the most famous loved to be seen. Their list of celebrities included the Beatles, who were conned into showing up one night in 1964 on their first trip to L.A., because publicity hound and club regular Jayne Mansfield set up her own photo op with the unwilling 'Fab Four' minus McCartney. Subsequently, the group left after an infamous George Harrison picture had him throwing a drink at the photographer, as they quickly escaped the joint (being lifted above the star-frenzied crowd by bodyguards).

Some, if not many, of my contemporaries were becoming rebellious about societal concerns and a potentially growing police state, but for me, it was simply about adapting to a new area, while growing into an adult without ever being influenced by those who tried to shape others' habits and lifestyles. I just wanted to take in how the world was evolving around me and moving up Doheny in the summer of '68 changed everything, including carpooling to school everyday with several other kids in a crowded yellow Volkswagen bug, who were all smoking wacky tobacky (when it was FAR from legal).

I would literally say out loud, "just get me there in one piece, PLEASE—and without getting arrested!" Any trip typically included groovy music blasting out of the small windows, like Spirit's 'I Got A Line On You' (some of their records were produced in psychedelic colored vinyl patterns—similar to those on some of my new neighbor's brains). It was common to hear many say they wanted to "blow your mind.' No thanks, blow your own...I just wanted to play ball and enjoy my new kaleidoscopic surroundings (besides, it's probably the reason why I remember so much to tell you about)... but it was 'far out man!'

So, here I was, regularly hitchhiking without any 'bread' in '68 from Laurel Canyon down the Strip past Gazzarri's, The Whisky, The Trip (the then recently closed musical nightspot next to the Playboy Club—and no relation to my brother's band), and my future hangout—the soon to be built and very much in demand Tower Records store. This was when a new teenage culture was being (somewhat) accepted by society. Individuals would roam the sidewalks (often aimlessly) on a nightly basis (weekend nights were insane), truly starting a new revolution in our community—full of musicians and actors and many more wannabes. I would just observe and wonder where we were all headed in this new 'flower power' generation?

I still have this card from my old hangout

One thing was for sure, the brilliance of Joni Mitchell, Carole King, 'Mama' Cass Elliott, and Linda Ronstadt, among other great talents in the neighborhood, slammed open the door for women to be much more respected and relevant in the music biz, as well as in society as a whole. Mores were changing faster than diapers, and they obviously made a huge impact on the guys, inspiring them to be better, which society all capitalized on—and thank God the ladies were finally getting accepted into the rock scene to sing and play their hearts out!

❏ YOUR SONG

With this grass-smoking culture surrounding me, the rest of my curiosity would take me to wherever it led—a different type of trip man! Just a gas! In 1970, I was regularly stopping in at Tower Records on Sunset Boulevard and spending hours just flipping through the record racks. I would drive past Tower almost daily on my way home and now just grin from here to the 'madman across the water,' when recalling the time while vinyl disc shopping somebody said to me, "Hey, Elton John is here!"

Not seeming so far-fetched then, I wandered through a few aisles, and there he was doing exactly what I was, just looking at records and more records (in the British Import section of course). It really was our candy store without the calories. But I was amazed to see Elton's earnest quote when Tower went out of business, that it was 'one of the greatest tragedies' of his life. One of mine at the time was not being able to see his first U.S. show at the Troubadour (the most crucial of his career) in the summer of '70, although a few of my friends who did, raved about this guy. I did, however, get to see Elton play at Dodger Stadium five years later—and that was totally far out!

❏ RUNNING ON EMPTY

After finally getting my first car—a '65 Chevy Impala, I couldn't help but cruise Sunset Boulevard (with seemingly the rest of the world), checking out the

As hippie as I got—Let it be!
Photo by Avery Helm

entire 'scene,' including some nights stopping to eat at Greenblatt's Deli or Ben Franks. The whole music world seemed to be truckin' there as well. I then drove a few blocks south past the 300-seat Troubadour club to people watch and see who might be playing there that week. Although still under age, I somehow got into a few of the open-mic 'Hoot Nights' on Mondays, once seeing Joni Mitchell near the bar around the time her 'Ladies of the Canyon' album broke big and thought how cool it was just to hang there truly feeling some youthful history in the room—although also totally out of place.

I didn't even drink and probably looked more like someone who should be selling popcorn on the crowded sidewalk in front of 'The Troub,' as a very un-hippy like human (although my hair was much longer then). I simply wasn't like most of those people but loved everything else about the music scene, when I wasn't engaged in my real passion of playing and watching sports.

❏ LET'S GET VERY SMALL

I was so lucky to have been raised during an era of all-time quick-witted comedians who influenced my own sense of humor and overall outlook on life—being able to laugh at our own stupidities—without today's unwarranted exaggerated guilt trips. Groucho Marx could ad lib like few ever, along with two of my other personal favorites—Steve Allen and George Carlin. This talented duo offered the most clever combination of self-deprecating and observational comedy imaginable (the healthiest of outlooks, if not abused). Subsequently, this newer generation of funny folk had one unusual act catch my eye from the start.

A special keepsake from the Sobel collection

—— **FUN FACT** ——

The great Steve Allen, AKA the everything entertainer who truly did it all and was brilliantly funny and clever once said, "I write in the first person, because I am the first person I ever met."

I had seen some young goofball make his 1968 TV stand-up debut on The Smothers Brothers Show and then later on the Steve Allen show, and thought this total unknown Steve Martin is making me laugh hard enough to hurt. As a result, I would try to get tickets to his show, when/wherever that might be locally. I then noticed that he was coming to the Troubadour for one of his first shows, having no idea at the time, 'The Troub' was where he hung out and where his career was about to really take off. The Troubadour, however, wasn't a comedy club, and Martin wasn't just a stand-up comic. His shtick also entailed playing banjo, while telling jokes via physical comedy. I was one of his earlier fans.

When my buddies and me got a table right in front (where we could easily touch the stage) in 1970, I found myself in Martin's act, when he playfully asked an all-too-popular question of those times, "What's your sign (horoscope)?" Feeling bold and frisky, I quickly shouted out "STOP!" Looking back, not only wasn't that funny—it was also a mighty weak heckle. The ham in me came out, however, when Martin immediately quipped while strumming his banjo and wearing a wild and crazy balloon headband, "I see it's the first time you've had a drink in public!"

Of course the audience laughed as much AT me as they did for Martin. I sheepishly giggled and shrunk back into my chair. Now I was 'The Jerk,' well before him, and Martin was enjoying using me as a prop—which he had many of that night. If only they had future bets then, my money would've been on Steve Martin's success. If so, I'd be almost as wealthy as he is.

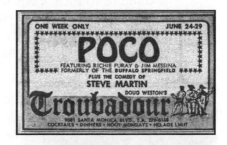

This was Martin as I remember him in 1969, taken at the Ice House in Pasadena—photo by Henry Diltz

❏ FOR WHAT IT'S WORTH

There was something happening here, as the sounds of my generation had come to be very clear. It became a part of me, and there was nothing I could do but embrace it and feel that Richie Furay 12-string acoustic guitar or perfect harmonization in my bones. I was mesmerized by the sound of the Buffalo Springfield, followed by Poco and then Crosby, Stills, and Nash. Add Neil Young into that blender and you just created musical nirvana. It was my only drug of choice, while the whole world still seemed to be getting stoned around me.

❏ DESPERADO

I got to see a barefoot and beautiful Linda Ronstadt (wearing a skirt shorter than my teeny resume) play at the Troubadour, belting out songs like none other heard before or since. I'd been hooked on Linda since her Michael Nesmith (of Monkees fame) penned hit 'Different Drum' with the Stone Poneys in 1967. But I was hardly alone, as every man alive fell in love with her (including our future

The Grammy Museum's own ode to Poco exhibit (absurdly STILL NOT in the R&R HOF)

governor) and that amazingly pure voice. And what fortunate timing seeing the now rising newcomer Steve Martin open for Linda's 'Silk Purse' tour stop on the Troub stage, with her own backup newbies Glenn Frey and Don Henley. These two future musical icons playing together right in front of my face just before they created The Eagles—who were influenced by Poco, who were influenced by Buffalo Springfield, who were influenced by the Byrds—when folk/country rock was born, which so much influenced my being.

Linda with The Stone Poneys at UCLA, Jan. 19, 1968—photo by Henry Diltz

It was an amazing time and place in my neighborhood and at The Troub, where Ronstadt once portrayed it as "responsible for the entire music scene here." Linda was on her way to becoming the only female to have five platinum albums in a row—and later the only woman to wear a little blue boy scout outfit in front of us at the Universal Amphitheater, followed by a Dodgers jacket, while singing the national anthem at the Ravine. Damn those were good times!

The nearby 1969 Manson murders, however, changed the scene in the area forever, and the innocence was gone. Suddenly, it was no longer comfortable to go from door to door, with everybody welcomed to come in. It affected mine and many others' free-wheeling hitchhiking habits in and around Laurel Canyon and the Strip. Paranoia ran deep, and into our lives it did creep...although the area remained funky, the golden age of music, creativity, and culture in the area had run its course, as that complex decade faded into history!

FUN FACT

Sixteen months after her 'Silk Purse Tour,' the Eagles opened for Ronstadt's concert at UCLA's Royce Hall. Each time I saw Linda in person or heard her sing a Karla Bonoff written song, I was more inspired than ever to join my musical friends Lobsenz, Gold, and Mendelson in a garage somewhere and just jam away, singing my ass off while slamming some bongos! Why can't someone write like that anymore?

My few minutes with Wilson—photo by Paul Olden

❑   GOOD AND BAD VIBRATIONS

In January 2009, I was invited to the brand new downtown L.A. Grammy Museum's inaugural public program 'An Evening with Brian Wilson' and to be a part of an intimate audience of 200. My buddy Paul Olden joined me there, as we watched this iconic musical genius and one-time Laurel Canyon resident get interviewed on stage and then perform solo. That's when I got to ask Wilson if he truly did first hear one of his songs on the radio on my KFWB? Wilson replied, "Yes"—making for a 'Fun, Fun, Fun' story to bring back to the station.

But what would've been even greater was a hopeful in-depth one-on-one with this gifted legend. Subsequently, Paul and I got a private invite upstairs to speak with Wilson. But Brian was no longer in the mood to chat—not fond of doing interviews anyway and glossed through a few of my questions, a bit disappointing to not give me much to share with our listeners. At least I got that rare opportunity to interact with the ultimate Beach Boy—another almost Zelig moment.

❏ RETROSPECTIVE: THE BEST OF THE CANYON

In May of 2014, via our mutual friend music/sports journalist Keijo Liimatainen, I got to re-live it all after receiving an invitation from legendary rock photog Henry Diltz to see the opening of his 'California Dreamin,' The Sounds of Laurel Canyon 1965-1977 exhibition also at the Grammy Museum. Keijo and another friend and colleague Gunnar Nordstrom were the producers of a wonderful 90-minute documentary on Diltz ("The Accidental Photographer"), so again, the timing was perfect.

Just a neato time hanging with Henry

An on-stage panel discussion featured Diltz, whom Garth Brooks once described with conviction: "He is God in this industry." And it truly was groovy getting to chat with the official photog of Woodstock '69 on his special night. Joining Henry were 'The Monkees' Micky Dolenz (who my brother Glenn briefly managed, when as a TV director), Danny Hutton one of the three lead vocalists of Three Dog Night, Art Podell (singer/songwriter) half of the iconic Greenwich Village duo 'Art and Paul' and an original member of the popular early folk group 'The New Christy Minstrels, Gail Zappa (Frank's widow), and others before I headed across the street to work a Clippers-Thunder playoff game.

Spending a very 'Pleasant Valley Sunday' speaking with Dolenz

Hanging with such vintage artists like Dolenz and Podell at the show's end was a blast, but an even bigger kick because remarkably both had a clue who I was, as longtime listeners to KFWB's rock and sports news formats, which I guess was just another sort of L.A. thing. Micky wanted to talk some 'WB history (as a SoCal native), while Art is an absolute rabid Dodger fan, growing up in Brooklyn. He saw Jackie Robinson play his first season, while living around the corner from the great Gil Hodges. He wondered when we ALL might get to see the Dodgers on local TV again? I

Talking baseball with Art, the longtime marvelous minstrel

told him to not hold his breath, and then six years later—it finally happened, on of course April Fool's Day during a pandemic.

The very personable Podell, with stories galore, talked of some of his days playing Greenwich Village in New York. He was the guy who recommended the beautiful melodious voice of Mary Travers to fellow folk singers Peter and Paul (and you know the rest—although he doesn't take full credit for that). Art also later disclosed to me his association with the recently deceased mega-star Kenny Rogers and how he helped to catapult the start of his career with 'The New Christy Minstrels,' Podell recalled, "I helped audition and hire Kenny, so I could leave the Minstrels. We found him in Houston playing bass in a jazz trio (The Bobby Doyle Trio). I informed him he was hired in the parking lot." What a great time to be an attendant in that lot! The rest is history. Who knows what direction Rogers' life may have gone without that gig?

Podell also described how it was being THE first folk singer to play the Troubadour (and unpaid). "He (club owner Doug Weston) couldn't afford to pay and was getting ready to close the place down. The only reason he would put me in there was because a good friend of mine in California when I first landed knew him, and he set us up. When I met him (Weston), he said to me, 'I don't even know if we can stay open. I don't know what to do?' Maybe jazz, but there was no folk music there. It was just startling." Almost 60 years later, the Troub is still standing.

DID YOU KNOW?

Legendary comic Lenny Bruce was once arrested on obscenity charges at the Troubadour for using the word 'schmuck' during his routine on stage. This schmuck should've been put away for decades for using far worse during my hockey broadcasts!

FUN FACT

Podell's early folk duo of Art and Paul, who recorded the classic 'Puff, the Magic Dragon' more than a year before the Peter, Paul, and Mary hit, made it easy for another New York folk-rock twosome to go with Simon & Garfunkel, when changing their name from Tom & Jerry in 1963.

To completely set the record straight, Art Podell was the earliest of them all to be a Laurel Canyon resident as he confided in me, "I moved up to Laurel Canyon in 1961 and I needed a roommate and grabbed some young kid named Jim McGuinn, who changed his name to Roger later (Yes, the same guy who co-founded The Byrds). He was my roommate because I couldn't afford the place all by myself. And McGuinn and I were the seeds who began the whole thing up there, because everybody else followed us."

How's that for a bit of mostly unknown history? This completed a special night for me with the Laurel Canyon dwellers. I lived it (to a point), and it was amazing to re-live it all over again in our own time-capsuled like museum! While many were really just California Dreamin', it was truly my reality LIVE AND IN PERSON, and I wouldn't have it any other way.

The End—photo by Henry Diltz

CHAPTER 6

EARLY VEGAS BABY

❏ THE SOUNDTRACK TO OLD LAS VEGAS

As a kid growing up in L.A., I would see most families take their usual vacations—to the lakes, the mountains, beautiful beach spots, the Grand Canyon, etc. But the Sobels? It was always through the middle of the barren Mojave Desert onto Vegas, Vegas, and more Vegas! Unfortunately, there was absolutely nothing for kids to do there in those late 1950s-60s. We had to kill time, while wondering if our parents were wagering away our hard earned silver dollars? They loved everything about the classic early Vegas experience, and we simply had to go along with it until later learning to appreciate it all.

———— (NOT SO) FUN FACT ————

WTF! My mother once deposited my entire Vegas collection of very old silver dollars in the bank—but NOT in a safe deposit box, meaning that they had vanished forever. I will never get over that, along with her not notifying me when tossing out my huge closet-full baseball card collection nicely stored in shoe boxes from the early 60s (which decades later could have bought us a house). She labeled it 'a fire hazard,' but silver dollars a fire hazard?

In the early 60s, we would mostly stay at the 'in' place of the time the Sands Hotel AKA: 'A Place In The Sun.' It was the coolest spot in town then, especially after the 1960 cult-like crime/comedy flick Ocean's 11 gave it iconic status. It was just like being in the movie, when we checked in a few times every year. As the frequent haunt of the famed Rat Pack (Frank Sinatra, Dean Martin, Sammy Davis, Jr., Joey Bishop, and Peter Lawford), the Sands had a mystique that could never be equaled before or since.

My day would consist of the same things each and every time visiting there—wandering the nearby grounds, which in those days, instead of giant hotels next door, there were only giant desert ants that I chased around their little barren sand dunes, as we

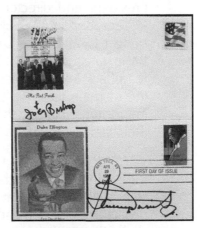

Joey Bishop and Sammy Davis signed first-day covers from my collection.

all tried to understand how a mirage could form in the street. I'd then linger at the Paradise Pool with my siblings, walk directly across the street to Bud's

Liquor Store (to get ANOTHER free miniature plastic slot machine given out with any purchase—which was mostly gum), and then went next door to The Castaways, a Polynesian-themed hotel/casino (now the Mirage).

With only time to kill, I would usually just hang over the lobby rail overlooking the glitzy Sands casino, checking out my parents at whatever table they would be playing at, while regularly having my hotel bellman buddy Bo Schneider drive me around in his snazzy electric tram. Bo didn't just regularly drive me anywhere between his duties of checking folks in, he was also my personal Rat Pack tour guide (well before it was popular), showing me where Frank and Dean and Sammy and the others stayed when playing the world-renowned Copa Room, a showroom that was the epitome of classic old Vegas. I wasn't even ten years old, but got an inside look that any Entertainment Tonight producer would've killed to be a part of. I might see Martin returning from a golf game or with his buddies in the fancy-shmancy Garden Room restaurant or around the popular Sunrise Terrace, overlooking the beautiful views of Sunrise Mountain.

SANDS FUN FACTS

This was all before the Sands had a high rise with a view, so there were no tower suites, just simple motel-like two-story wings with nice bungalows, each named after a famous thoroughbred racetrack as in Hollywood Park, Aqueduct, Belmont Park, Garden State, and Arlington Park. Each bungalow had its own different amount of prestige. I would often just sit outside at night and watch the big neon Sands marquee light up the desesrt sky in script form.

❏ THE MAN WHO MADE IT ALL HAPPEN

My father somehow knew Mr. Jack Entratter, who was the longtime Sands president and director of entertainment after his years running the famed Copacabana in NYC. He oversaw their main showroom and had the biggest budget to attract the biggest names often in the earlier days, with the Count Basie Orchestra behind them. For years, the Sands main marquee always read 'Jack Entratter presents.' One time in bold letters, the marquee featured the ultimate tease of 'DEAN MARTIN—MAYBE FRANK, MAYBE SAMMY.' Their impromptu sold-out shows would attract even some individuals who slept in their cars just to be on the grounds when no rooms were available.

Dad would stress that Mr. Entratter was the one man most responsible for putting Vegas on the map, with his show biz contact list longer than the strip itself and with that amazingly high entertainment budget of over a million dollars a year in the early 60s. As such, he always made it a point to have me shake Entratter's hand whenever making contact there—the perfect example of 'it's who you know baby!' The Copa Room became THE place for any big-name entertainer to show off their skills. It was easily the best part of my stay there getting to see them all perform.

The Sands is where Dad taught me how to hand the maitre d' a tip (at the Copa Room entrance) by calmly rolling up the bill and shaking his hand, while requesting the best table possible, which for us was most often at the stage or very close to it. That always made this little kid feel like a big shot—in a fun way!

── **DID YOU KNOW?** ──

U.S. Presidents couldn't resist The Sands then, with John F. Kennedy a visitor just three months before his assassination, and Harry Truman being seen playing piano with the great Jimmy Durante. Also appearing at the Copa Room in '63 was Joey Bishop when teaming up with Dodger stars Don Drysdale, Frank Howard, Tommy and Willie Davis, Ron Perranoski, and Bill Skowron—my kind of show!

From the Sobel collection

❏ RAT TALES

The Rat Pack era was simply the greatest to see the top entertainers of all-time, many of whom appeared at the Sands and Sahara hotels at the time. When I was about eight years old, my mother and I were walking through the Sands casino and coming our way was the least known of the Pack, Peter Lawford whom I had previously asked why was he famous? (We later saw him perform his song and dance show on stage.) Actually, I had seen him wandering in the casino a few times. Mom said he was simply an actor turned socialite, who got connected with Sinatra when he was married into the Kennedy family, before becoming the brother-in-law to JFK. Was that a good reason?

My mother watched as I approached Lawford, when he bent down to put his hand on my shoulder and said, "Hi pal." Mom quickly introduced me to him, and he smiled back and with that smooth British accent replied, "It's so nice to meet you Teddy." I shook his hand and he walked away. I then soon asked Mom again, "I still don't understand what makes him famous?" She laughed, as we moved on and never let me forget that moment—which is why it has stuck with me all these years later. Its been said that Lawford was 'famous for being famous' and now I get it—sort of like one of the Kardashians (except with SOME talent).

With my father often introducing me to his influential friends he would always repeat, "you never know when they might be in your life." This advice was on my mind when he was walking me over to Joey Bishop, after a function at the Friars Club. That meeting turned out to be a nice interaction with one of the Rat Packers.

DID YOU KNOW?

The original Rat Pack group began in the Holmby Hills (West L.A.) home of Humphrey Bogart and Lauren Bacall. This iconic group started performing together in 1960, which was great timing for this little six-year old, who found himself in Vegas more often than many gila monsters.

FUN FACTS

Lawford's first appearance with Sinatra was in a 1947 musical film "It Happened in Brooklyn." He was also the guy who first brought the "Ocean's 11" concept to Frank, which cemented the Rat Pack for eternity (although Lawford initially had William Holden in mind for the lead roll of Danny Ocean!) Also in "Ocean's 11" was a scene with Dean Martin singing in the Sahara lounge. Alongside him, playing the xylophone, was the great Red Norvo, whom I loved to watch pelt his mallets on those keys like a magic wand behind Martin and Sinatra at the Sands. Check him out in one of his old jazz sets online sometime.

Dad, a gambler and a regular who again always seemed to know the right people everywhere, got us in to see most of the greats perform. Just a magical time to get to be in the same showrooms as the inimitable Bobby Darin, Andy Williams, Louis Armstrong, Ethel Merman, Jerry Lewis, Red Skelton, Danny Thomas, Mitzi Gaynor, Wayne Newton, Liberace, Milton Berle, Jimmy Durante, Harry Belafonte, Lena Horne, Don Rickles, Steve & Edie, Edgar Bergen and Charlie McCarthy, Shecky Greene, Buddy Hackett, Alan King, Debbie Reynolds, Vic Damone, Rosemary Clooney, George Gobel, Hines Hines and Dad, the Four Step Brothers, Abbe Lane, Juliet Prowse, Paul Anka, Robert Goulet, Joe E. Lewis, Allen & Rossi, Buddy Greco, Jack Carter, Corbett Monica, Jan Murray, Buddy Lester (my buddy Paul's dad), and Dinah Shore (whom I would later get to meet and greet at her golf tournament.) This long all-star list of extreme talent was never too much for this kid to feel like a big-leaguer in their presence. And that will always be a part of me.

You haven't lived until you've locked eyeballs with sultry entertainers like Mitzi Gaynor and Abbe Lane flirting from just a few feet away on stage. As a 10- or 11-year old, they brought out feelings I didn't even know I had, when Mom proudly said, "Teddy, she REALLY likes you!" I was just sitting there smiling and thinking, "I've gotta have that someday!" Where the hell was puberty when you really needed it?

Abbe left me an indelible memory with a perpetual smile :-)

Besides frequently staying at the Sands and the Riviera during the early 60s, we were also regulars at Wilbur Clark's Desert Inn, the Dunes, and occasionally the Sahara—one of the earlier Strip hotels, where I would roam the casino at night (avoiding security while in my pajamas), sneaking slowly past the old Casbar Lounge to get a close up glimpse of Louis Prima, Keely Smith & Sam Butera, wailing away with some of the most amazing music. I would hide behind a post and take it all in. That was the same spot where the Vegas Lounge act was born. Dad took us to their big Conga Room for shows featuring Ann-Margret and Tony Bennett. Even the Beatles stayed there in 1964.

❏ NEW JACKPOTS ON THE STRIP

In 1966, Caesars Palace opened, and to walk into that glamorous new Roman Empire was a unique experience during a time when the large neon signs began to dominate the Strip. This was also the same year that the Howard Hughes era began in Vegas, when he checked into the penthouse at his Desert Inn and never left, preferring to buy the hotel instead of facing eviction. The Sobels stayed there a few times. I always wondered if we might ever see the world's most famous recluse, but it never happened.

In 1989, longtime developer Steve Wynn opened the city's first mega resort The Mirage. Years earlier, my mother had moved to Vegas and worked for him in his downtown casino at the Golden Nugget, before he became a big shot. She had learned from my father the ins and outs of being a good gin rummy player and worked as a shill in Vegas (which I always joked that she got paid for sitting at a card table to attract other players, instead of potentially losing her own money).

Popular Vegas comedian Shelly Berman signed this Sahara show card for my mother.

Mom would tell me stories that Wynn was a nice man at the start, but how he had changed. Subsequently, she became miserable as part of a negatively changing work environment. She was much more complimentary about doing the same work for Vegas legendary owner and friend Jackie Gaughan at his downtown Union Plaza, where she stayed for a few years, after an unsuccessful yet relentless run with her own women's clothing boutique called Clothes Quarters on Maryland Parkway, which closed sooner than hoped.

The Sobel family at the Dunes dinner show

The Sultan stood tall looking out over "The Strip"—from Sobel collection

When staying at the old Dunes Hotel, I would love to stand outside and stare up at the immense 35-foot tall fiberglass Sultan statue above the main entrance. He was clad in a turban and cape (seemingly daring you to stay at his hotel), before eventually being laid to rest in the middle of the desert at the base of the mountains, which you could see off in the distance for many years, while driving to and from L.A. Wynn bought the Dunes and involuntarily imploded it on my father's birthday October 27th 1993 (replacing it with the Bellagio), symbolically ending the mob-controlled era in Vegas. Three years later with the demolition of the Sands, there went my childhood and instead of Sinatra and Martin, it's now the site of two other Italianos named Venetian and Palazzo.

❏ PARLAYING HISTORY

My parents wanted to expose us to the best in the entertainment world, with my mother loving the big band sounds and the old classics, while my father appreciated his own sounds, specifically watching Louis Armstrong play the trumpet and belting out his songs. Every time 'Satchmo' would open his mouth and sing, while wiping his brow with that handkerchief, Dad would cry tears of passionate joy. When I was younger, I would tease him about it and ask, "why are you crying?" and he would say, "because this man is the greatest." I teased him one too many times, when he then told me to leave the room and let him enjoy Louie to himself, an event that NEVER happened again! Now, I can't get enough of Armstrong myself.

My current version of Louie Armstrong is Alicia Keys. I fully get the passion that Dad had when her music hits me right to the core. She has the same affect on me, when sitting at her piano and belting out OOOOH NEWWWW YORK...I'm totally done, with tears pouring out like a volcanic eruption!

❑ A SOULFUL ERA

Sadly, Las Vegas was almost as bad as the deep south, when it came to segregation and racial issues until 1960, when the influential original publisher of the Las Vegas Sun newspaper Hank Greenspun helped to end segregation in all of the town. Concurrently, Sinatra insisted that Sammy Davis get treated like royalty at the Sands. Dad exposed us to all cultures, wanting us to see the likes of Nat King Cole, Lena Horne, Pearl Bailey, the tap-dancing family of Hines, Hines and Dad, and of course the amazingly talented Sammy D. Each time we saw the Mills Brothers croon out their perfect harmonies, my father would be singing Up a Lazy River for days. Then, there were the incredible Nicholas Brothers, who by anyone's standards were the greatest dancers EVER!

DID YOU KNOW?

The Nicholas Brothers had once taught dance master classes at Harvard University, where two of their students were named Michael and Janet Jackson. Another mostly unknown Vegas fact, there are several streets that run north-south on the west side just east of Interstate 15, which are alphabetized honoring black historical figures. The last one starts with an N—for the Nicholas Brothers. If you've never been exposed to those out-of-this-world dancing siblings, looking up their videos is a must!

❑ MORE MAIN EVENTS

Of course, Vegas also became the site of some of the all-time great boxing matches. One of its earliest was a young and new heavyweight champ Muhammad Ali against the ex-champ Floyd Patterson in a battle of Olympic gold medalists two years to the day after JFK was assassinated. As someone my father greatly admired, Patterson was one of Ali's early boxing inspirations. Subsequently, Ali became a polarized figured calling Floyd an Uncle Tom, due to Patterson not accepting Ali's name change among other differences. Ali retained his belt after 12 rounds, toying with an older and injured Patterson, who was also dealing with a slipped disk in his back that he had kept quiet.

It was only a few years after that when I ran into Patterson in a local barber shop near Culver City adjacent Rodeo Bowl, recognizing that face from his fights on TV. Sitting in the barber's chair, he suddenly stood up and as he began to walk away, I stopped and asked if I could shake his hand, while saying how much I enjoyed his fights. Mr. Patterson gave me his autograph and was just so friendly and soft-spoken—not knowing what to expect from a man who used his fists for a living? It was my first interaction with a boxer (which excited my father) and nice to know that he could be just as charming to a stranger as being brutal in the ring. After he called me "Champ," I was a Patterson fan forever!

Among the fights I later covered in Vegas was Manny Pacquiao vs. Shane Mosley when I interviewed Pacquiao right after his win and of all people Paris Hilton. I felt a little sleazy that night lowering myself to that level...but my station was happy for getting comments from someone who nobody knew why she was famous either? My personal involvement with Mike Tyson's comeback from prison is detailed in a later volume.

So many memories from my days in Vegas that will always linger, despite the Rat Pack and the old mob being long gone (or as the Pack would call it, "Splitsville"), as are The Sands, the Sahara, the Desert Inn, the Dunes, and the Riviera. However the cards are shuffled, those early times in 'The Miracle in the Desert' will stay with me for as long as they call it 'Lost Wages.'

CHAPTER 7

THE MOB AND THE SOBELS?

I must first emphasize that my family was NOT AT ANYTIME, EVER involved or associated with any mobsters or the underworld—NOT EVER! Now that I got that out of the way, the following is simply about how some of those folk affected the Sobel family's existence—stories that are a must to share.

Since my father was born in 1917, he was 11 years younger than the first prime subject, the late Benjamin 'Bugsy' Siegel. Siegel was one of the most feared and infamous gangsters of his day and right there in the same city as my father. I could only snicker when learning that Siegel's family emigrated from the same Galicia region in then northern Austria as my paternal grandmother Minnie…but I digress.

It was sometime during World War II (likely between 1940 and '44) when Dad was being tempted by some who he hung out with in New York City to invest his money in a small desert town you may have heard of called Las Vegas. Vegas was not always a mob run town specifically in those earlier days, confirmed to me by its most well-known native from that period the legendary tennis icon Jack Kramer. He was born there in 1921 and lived near where the strip is now until 1934. It's common knowledge that Siegel's business dealings didn't start until 1946 when he built the Flamingo Hotel. This started the glitz and glamour era of the strip—which should never be forgotten despite the city being aesthetically built-up by mob money.

My father told me that he never met Bugsy Siegel, but I wouldn't be surprised if some of Dad's friends (when in his 20s) were either potentially somewhere down the food chain involved with Siegel's group or just had influential money to invest and create their own secluded desert resort town, attempting to cash-in however possible. Despite how he dressed, Dad was as much of a mobster as your favorite Aunt Bea. As you may recall, his motto was always, "it's who you know in life," so obviously he knew somebody who wanted him to partake in this venture that would eventually turn into the famed 'Sin City.'

My dad certainly had the look when he hung with these interesting types of their day, but that was simply New York City in the 1930s and early 40s, so it's much too easy to make snap judgments about the character of his group of friends. The bad news: my father never did buy into getting a piece of one of the richest cities in the world. But BY FAR the best news and due to that same decision, I would have never been born in the first place (he likely never would've met my mother), as I write this with one huge sigh of relief.

Put yourself in my father's shoes as to why he decided not to invest in Vegas at that time? It seemed too irrational that resorts and casinos could flourish in the middle of nowhere (the desert) far from a much greater populated civilization and more than a six-hour drive from L.A. at the time, well before the highways were fully developed. As a guy in his early to mid-twenties, Dad was asked to enmesh with the big shots far away from his home in the Big Apple with a totally unknown future? If you could only see the 'if only' $$$ look in his eyes, when we talked about it. Obviously, it was a different world then, but the what ifs were larger than the universe to all who thought about the riches that were never to be for Mr. Sobel.

——— (NOT SO) FUN FACT ———

I was curiously intrigued to much later learn that Siegel is interred at Hollywood Forever Cemetery, just a short walk from the mausoleum that holds my grandparents (the Foremans) and where George Harrison's body was cremated.

❏ THE FRIARS DEALT DAD A GREAT HAND!

Little Santa Monica Blvd. the way it used to be

In the mid-1960s another well-known mobster very much affected my family and some of the special last few years of my father's much too shortened life. This all encompassed the famed Friars Club of Beverly Hills, which was only about a 700 member private club at 9900 'little' Santa Monica Blvd. The club consisted mostly of elite show business old-timers or those who had very influential money until it opened up to respected business professionals—which is how my father fit in.

FUN FACT ———

The Friars Club is likely the site that the legendary 'Groucho' once coined the classic quote when writing his resignation from the club (a few years before I was born), "Because I don't want to belong to any club that would have me as a member!"

Some background on this Friars, it was founded in 1947 as a west coast branch led by the old vaudevillian AKA 'Toastmaster General of the U.S.' George Jessel who enlisted such well-known members as Bob Hope, Bing Crosby, Jack Benny, Jimmy Durante, and George Burns as its inaugural officers. Their original location was perfect for how it evolved into its high-stakes card room, at the old Clover Club which was a Sunset Strip night spot where Hollywood's stars had gambled to their heart's content in the 1930s.

If you're wondering, of course it was illegal to have such card games as per state law. It still went on, however, in most of the fraternal clubs from those days...with some of that 'under-the-table' money greatly benefiting worthy charities that helped to keep the authorities away.

The following Friars story stems from a man named Johnny Roselli, the west coast representative of the 'Chicago Mafia' sent to L.A. by Al Capone and later working for Sam Giancana. Among other much more prominent international incidents, Roselli was involved in L.A.'s big money gambling scene and, in 1963, Frank Sinatra sponsored him for membership in the exclusive Friars Club. Soon after his acceptance in the club, the guy known as 'Handsome Johnny' discovered an elaborate card-cheating scam run by one of his Vegas friends Maury Friedman. Before long, Roselli was getting a cut (even though he rarely played gin rummy).

FUN FACT

One urban myth had Roselli, via his Hollywood ties, help Sinatra when at the bottom of his career get the lead role in 'From Here to Eternity' (winning the Oscar for Best Supporting Actor). Also, through reported strong-arm tactics, Roselli got his lover Marilyn Monroe her first Hollywood contract and was also suspiciously linked to her demise.

Initially, it was thought that there were well-placed cameras in the club's ceiling above the upstairs room full of card tables at the Friars so the cheaters could see everyone's hands (some of the best gin players in the world played in those high-stakes games, with as much as $100,000 on the table at any one time). But it was later learned that a 'mechanic' was looking through drilled peep-holes from above as the 'eye in the sky' and had a tiny radio transmitter device (strapped to the cheater's stomach inside his shirt) to alert them on when to hold 'em or fold 'em. It took until July of 1967 (a five-year conspiracy), when the rigged games were finally discovered by FBI agents who were tailing and wiretapping Roselli for more than just this scam.

This whole crooked card game scandal, led by various undesirables, affected scores of notable wealthy men including, Groucho's other gambling brother Zeppo Marx (Chico also loved the ponies), comedian Phil Silvers, singer Tony Martin, millionaire shoe magnate Harry Karl—the husband of actress Debbie Reynolds and owner of Karl's Shoe Stores, once the largest chain in America (club president Milton Berle then jokingly called Karl 'Friar Took'), and others who were bilked out of hundreds of thousands of dollars.

After a long six-month trial, a Federal grand jury indicted six men for card cheating, with Benjamin Teitelbum receiving up to 83 years for his role in the scam. Roselli (AKA Filippo Sacco) was originally sentenced to 43 years behind bars but got it reduced to four for the Friars incident, another year for being an illegal from Italy, and a $55,000 fine (pretty good cabbage in those days). But, he only had to serve two years and nine months.

DID YOU KNOW?

U.S. District Judge William Gray, after Roselli's friends sought a more lenient sentence for previously serving his country, replied "I am just not able to conclude that Mr. Rosselli is entitled to brownie points for having tried to assassinate Fidel Castro."

A bit more on this Roselli character—he testified before the U.S. Senate Select Committee on Intelligence in 1975 about the CIA's plan to kill Castro (called Operation Mongoose). The next year, Roselli was called before the committee to testify about a conspiracy to kill President Kennedy (one widely considered theory had Roselli as the second shooter in Dallas with Oswald). Three months after his first round of testimony on the Kennedy assassination, the Committee wanted to recall Roselli, but he had been missing for days and was simply a man who knew too much (including possibly bringing down his Vegas connections) and was about to pay the price!

DID YOU KNOW #2?

In 1931, Johnny Roselli was said to be part of a duo who bribed the Nevada Legislature into legalizing gambling (with Al Capone's money). Much later, he was a key figure in the negotiations for Howard Hughes buyout of mob casino interests in the Desert Inn Hotel on the Vegas strip, as well as subsequently helping to engineer Hughes' purchases of the Sands and Frontier Hotels. If all true, Roselli actually started the gambling era in Nevada while also ending the mob era in Vegas (over a 45-year stretch).

In 1975, after a series of giving testimony before the U.S. Senate Committee on Intelligence about the purported plan to assassinate Fidel Castro, Roselli disappeared. The FBI investigated Roselli's disappearance, learning he had been living in Miami and left his home one day to go play golf...and 10 days later, they found his decomposed body in a 55-gallon steel fuel drum, floating in nearby (appropriately named) Dumfoundling Bay.

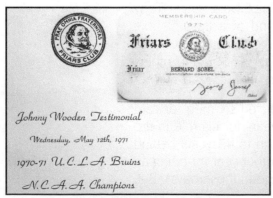

Dad's last membership card—better than any Ace of Spades

❑ PLAYING HIS CARDS RIGHT

The bottom line to this story is that, thanks to Roselli and his buddy's shenanigans, when the publicly disgraced Friars Club's card room was ready to reopen, it needed the most trustworthy card-playing member to oversee everything, including all of those celebrity gin rummy games. So, sometime in late '67 or '68, the club took a vote, and it was my dad, Bernard Sobel, who stood the tallest as the man who would be entrusted with the responsibilities as the new president of the Friars card room. I still remember his prideful smile, when he told us about this esteemed honor, and I was in awe again.

Meanwhile during the time when the cheaters were convicted, most of the names involved in this scandal were regularly brought up at our dinner table. It was strange to watch the news and then get some of the inside stuff from my father of all people. Dad was also an outstanding card player, as someone who passed his calculus class with flying colors, while I could barely count to 10. And he would never hesitate to tell me his own feelings on some of the best known and generally beloved celebrities who were the biggest financial losers in the scandal, when I asked.

My father would look me straight in the eye and make statements that were sometimes disappointing to hear, but simply sincere, "I don't like Phil Silvers, he's such a poor loser with a temper—and really cheap," making me think of his card playing character on his own Phil Silvers Show, which I totally had always enjoyed so much. But this was the real world, and Dad never pulled punches. He also couldn't stomach Tony Martin, who he thought of as one of the cockiest men you'll ever meet, which seemed most obvious when seeing his TV appearances. And as much as I LOVED the Marx Brothers, hearing about a constantly whiny and miserable 'Zeppo' sitting at the card tables was also quite disheartening. But he wasn't Groucho (my comedic idol), so I could live with that.

FUN FACT

At a January '68 Friars roastmaster dinner, comic Corbett Monica (whose stand-up routine I'd enjoyed a few times in Vegas) stood at the dais and joked, "This dinner is so packed that a lot of Friars couldn't get in. They are watching the show through peepholes in the ceiling!"

❏ NOW FOR THE REAL SOBEL RUN-IN WITH THE WRONG CHARACTERS

Then, there was my brother, Richard, an accomplished writer, who had some most unexpected dealings with those who we'd all prefer to avoid. I asked him if he could share some of his story recalling his time in "Sin City," and he offered up the following excerpt from his own memoir:

In Another Life
By Richard J. Sobel

By the end of the 1970s, mob infiltration of Las Vegas casinos had begun to give way to corporate control, but it was not a clean and orderly transition. I arrived on the scene in the midst of a storm of illicit activity, unwittingly bound to bear the bumps and bruises from the last years of that turbulent decade ….

I was knuckling down at my typewriter one evening at my townhouse in Las Vegas, Nevada—fingertips blistered after a lengthy reacquaintance with my guitar, which had remained idle in its case for the last few years—when my uncle, Carl Foreman, phoned from his home in Beverly Hills, California.

Word had reached him that I might be the target of a mob hit, and he wanted to hide me out. He wasn't at all put at ease by my recounting of the events leading up to the explosive final moments of my job, nor was he amused by the parallels between the way things went down and the storyline of the movie, *High Noon* (he wrote the screenplay, which would be his last Hollywood film before his historic blacklisting in the 1950s). I mention his blacklisting and the parallels to *High Noon* because if you look closely at some of the details soon to follow, they read like an old-Vegas-style version of that story—even down to the time of day and the badge-drop!

My uncle had recently returned home after basing his long, distinguished career in London, England, and was branching out, building a television production company; and intrigued by my unique experiences and real-life glimpse into the too-often romanticized world of gambling and gangsters, he'd previously proposed that I write a story treatment about my Vegas experiences for a potential TV project. I accepted his proposal, noting that politics, too, is a gangland; and he, too, had a unique insight into the workings of these kinds of bullies—such as "Tail Gunner Joe," "The Duke," and the like—who, by their nature, didn't have the backbone to stand up alone, at great stakes, like he had done.

Given the real time prospect that a contract had been put out on my life, I'm thinking we had our third act for the TV story now. But fearing my life was in danger, my uncle's only concern at the moment was my safety; and though I didn't share his alarm, I was glad to have him in my life, after what was for him an exile, but for me, an estrangement.

So how did I arrive at this point, where it was believed I had a price on my head—my uncle, a Commander of the Order of the British Empire, desperately trying to save my life—when it seemed like such a short time ago that I was practically just a kid, sitting with my rhythm & blues band in the Baldwin Hills, California, home of Robert "Bumps" Blackwell, within reach of a buffet table spread with pizza, coffee, and contracts for a record deal and a planned tour with Little Richard? Well, it all began after those papers went unsigned, thanks to a no-show by a couple of my drugged-out bandmates; and during an extended period of disillusionment with the music business, I was persuaded by a family friend to move to Las Vegas, where he could help me get a job as a casino dealer.

In short, I got into the gambling business. Like my father, I excelled as an oddsmaker; and I would become a frequent guest expert handicapper on radio, while working full time as a 21 dealer at the Tropicana Hotel & Casino.

It was the mid-1970s, and the Trop was a hotbed of mob meddling, teeming with competition for control of the property and many hands trying to reach into the pot to skim profits. Amid the turmoil, a growing mystique surrounding my hiring (these were coveted jobs usually reserved for people with special "connections") fed the paranoia and assumptions among the old-timers in this hidebound environment—and a mythology about me began to emerge: Who put me here to look after their interests? Was it "Cork" or "Tuffy" from the Kansas City crime family? Frank "The Mad Bomber" from Milwaukee? Joey "Doves" or Tony "The Ant" from the Chicago outfit? Or might it have been the enigmatic chemical company heiress (who was suddenly investing millions of dollars into the property), or the landlord brothers (who were fighting to retain control)? (It didn't help matters that I looked like I could have come straight out of central casting for the role.)

My increasing prowess as a dealer soon earned me the nickname, "The Windmill," and before long came the inevitable whispers, effectively branding me "Richie the Windmill Sobella from Palermo"—a lovely surname, but not mine. I'd never even been to Sicily; the only nickname I'd ever used was my pen name, R J Sobel; and the closest I'd ever been to organized crime was perhaps when I conspired with myself to steal a line from a Wordsworth poem (ultimately thinking better of it). I was now living in another world: a ridiculous—yet ominous—anachronism.

That I later worked my way into the position of Baccarat croupier—one of the most prized and lucrative jobs in town at the time—only fueled the fiction, heightening rumors about who my "juice" was and what management position I was being groomed for. I didn't put much effort into trying to quell the gossip, as I mostly kept to myself and wasn't one to suffer such nonsense.

With the seat of power seeming more like musical chairs, another in a rocky succession of casino managers had been put into place; and the buzz was he was looking to clean out people who might be connected to any competing groups. A mistake by my Baccarat crew, involving not collecting a player's $8,000 losing bet during a hot and heavy game, quickly brought things to a head: the Casino Shift Boss informed me that the Eye in the Sky recorded the error and he'd been ordered to have me sign a warning notice that singled me out as the one responsible for the casino's losses. He put the paper in front of me, but I told him no, I don't make those kinds of mistakes, and I'd have to see the recording; and after much fuss, I sat in the "Eye" and viewed the tape, along with the Pit Boss who had supervised the game. "Stop the tape!" I said, "Rewind it … right there!"—the tape clearly showing the mistake was not mine, but was the fault of another dealer on my crew (who was untouchable because of his connections). I told the Shift Boss that the recording vindicated me, but he said there was nothing he could do and I'd have to sign the paper by noon on Monday. I went home for the weekend, knowing this fight could not be won alone—and one wouldn't need to be an oddsmaker to know that refusing to sign would, in all probability, mean the end of my job.

The Pit Boss called after getting off shift that night, regretful that his failure to catch the other dealer's mistake set the stage for this injustice, and indignant himself, having been told that, as my supervisor, he'd have to sign off on the paper. I made it clear that, regardless of the consequences, I would not sign it. He expressed he also wanted to do the right thing and back me up—but withered over the weekend, calling back on Sunday to say he has a family to think about and a kid on the way, and couldn't risk losing his job, or worse.

Monday came, and I showed up at the Baccarat pit in my black tux uniform for my regular shift at 11:40 a.m., but was met by the Shift Boss, who again put the paper in front of me. And I again refused to sign it. He said in that case I was to report to the Casino Manager's office at noon. The tension was high at the Baccarat table those next 20 minutes—the dealers, bosses, even the shills and pit clerks shunned me, their eyes on their watches, counting down to the anticipated showdown between the Casino Manager and me.

The clock struck 12:00, and I went to the Casino Manager's office, where the Shift Boss and three armed security guards were lined up against the wall; the Casino Manager, eyes down, at his desk. I sat facing him, ready to state my case; but he disregarded me, only uttering out of the side of his mouth: "Did he sign it?" "No," replied the Shift Boss—and without looking up, the Casino Manager said, "Terminate him!" Furious over not being given the opportunity to defend myself against the false accusation and well aware that there would be no recourse in this corrupt atmosphere other than to stand up to this jerk and his spectacle of intimidation, I came out of my chair, railing at him, challenging him in front of his underlings: "Look me in the eye, coward …!"—but was summarily separated from him by the guards. Was I subconsciously thinking of Marshal Will Kane (in the final scene of *High Noon*) when I took off my name badge and dropped it to the floor before turning and walking out of the office, down the stairs, through the basement catacombs, and out the employees exit for the last time?

Chatter about my encounter with the wiseguy spread up and down the Las Vegas Strip: "He's blacklisted in this town" and "His days are numbered." It was often said that there were a lot of bodies buried in the desert. Was I going to be next? After all, it was the Mad Bomber himself who notoriously once said after a particular hit was carried out: "He called me a name—to my face—and now they can't find his skin!"

Not fazed much by the implicit threat (nor thrown by the loss of my job—I was planning on getting out of the business soon anyway to pursue my writing interests), I turned down my uncle's offer to hide me out. However, several months later I sold my home and, unscathed and story treatment in hand, moved back to Los Angeles, where over the next decade I would write original screenplays—and collaborate on projects with my uncle and other eminent writers—including that Centerpoint Productions TV pilot based on my storied time in Vegas.

But unlike those three-act dramas, the story doesn't end there— as between my stint as a screenwriter and the life I live today as a writer and poet, unexpected circumstances would lead to my (somewhat triumphant) return to Las Vegas, years after federal agents took down all the principal crime figures of that infamous era. I became a casino executive at a number of properties, where I made my mark upgrading the ethics and image of the industry. And it was during that period—while working as a casino manager at the highest stakes casino in the country—that an associate told me he'd just spoken with a friend, the Tropicana Shift Boss from those earlier years, who told him the story of what he called my "legendary confrontation" with the heavy-handed casino boss, saying that he never did learn what "family" I was connected with [hint: it was, of course, none other than the Sobel/Foreman family]; but he never forgot what he witnessed in the Casino Manager's office that day, and I was his "hero" for standing up to the guy the way I did.

I discovered that—even after all those years—the mythology, like me, still lived on.

Welcome to old Vegas folks...Only in my family? No, not even close. But it's the only family I'm aware of these types of goings on occurred...and I'm content with sharing for all to chew on.

❏ SPECIAL PERSONAL FRIARS MEMORIES

The Friars wasn't only a club for its big money members to play cards, get a relaxing steam bath, and shoot pool (and the bull), they also raised millions for charitable causes, including numerous hospitals benefiting kids. A chunk of those funds came from their famous celebrity 'roasts' (most people are familiar with the similarly formatted Dean Martin Roasts on TV). Unfortunately, I was too young to be allowed to attend those full of adult-talk parties, when my

Friars staples: Sinatra, Youngman, Berle, and Murray— from the Sobel collection

father was a member, but he did invite me to some of my favorite moments ever at the club, which were sports-related roasts.

I always seemed to be the ONLY kid in the room there, which felt a bit awkward—as Milton Berle once called the average age of their members 'Deceased'! I also felt like the ONLY guy who didn't have a cigar in his mouth—as my father often did. But I could care less when he would introduce me to his friends and co-members, and he would proudly hear 'nice to meet you Teddy' from familiar prominent faces, like comedic pioneers Milton Berle AKA 'Mr. Television,' Red Buttons, Jan Murray, and the king of the one-liners Henny Youngman, who only needed to say, 'Take my wife, PLEASE!' to get laughs.

FUN FACT

An older 'Uncle Miltie' Berle became 'Abbot Emeritus' at the Friars, passing along his abbot (presidency) title to a younger Steve Allen whom he baby-sat as a teenager, when playing in Vaudeville.

DID YOU KNOW?

Famed showman Mike Todd was killed in a plane crash on the way to his own Friars Testimonial Dinner, while his wife Elizabeth Taylor had to stay home with a cold—or she would've been on that fateful 1958 flight with the third of her seven husbands! And Hollywood history would've also been much different as Todd's close friend and tennis playing buddy Kirk Douglas was talked out of being on that flight by his wife, Anne, or else no future Douglas classics, such as 'Spartacus' and no ending of the Hollywood blacklist in 1960 when Kirk gave full credit to his screenwriter Dalton Trumbo on that film.

Mr. Goodman made me the happiest new teen on earth

❏   MEETING THE SOUVENIR KING

With all of those gigantic show business names, the most important man for me to meet and greet was easily Danny Goodman, who was on the board of directors of the Friars Club for more than 30 years and the Dodgers VP and director of advertising and promotion. He's the person who virtually invented the sports souvenir marketing industry as the longtime concession chief during the old Hollywood Stars era at long-gone Gilmore Field. And I still have the Dodger jacket that he'd given for my 13th birthday, along with vintage Koufax and Drysdale signed baseballs. In the package there was a note that read, 'Happy Birthday, Teddy. Danny Goodman.' THE BEST birthday gift of my life!

Mr. Goodman was the man I requested my father to have him ask Mr. Koufax if he could attend my bar mitzvah? I don't know if that actually ever occurred, but Sandy never did show up—at least I tried!

Making Sandy laugh as if he was at my bar mitzvah after all

Through Danny Goodman, several familiar athletic greats, like Arnold Palmer, Bill Shoemaker, Stan Musial, Leo Durocher, and even Vin Scully became members of the Friars (the first place I ever met Vin). My father was sure to get the always limited tickets to any Sports Roasts with two of my favorites (within a few months span in 1969) being Elgin Baylor, Jerry West, and head coach Butch van Breda Kolff after the Lakers lost the '69 Finals to the Celtics AGAIN, as well as USC football legends coach John McKay and O.J. Simpson. This was O.J. the kid star running back and not the one you saw everyday on your TV for the wrong reasons. They were all incredible to meet for this sportsminded teen and the roasts were great too (once I fully understood the dirty jokes).

Among others who were important players in Hollywood then and whom my father very much wanted me to know were Mike Frankovich, the chairman of the board of Columbia Pictures and vice president of Columbia International, and Irving Briskin, who produced 82 movies, mostly for low-budget B-movie 'quickies,' with his strict rule of "do it in one take." Irving's brother, Samuel, who was the more well-known Briskin, produced over 60 films and was considerably involved with my uncle Carl's 'The Guns of Navarone'—more on that later.

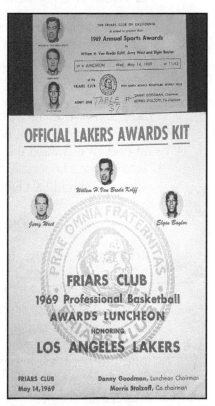

My ticket to this Lakers roast, when every comic gave it to the guys for how they had just lost AGAIN to the Celtics only nine days earlier

When I met Mr. Briskin he was Debbie Reynolds' business partner and manager. Reynolds lost millions of dollars for her investment in a video machine called Scopitone (an early version of MTV but, as Debbie later wrote, "The Scopitone Machine was 25 years ahead of its time, so far ahead no one bought it."

Another Debbie Reynolds story, she bought a small establishment just off the strip called the "Paddlewheel Hotel Casino" in 1992 and reopened

A polaroid taken of Coach VBK signing his autograph in front of me and my father

it a year later as "Debbie Reynolds Hollywood Hotel," which included a museum featuring her collection of movie memorabilia. I remember my mother laughing about inquiring to get a job there after often being called a Debbie Reynolds look-alike, but it never happened. Maybe to avoid any confusion? Which was just fine as the hotel struggled, and Reynolds filed for bankruptcy in '97 and then sold it two years later.

❏ FROM THE FRIARS TO THE WHITE HOUSE

Ronald Reagan was the governor of California during the last six years of my father's life. He was also a longtime member of the Friars Club, where I once met his agent, one of the last of the movie moguls and Steven Spielberg's mentor Lew Wasserman. An amazing success story, Mr. Wasserman began as a theater usher to become THE most powerful and influential in all aspects of show business, including being the man who thwarted Donald Trump's attempted 1988 takeover of MCA Universal. The grandfather of Casey Wasserman (who at one time owned the Arena Football League's L.A. Avengers), Mr. Wasserman actually got a financially strapped Reagan a four-week $60,000 deal to do a Vegas show at the old Last Frontier Hotel, the only time that he was on stage in Vegas.

❏ THE FRIARS AND OUR FUTURE PRESIDENT

The previously mentioned Johnny Roselli arrived in Los Angeles around 1930 and worked in the illegal gambling wire service operated by Moses Annenberg, the former circulation manager for the Hearst newspapers, who also had supplied information to bookmakers across the country. Annenberg owned several publications, including the *Daily Racing Form*. And yes, the same Annenberg, who was the father of Walter who went on to be quite a philanthropist, including wisely investing the 'well earned' family money and then later establishing his Annenberg Foundation, which eventually led to the impeccable Annenberg School for Communication and Journalism at USC. Not coincidentally Walter was given a presidential medal of freedom in 1986 by who other than Ronald Reagan.

Remember how I opened this book with my dad saying it's all who you know? Is that now sinking in so deep that you'll need an excavator to get out of?

❏ THE FABULOUS FRIARS FRATERNITY

I had some awesome encounters with a few of the big names of the day back in the late 60s and none better than with the then notables David Janssen and Dr. Giovanni. For four years, the TV drama 'The Fugitive' was among the most popular shows of its era for its cult-like viewing audience. In fact, it invented the television series 'finale' and changed that genre's history forever. In August of 1967, the show's special two-part final episode held the record for the most watched episodes in history for more than a decade (until 1980, when America learned who shot J.R. on 'Dallas,' and later the final episode of 'M*A*S*H').

They got a 72 share—meaning that about three-quarters of all TV viewers that night (78 million people—including me) were watching 'The Fugitive,' even more than when The Beatles played the Ed Sullivan Show three years earlier.

Janssen's character —the falsely convicted Dr. Richard Kimble— was always on the run during the 120 episodes, after his train (on its way to death row and the electric chair) was derailed allowing him to escape and begin a long cross-country search for the 'one-armed man' who murdered his wife. Although dropping in popularity at the time, that final show was simply a MUST WATCH for a public that craved a great dramatic finish.

And it was not long afterwards, when I entered the Friars Club with my father, for about an hour (where I wasn't supposed to be, due to being under age). He told me to relax and take a steam bath to kill time—what 15 year old really wants to sit in a sauna? But I did so and walked into the empty steamy room, picked up the newspaper and waited for the clock to tick faster to get me out of there.

Several minutes went by when the sauna door opened and there stood the dark haired David Janssen, with a big white towel wrapped around him. He looked exactly like the guy the whole country regularly saw on TV, but he seemed a bit bewildered that a kid was in the Friars steam room. And before opening his mouth, I quickly blurted out, 'OH, SO THIS IS WHERE YOU HIDE OUT!'—of course referring to his role as Dr. Kimble.

Janssen, who always seemed so serious in most of his acting roles—let out a huge belly laugh. He fully got it and seemed to enjoy my sense of humor— and then sat nearby, as we talked a little baseball and his show, as I sweated my ass off. He was actually quite funny to hang with, and of course, little did I know that I was about to go to the same Fairfax High School that he had graduated from. Once ranked 36th by *TV Guide* on its 50 Greatest TV Stars of All Time list, Janssen sadly died much too young at only 48.

❏ CHECKING MY POCKETS

In another random event at the Friars, we were walking through the club, when Dad stopped, looked towards an older man sitting there and said, "You know Dr. Giovanni, the World's Greatest Pickpocket? I want you to meet my son Teddy, and maybe you could show him a little of what you do?" I had only recalled the name of this well-known comedy magician from 1929 into the 1970s, but I had no idea that he was the most famous pickpocket artist in the world, who'd entertained royalty and world leaders with his comedic charm. And of course, he was sitting where else but in the card room for our introduction.

Dr. Giovanni had became legendary for entertaining, while stealing jewelry, wallets, and wardrobe from the world's elite right in front of their faces. He took President Roosevelt's watch from him four times, and stupefied Winston Churchill and the head of the FBI J. Edgar Hoover by swiping their suspenders right off of their bodies…etc. etc. Now it was my turn, and as a skeptical teenager, he just toyed with me from less than two feet away.

This all-time magician's credentials were supernatural

Then in his mid 70s, Dr. Giovanni quickly opened up, as if we were together on stage—and asked me to sit down in front him so he could show me his stuff. He first placed three coins on the table and asked that I choose one coin and to follow it as he moved them around with each hand, and I watched them like a hawk! With his hands covering all three, he then asked where was my coin of choice? I said that's easy—and picked its location. The good doctor (which he wasn't—while not even being Italian) then showed me both sides of his hands so he couldn't hide anything, and all three coins were gone.

Totally baffled, I tried to come up with an answer as to where they had gone? And he just smirked and said—"You want to know where it is?" And he reached out to pull it out of my left ear. C'mon! That was too wild, and I just had to get another try at this guy who grinned at me as just his latest victim. He then did a card trick inches away from my eyes and again made me look silly—which is what he did to and with everyone. As we parted, both of us stood up and while thanking the best of the theatrical thieves for a wonderful personal show by shaking his hand—with his other hand he gave me my wallet back, which I never knew was missing. That was an awesome experience to be played by the mesmerizing King of the Pickpockets and in front of my laughing father—a memory never to be forgotten.

And then there was the time Dad introduced me to actor/dancer George Raft (a childhood friend of Bugsy Siegel, who else?), while proudly going with the usual greeting, "I'd like you to meet my son Teddy." And the surprisingly humble and soft spoken Mr. Raft kindly replied, "I loved working with Jimmy Cagney and Spencer Tracy, but this is a true honor!" Of course it wasn't, but I was smiling from me to you anyway.

DID YOU KNOW?

George Raft was the first to ever say in a movie (as an adlib) "This town isn't big enough for the both of us"—which would've been funnier, if he'd said that to me.

My father did regularly play cards with or had meals alongside so many well-known names and became a part of the Friars' folks family despite having absolutely nothing to do with their world, I only got to join him there on mostly special occasions. I was only about 14, when he got more involved at the club and was just trying to comprehend what had really gone down there? But after all that crap, HE got the honor of being president of the once nationally disgraced card room? Now that's being trusted, and it'll always be pridefully gratifying knowing how those people felt about Dad.

Milton Berle once said about the Friars (when he wasn't mocking fellow members), "aside from my family, it's one of the closest things to my heart. And I'm proud, PROUD to be a Friar." The windowless Friars of Beverly Hills, with its 60s space age facade was demolished in 2011, 50 years after its opening. But to me, it will always be right there on little Santa Monica Blvd. for as long as I can say, "I can't belong to any club that would have me as a guest!"

CHAPTER 8

DRYSDALE AND CAMELOT: A DYNAMIC DECADE

❏ WHERE WERE YOU WHEN JFK WAS KILLED?

The 1960s was an amazing decade, full of so much change for the good but also very turbulent, tragically losing three prominent men who tried to change the world for the better. JFK, RFK, and then MLK were all taken from us, and much of the innocence in this country was gone forever. And I personally lost my Grandpa Izzy in 1960, when he was too stubborn to get medical attention after a car accident. I came home that day from Linda Vista elementary school to a mother who was uncontrollably crying...something I'd never witnessed before.

Three years later on Friday November 22nd, I was at the same school, when something obviously serious was happening, but all we were hearing were a bunch of whispered rumors in our class. You often hear the question, "Where were you when JFK was killed?" Well my recollection at 10 years of age was about a weekend that instantly took away some of my own innocence, and my 'Leave It To Beaver' days were done.

About 1500 miles away from Culver City at 8:30am pacific time, President Kennedy remarked to America's first lady Jackie, "last night would've been a hell of a night to assassinate a President" (referring to their late night motorcade through Fort Worth).

9:40am: Another Presidential motorcade leaves Love Field for a little procession toward Dealey Plaza through downtown Dallas.

10:30am: Shots are fired at President Kennedy's head just after the motorcade passes the Texas School Book Depository—but we were totally unaware of all of this while sitting in class.

While sitting in class, and sometime before lunch, everyone in our little school were told to go into the main auditorium/dining room, where there was a black and white TV on the stage, with a very long rabbit ears antenna. THE news voice of America Walter Cronkite was keeping us updated on the latest from the shooting in Dallas. It was a nervous time that we'd never experienced before. It had been 62 years since a U.S. President was assassinated, something at the age of 10, I wasn't aware of yet.

At 11:26am we received the official announcement, and we all know how this story ended. My personal experience was coming home early to a mother, who again was in her bedroom crying, but this time at our nation's tragedy.

I wasn't sure how to react, but our newly sworn in President Lyndon Johnson told us by declaring that Monday would be a national day of mourning. Although realistically that had already begun, I was glued to the TV all-weekend long, without any of my usual shows. Most stations were showing something regarding the loss of our President, which surprisingly kept my youthful attention throughout. I had never felt so serious for such an extended period of time in my young life (besides my grandfather's earlier death), but was suddenly welcomed to the harsh real world.

It seemed as if that Sunday's funeral procession, with a caisson carrying the body of our president rolling through the streets of Washington DC, lasted forever, which kept me recalling 'The Caisson Song.' This was the official song of the U.S. Army, with the repeated lyrics 'as the caissons go rolling along.' The song was one of my favorites that I had learned to play by ear on the piano a few years earlier. But, the words now had a totally different meaning.

And so did this day—because soon after I woke up that Sunday morning, I wandered into my brother Richard's room where he was randomly recording (via reel to reel audio tape) a live event with the President's accused assassin Lee Harvey Oswald being led into the Dallas Police headquarters basement. He asked that I keep quiet, while recording this off of the TV, when suddenly at 9:21am, I heard a loud car horn sound and then a bang that I'll never forget. The TV reporter blurted out shockingly, "He's been shot, he's been shot. Lee Oswald has been shot!"

Out of nowhere, Jack Ruby gunned down Oswald on live TV. This was another hard-to-believe moment. What were my virgin 10-year old eyes watching again? Did we actually just see that? And soon after, my brother kept repeating the audio he'd just recorded. He couldn't believe that he had recorded such history in such a random fashion.

First-day cover signed by Nick McDonald the Dallas police officer who captured Oswald in the Texas Theater 90 minutes after JFK was shot—and by Officer James Leavelle who was handcufffed to Oswald when killed by Ruby; from the Sobel collection

For the rest of that day—and even much longer afterward, I would hear those sounds in my head (specifically the car horn quickly followed by the gun shot). Although it wasn't eternally damning, it was something that stuck in my brain, and some of those same feelings come back every time that event is brought up.

Another five years goes by, and in April of '68, the man who stood for non-violence like few others Martin Luther King is shot and killed in Memphis. In the process, more hopes are killed with him for all races. MLK once said, "The time is always right to do what is right."

As this country tried to somehow come together and live up to those words, it was only two months later that we would once again feel a national sadness that would make us doubt so much more.

❏ L.A. GETS NATIONALLY SHAMED

So, here we go again, but this time it wasn't thousands of miles away, but in our own backyard. Now as a 15-year old in June of '68 and with Simon & Garfunkel's 'America' appropriately a huge hit, and while I was often laughing on the bus, wondering what Mrs. Wagner's pies tasted like and playing games with the faces. It was right after listening to Vin Scully give me his words-eye view of Drysdale's record-breaking latest shutout and wrapping up his postgame show, I checked out some late night TV, when Robert Kennedy happened to be accepting his win in the critically important California Democratic presidential primary at the old Ambassador Hotel in the heart of L.A. on Wilshire Blvd.

While beginning his about 10-minute speech to claim victory over Senator Eugene McCarthy, RFK (who had become sort of a national rock star) immediately refers to my baseball idol by saying. "I want to first express my high regard to Don Drysdale." (getting huge cheers from his partisan L.A. crowd and with a big smile from Bobby), "who pitched his sixth straight shutout tonight, and I hope that we have his good fortune in our campaign" (followed by another loud roar). If I was only old enough to vote, I would've easily leaned toward RFK for sure—what an emotional night it was for me. The 'Big D' was on top of the world...but sadly, the real world would soon suddenly change again.

❏ RFK AND THE DODGERS

My favorite Dodger outfielder Ron Fairly filled me on his recall of being at the same Ambassador Hotel just two days earlier for an RFK rally—standing just a few short feet away from the Senator, but he never got to meet him. Fairly added that Drysdale had left his Dodger team at least twice, after east coast starts, to likely visit with Kennedy in Washington. We knew that RFK was a sports fan and that it was his strong will to win at anything that attracted many athletes to him and his causes.

Coincidentally among RFK's last words spoken that night and forever were in jest, "Rosie Grier (the immense L.A. Rams great D-Lineman) said he'd take care of anybody who didn't vote for me!" And Kennedy's final words in front of his celebratory Embassy Room were again jokingly—"Mayor Yorty has just sent me a message that we've been here too long already...So, my thanks to all of you and now it's on to Chicago, and let's win there..." and then he headed off stage with everyone assuming that it was the end of just another big night in L.A.

Before I could turn off the TV and head to bed, however, a few short minutes later (just past midnight June 5), there was another news bulletin from the Ambassador and another Kennedy tragedy. RFK had been shot in the kitchen behind the ballroom on his way out to meet with the press. Of the several individuals surrounding our possible next president whom I was quite familiar with were Grier (assisting Kennedy as a bodyguard), who tried to tackle the assailant Sirhan Sirhan, along with Gold Medal-winning Olympic decathlete Rafer Johnson, and journalist George Plimpton (of *Paper Lion* fame). They were all credited with capturing the gunman.

All hell broke loose and with the wounded Kennedy lying on the floor (and being more concerned for others), he reportedly asked the same kitchen bus boy who had given him room service there the previous day (and was the last person who's hand he shook) and now kneeling beside him if, "everyone was ok?"

Unfortunately, not. Those were the reported final words of his shortened 42 years on this planet. RFK died the next day. Somehow, Teddy Kennedy's mention of his brother's popular quote at his services has always stuck with me..."Some men see things as they are, and ask why. I dream of things that never were, and ask why not?" That sounded so much like how I was trying to live my life and the way my brain worked. But again, what the hell is going on in this country? How could this violent act happen again? And in my city?

Now, I was feeling some of the same sense of community embarrassment that very possibly many individuals in Dallas had felt five years earlier. But, it did happen here in L.A., however, and it was time to gather our thoughts and move on. Maybe it came a bit easier to me as a teenager, because I had an important event to attend just three days later.

Sadly, despite 68 years in business for so many wonderful reasons, the Ambassador became best known as the location of the RFK assassination. As the singing group The Rascals once put it, 'People Got To Be Free,' with a plea to all for more tolerance and freedom, with an even greater societal test ahead.

❏ DRYSDALE GOES FOR THE RECORD

1968 was also 'the year of the pitcher' in baseball. HOFer Bob Gibson, one of the absolute all-time greats and the ultimate mound antagonizer, finished that year with a ridiculously low 1.12 ERA. Several other long-established records were also being blown-away, which got league officials the following season to lower the mound by five inches—AKA 'the Gibson rules' (along with reducing the height of the strike zone back to the jersey letters), which affected the dominance by pitchers forever.

My father drove me to Dodger Stadium one night to watch my favorite pitcher achieve something that would live on for all time. He had gotten me a ticket to the most anticipated regular season game in years. On occasion, Dad would ask his very well-connected friend Mr. Frankovich, if his amazing season seats might be available for his son Teddy to use? And even though he knew what this game meant to me, I still couldn't believe that they were gladly offered, and I was certainly in baseball heaven leading up to that night.

It was only three nights earlier when I was listening to Vin Scully call Don's 5-0 shutout of the Pittsburgh Pirates, when Vinny said, "Big D now has '54 pearls on a string." (Are you paying attention, current pitchers? Six straight COMPLETE GAME shutouts? The way the game is played now, that record may last into extra innings of eternity!)

——— *FUN FACT* ———

Most credit William 'Refrigerator' Perry for scoring a touchdown or not in Super Bowl XX as the original proposition bet in Las Vegas, with the odds dropping from as high as 75-1 to 2-1 at kickoff. But nobody EVER mentions all of the odds posted on Drysdale getting his 6th straight shutout 17 years earlier (at 9-1 odds). They actually took bets on each inning—Big D was favored at 3-1 to blank the Pirates in the first, 3-2 in the second. And then starting with the 3rd inning, the odds were against Drysdale the rest of the way at 4-3 in favor of Pittsburgh scoring, followed by 2-1 in the 4th, 3-1 in the 5th, and all the way up to 9-1 in the 9th.

Drysdale signed collage of his shutout streak record—from Sobel collection

Drysdale's streak began on May 14, when he was off to a dismal 1-3 start to the season (his lone win being an April 13, 1-0 shutout of the Mets) and coming off his worst overall season at 13-16. But Don then went on to break 'Doc' White's 64 year old mark of five straight shutouts and in the 2nd inning against the Bucs, besting Carl Hubbell's N.L. scoreless inning record of 46 1/3. In the process, Drysdale continued to modestly credit the defense behind him, without any changes in his pitching.

And that last bagel around the Pirates' neck was easy compared to shutout #5 of Drysdale's streak—which was against the hated Giants. It will always be remembered as one of the whackiest 9th innings EVER, when Drysdale hit San Francisco catcher Dick Dietz in the elbow with a 2-2 pitch that walked in a run with the bases loaded and nobody out. As I nervously listened intently to Scully's radio call, it was definitely the end of the streak, and my heart fell to the floor—for about two seconds!

But I guess home plate ump Harry Wendelstedt heard my pleas all the way from my bedroom and immediately ruled that Dietz intentionally didn't try to get out of the way of the pitch (a VERY rare ruling indeed). And with such a prestigious record on the line for my baseball hero? Could this be true?

Scully yelled out, "Did it hit the bat? It HIT the bat said Wendelstedt. HOLD EVERYTHING, and the Giants are all over the plate umpire!." My shattered hopes were suddenly still alive. The right fielder that night was of course, good 'ol Ron Fairly, who told me that S.F. Manager Herman Franks was literally jumping up and down like a crazed person, arguing the call. A Dodger scout at the time (and in attendance for that one) Tom Lasorda once said "I'd never seen that call before in the big leagues, never had seen ANYONE make it."

FUN FACT

Ironically, also against the Giants, Orel Hershiser established the current record for consecutive scoreless innings pitched (59) with the benefit of an interference call against San Francisco's Brett Butler for breaking up a double play.

So, maybe just maybe there could be a mini-miracle happening through my transistor radio. There was also quite a delay in the game, with all the arguing on the field over the call. Drysdale later admitted that he needed that extra time to rest his weary arm—before finally gathering up enough energy to get Dietz to hit a short fly out. Subsequently, Drysdale then got the next two batters, and his streak was still alive. I was cheering in my bedroom like I was at the game. My parents, who came running in, got all excited for me too.

Then eight nights later (June 8), I really was at the stadium when Drysdale was going for a scoreless inning record that had lasted for 55 years, set by the immortal Walter Johnson, who was well known for being the All-American good guy. Johnson's favorite cuss words were: "Goodness sakes alive!" Yes, 'The Big D' was about to derail 'The Big Train,' and I was the one loving being alive. With so many variable happenings that night, I just have to preserve them for everyone or at least anyone interested to read what's next?

—— *FUN FACT* ——

Johnson once had the greatest weekend in pitching history throwing shutouts on Friday, Saturday, and Monday. What happened on that Sunday? There was no game...he was probably eating bagels that day!

Playing the outfield at Dodger Stadium in a media game with Don looking over me

❏ THE BIG D DOES IT RIGHT IN FRONT OF ME

Wearing a black armband (along with the entire Dodger team) in honor of his friend RFK, who was buried that same day, Drysdale was in the national spotlight, and I was there to watch him break that all-time record, sitting in the first row behind the Phillies dugout, thanks to my father's friend, film producer M. J. 'Mike' Frankovich.

Mr. Frankovich had befriended my dad at the Friars Club (my mother also regularly played cards with 'Big Mike's actress/wife Binnie Barnes), and he was always extremely nice to me. He specifically knew how big of a sports fan I was and, in this case, such a Drysdale admirer. We got to speak about sports a few times and he knew everyone who was anybody in L.A. (and well beyond) in many fields. At the age of 15, I ate that up like a chocolate cream pie.

Just so you know how special Mr. Frankovich was in our town, he became president of the L.A. Coliseum Commission, where he was heavily involved in bringing the '84 Olympic Games and the Raiders NFL team to Los Angeles. It also didn't hurt that he was friends with team owner Al Davis.

Frankovich was also an adopted son of the extremely popular film funny man Joe E. Brown. After being an All-American quarterback at UCLA and star Bruins baseball player (later in their sports Hall of Fame), Mike signed as a catcher for the Mission Club of the Pacific Coast League, with hopes of becoming a big leaguer before developing into a radio sportscaster (he even spoke seven languages). Subsequently, he later received an honorary Oscar for his humanitarian deeds. What a life!

This stadium giveaway had Don almost as excited to hear my story about that night, as I was when telling him

Back to Dodger Stadium on that Saturday night, I couldn't wait to witness history as Drysdale began to face the Phillies and leadoff man Cookie Rojas. I'll never forget the late-great stadium announcer John Ramsay's booming voice finally belting out the words, "Leading off for the Phillies, Number 16, 2nd baseman—Cookie Rojas." There was a sudden hush in the crowd as Rojas approached the plate to get this game underway.

Rojas is the father of veteran Angels broadcaster Victor, who recently connected me with his then 79 years young proud Cuban born dad. We chatted about this game and so much more as just two guys who love talking baseball. Cookie first remembered how the RFK killing created chaos throughout the nation that week. We then discussed this game, and I reminded him that he had led off with a lineout to centerfielder Willie Davis, as Drysdale then needed just two more scoreless innings (six outs) for the record. But Don started out by looking shaky and hittable, throwing only one strike in his first eight pitches, but Rojas was more about recalling to me how intimidating the 6'-6" Drysdale was, with his sidearm and leg kick motion, calling him "one of the greatest pitchers of all-time."

The Dodgers grabbed the early lead on a two-out first inning rbi single by Ken Boyer, but for the first time in memory, the score didn't seem too important as there was much more at stake. After a pair of back-to-back hard hit outs by Tony Gonzalez and Johnny Callison, the 'Big D' began to settle down and then tied Johnson's 56 consecutive scoreless inning mark to end the second inning by striking out Clayton Dalrymple on a 3-2 fastball. Just tying the record wasn't why we were all there, however. Only one more out, but we had to wait a little longer...

The top of the third came and on Drysdale's 1-2 pitch to leadoff man Roberto Pena, it was a slow chopper hit to Dodgers 3rd baseman Boyer, who charged in front of shortstop Zoilo Versailles (I watched, as if it was in extra slow motion). Seemingly taking forever, he flipped it to first baseman Wes Parker, and WE did it! "Big D" had the new major league record (and he wasn't done yet). I can see that play in my head just like it was yesterday.

At 8:45pm, Don Drysdale had become the greatest shutout pitcher in the history of baseball, and I was trying to hide my tears of joy, watching this in front of my own eyes. I couldn't believe how close to the field I was and that I was actually there. I looked around the stadium as if wanting to take every second of this moment with me forever. And here I am, writing about it exactly 50 years later and loving every morsel of those memories.

I also can't help but think that if this had happened these days, MLB Network would be breaking into the game to cover every key out. But in 1968, it was just a nice standing ovation, with a very brief acknowledgment of the record shown on the scoreboard (in front of over 55,000 screaming faithful) as Parker tossed the ball back to the dugout for the ultimate Drysdale keepsake. Don wasn't celebrating at all (never looking for any attention), but just rubbed up a new one behind the mound to keep on plugging along.

My scorecard of that game that remains a special keepsake

Nothing comes easy, however, and at the end of the Phils' half of the third inning, Philly manager Gene Mauch complained and demanded that the home ump Augie Donatelli check to see if the Dodger righty was using a foreign substance on the ball (making it a slippery situation to say the least). This was nothing new, as I'd heard many more similar accusations than I'd like to admit. At this point, I'm passionately booing like a crazed maniac, especially when Mauch walked back toward his dugout right in front of my angered face. There was no way he didn't notice me in that front row—I made sure of that!

After the inning and with the record now at 57 straight blanks, Donatelli stopped Don in his tracks on the way to the dugout and inspected the bill of his cap (which he habitually touched before almost every pitch), and firmly grabbed him by the left wrist to examine it. Then, the ump ordered Drysdale to take off his cap and rubbed his hands through the Big D's hair like a shampoo boy.

He must've found some kind of 'greasy kid stuff,' as he then warned Drysdale not to touch the back of his head the rest of the game {which was just fine by me), or he would be tossed. Could you imagine the star of the night getting ejected during this momentous game? Or how many replays we would see today from several different angles? Would Don's hair have shined enough to be guilty?

So, it was back to work and with every out, Don extended his record even after Donatelli and third base ump Paul Pryor made another inspection at the mound (cap and pockets) at the start of the 4th (which was personally annoying, so I can only imagine how Drysdale felt!) Mauch requested they check Don AGAIN at the start of the 5th. This was not just another ho-hum record-breaking game!

Among the many accusing Drysdale of using some foreign substance on the ball was Giants Manager Herman Franks, who claimed that the entire Dodger staff were throwing vaseline balls. According to Franks, "I never saw so many pitchers who plaster their hair with vaseline." Houston Manager Grady Hatton claimed that Don was definitely loading the ball, "He's using something, but if he can get away with it, more power to him." And Astros slugger Rusty Staub added, "Drysdale doesn't throw a vaseline ball, he throws a toothpaste ball. He puts toothpaste on different parts of his uniform. No runs, no hits, no cavities!" No kidding here folks!

Although the fifth inning came without any proof of Drysdale doctoring the ball, it did prove that all good things must come to an end. Phillies slap-hitting third baseman and tremendous all-around ballplayer Tony Taylor (Cookie's Cuban amigo) opened the inning with a single to right and raced to third on another single to left center by Dalrymple. My nerves were really getting frayed, hoping and praying that the now emotionally weary Drysdale could somehow find a way to stop this first and third—nobody out rally. First he did his usual, making Pena hit the dirt with a high hard one before striking him out. Now all we needed was a nice double play, and we're out of this serious jam!

Then walking up to the plate was a 32-year old journeyman, whom I'd never heard of before—Howie Bedell and was set to pinch hit for starter Larry Jackson (a 5-time all-star, longtime Dodger nemesis and former roommate of Boyer's in St. Louis). Bedell had just been called up from the minors, where he was a player-coach the previous week so he SHOULD BE the latest 'Big D' victim, right? Well not according to his new manager Mauch, who had earlier told Bedell that he was going to use him to end the streak that night.

Howie got up there and battled the ol'sidewinder by running the count to 3-1, fouled off a couple more pitches, and then it happened. A well hit fly ball to left-center field that the lefthanded Len Gabrielson (ironically Bedell's former roomate with the Braves) ran down to his left, caught it and then quickly gave everything he could with a high off-balanced throw to his close buddy and catcher Tom Haller who leaped to catch it. But the hustling Taylor had already perfectly tagged up and easily slid in safely, and the streak was OVER. It was the only rbi for Bedell in seven at bats that season, which was his third and final big league rbi after getting just two with the Braves six seasons prior. The rest of his 13-year career was spent in the minors. Good for him, getting to be a great trivia answer to history the hard way (although he went on to a highly respected player-development career and once had his own 43-game hitting streak in the minors).

My heart really did sink immediately when the streak ended. For a few moments, I was sick to my stomach. Although it didn't feel good, the record of 58 2/3 'pearls on a string' was now Drysdale's, and I began to appreciate it all, and so did the packed stadium with a fantastic ovation.

The guy waiting in the on-deck circle again during that historic at bat was who else, but Cookie Rojas (who followed with a single to right in front of Ron Fairly). Rojas recalled how much of a special memory for him it was to be a part of history that night (although it was the most depressing sacrifice fly I'd ever witnessed).

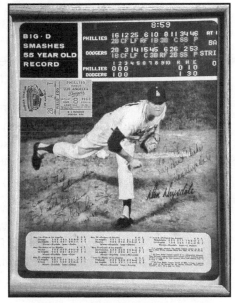

Rojas impressively also remembered that it was 20 years later, when Orel Hershiser broke Drysdale's streak with 59 scoreless innings—and that the "Big D" was there as a Dodger broadcaster to greet and congratulate the new record holder as he walked off the field in San Diego.

Record streak poster signed to me by Drysdale and Hershiser, with my ticket

After the record-breaking air was out of the balloon in the stadium, suddenly it was just another game, with my idol starting to falter, giving up a two-strike homer to slugger Bill White in the sixth, and the Phillies finally chased Drysdale in the seventh. It was fun to remind Cookie of how that ended with him (of all people) being the guy at the plate with runners at the corners and one out.

I asked Rojas if he remembered that moment, and he totally guessed, "I probably struck out?" I said NO, you singled to right again for the second Phillies run, and YOU are the one who sent Drysdale to the showers. He then started laughing and replied, "That's amazing!" Rojas continued, "And besides being such a great pitcher...he was a personal friend. When I was scouting after I was playing, we talked baseball all of the time and how great this game is. I felt that I was the lucky one to be so close to him and admired him in anyway possible. It was great great times!" Subsequently, I was the individual who got to pass along Cookie's well wishes to Don's widow Ann, as he had become a good friend of the Drysdale family over the years.

Don Drysdale went on to get the 5-3 win with the thought-to-be washed up new National Leaguer Hank Aguirre surprisingly shutting down the Phils from the seventh on for a rare save. Aguirre was the postgame comedian with his comment, " I can't understand how these umpires can grab hold of a guy and run their hands through his hair. I guess the next thing, the umpires will be bathing us!" As for the humble Big D's thoughts right after the game? "I'm glad it's over. I'm really very much relieved. I'm very pleased and lucky to have been able to get as far as I did. I do feel a little let-down, but it had to happen."

I knew that same feeling SO well and shared it with Don one night at the stadium a few decades later. He gave me that big smile with an aw-shucks type look, and thanked me for being such a big fan. Believe me, it felt strange to admit to him that I had written his #53 on all of my t-shirts and underwear, and now we were colleagues (which earned another "Big D" LOL). And it truly was surreal to get to interact with him over the years.

Also in his postgame comments, Drysdale admitted that he and his family were still badly shaken by the death of RFK in this obvious whirlwind several days for sure. "I felt like I ran out of gas. The whole thing finally took its toll. I've been depressed the last few days anyway. I never gave baseball a thought since this (RFK) tragedy. Baseball has been the furthest thing on my mind."

To explain just how this affected the rest of baseball and other pro sports were at the time (it wasn't about politics, but values and paying respect), Cincinnati pitcher Milt Pappas resigned from being his team's player rep that same Saturday, following an argument with his manager Dave Bristol over whether the team should take the field against St. Louis.

Pappas said the players preferred not to play, since the funeral proceedings for Kennedy had not been completed by game time. Other games were already postponed or ordered delayed until after the start of the funeral, but Bristol told Pappas the game would go on, if he could field just the minimum of nine players. The pitcher then said he wouldn't give his manager the satisfaction of going out with anything less than the full team. Some clubs voted not to play at all. This for someone who wasn't even president? Imagine that happening today? NO WAY!

Meanwhile, after losing his game to the Dodgers and with all of his shenanigans of harassing the "Big D," manager Mauch honestly confessed, "There are some great ones around, but if I had my choice of one pitcher, it would be Drysdale. He's the complete professional!" I seriously doubt if he was thinking that, when I was yelling at him to get back in the dugout after bothering my hero all night!

FUN ANIMAL FACTS

That same day, the appropriately named Gamely (the magnificent huge daughter of Bold Ruler) outdueled 11 male rivals to win the 28th running of the Inglewood Handicap by a nostril over Rising Market in front of over 40,000 at Hollywood Park, a location very familiar to Don. I wonder if he had something on that future Hall of Fame mare. That same night, the Drysdale's runaway dog ironically named 'Shutout' (I couldn't or wouldn't make that up) was found wandering the hills near their home and was fortunately returned by a neighbor.

❏ THAT RECORD MIGHT NOT LAST VERY LONG ANYWAY

By chance during Don's record streak, the amazing Bob Gibson had me really 'worried' with his own sudden stretch of shutout innings, which began on June 2 before blanking Houston 4-0 four days later. Then it was three, four, and five straight after a 3-0 whitewash of Pittsburgh. So, the perfect Hollywood script was being written, he could tie Drysdale with a sixth straight shutout, naturally, at Dodger Stadium, and, of course, against the "Big D." (I don't make these things up folks—this really could be its own movie, which is why I'm writing so damned much about it to remember it all!)

It didn't take long on that July 1st for that growing suspense to end at the Ravine (just 18 minutes after first pitch). Bottom of the first, two-out singles by buddies Gabrielson and Haller brought up who else, but again my guy Fairly to the plate.

The 1-1 pitch to Ron was a low fastball that hit the dirt, deflected off the catcher's bare hand and bounced off the ump's shinguard towards the Dodger dugout, and Gabrielson hustled home—stomping on the plate with both feet as a perfect exclamation point to end Gibson's streak at 48 2/3.

Fairly then meekly grounded out, and Gibby cruised to an easy 5-1 win, while starting another streak that went 23 innings (allowing just two runs in 71 total innings). He truly was just 'a game of inches' away from throwing 10 straight shutouts and was literally unbeatable for three months, reeling off 15 straight wins, something we'll very likely never see again!

My Gibson ball and signed first day cover—from Sobel collection

Drysdale said afterwards, "It's too bad the way it happened, he's a great pitcher." But I thought it WAS FANTASTIC how it happened. Later, Cardinal great Stan 'The Man' Musial dropped by the dressing room and stated my feelings perfectly, "That's the breaks of the game."

Gibson finished with an amazing 13 shutouts in 1968, but I could finally take a deep breath again. He later won league MVP honors and struck out a record 17 in game #1 of the World Series. That was after the fact, however, which was just fine with me.

FUN FACT

'Bullet' Bob Gibson got his nickname when he started his brief two-sport career with the Harlem Globetrotters. He was very special athlete who recently passed at age 84.

All of this acclaim for Drysdale was of course extremely personally satisfying. It all came to an immediate halt the following season, Dons's 14th and final—as his nagging shoulder injury forced him onto the disabled list twice before one final effort. On August 5, 1969 against Pittsburgh at Dodger Stadium, Drysdale got a no-decision in a ho-hum 11-3 loss, allowing two earned runs on eight hits in six innings.

Dodger team physician Dr. Frank Jobe prescribed complete rest for the "Big D" but to him, that was only postponing the inevitable. Dr. Jobe once told me how it may have been different, if treatment was more like it is today.

Reality set in, however, and six days later Drysdale held a press conference at the Stadium Club and announced his retirement at only 33, which had me stunned in disbelief (less than three years after Sandy did the same). It just didn't seem right that I could never watch #53 pitch again—and that I would just have to settle for doing a perfect imitation of his sidearm motion in front of a mirror or on a mound near me.

Don Drysdale finished with 209 wins (167 of them complete games), a lifetime ERA of 2.95, and was a participant in nine All-Star games. He also led the NL in games started four times, strikeouts three times, and innings pitched twice. All were highlighted with three World Series rings, his incredible 1962 Cy Young Award winning season of 25-9, and that record scoreless string that I couldn't have been more proud of and to see it live. Don was also one of the great streaky hitting pitchers of any era, actually leading the 1965 Dodgers with a .300 batting average, while belting 29 career home runs, several of which were in front of my joyful being.

Somehow, it took 15 absurdly long years until Don was elected to the Hall of Fame (when this time, the voters needed to be drug tested). Don't try to explain the delay in his election to some of the greats who also remembered Don as one of the most intimidating pitchers ever. Mickey Mantle once said, " I hated to bat against Drysdale. After he hit you with the ball, he'd come around, look at the bruise on your arm and say, 'Do you want me to sign it?'"

Eight time All-Star shortstop Dick Groat once said, "Batting against Don Drysdale is the same as making a date with a dentist." Furthermore, the great L.A. Times columnist Jim Murray once wrote during Drysdale's scoreless inning streak, "The old convincer in the Don Drysdale repertoire is the 'anatomy' pitch. You don't hit it, it hits YOU!"

Enough said. And it was always funny to get Don's reaction to the game of today with so few throwing inside much anymore. He despised that and had plenty of names for that type of 'wimpiness' saying, "I hate all hitters. I start a game mad, and I stay that way until it's over. If they knocked two of your guys down, I'd get four. You have to protect your hitters."

I always loved Don's openness about this and in his book *Once a Bum, Always a Dodger* (which thank God was released just a few short years before his sudden passing in 1993), his exact words to describe those deep feelings were, "I always believed that it was them or us, and nothing was going to stand in my way. Take no prisoners. If you were going to lose, take down the son-of-a-bitch who beat you, too. Make him feel the cost of victory." Wow, now that's the "Big D" whom I knew and admired. He finished his career with 154 hit batsmen. No political correctness in those days!

Photo by Paul Olden

Don was the opposite out of uniform, which is why he had so many great friends in the game who hated him, when he was on the mound, until they got to know him away from it and his earned respect as a man was off the charts. In reality, they just don't make 'em like Don Drysdale anymore!

FUN FACTS

Don's hometown school Van Nuys High won the San Fernando Valley League championship in each of his three years there. Upon graduation, he immediately signed with the Brooklyn Dodgers for a whopping $2,200 bonus and was pitching in the big leagues two years later. In 2004, after 89 years without an on-campus field, the school dedicated 'Don Drysdale Memorial Field' in front of his awesome family. Meanwhile, the myth that 'The Natural' star Robert Redford played with Don there is simply that. They did graduate together in 1954 and likely played together at a local ballpark somewhere, but never on the school's varsity team. Don was always a gentleman about that rumor and just went along in order to not hurt anyone's feelings. Rock star Alice Cooper once told me in a phone interview (and then again at the Masters) that he loved the one year he went to Van Nuys Jr. High—not quite at Van Nuys High, which to him always meant the home of the Wolves and Don Drysdale.

❏ THE TOUGHEST BROADCASTS OF MY LIFE

Don Drysdale lived a great life, which was too unfairly short (not unlike my own father). I remember watching him on my all-time favorite game show "You Bet Your Life." Host Groucho Marx asked a very young "Big D" what he wanted to do when he was through playing? Don replied that he wanted to get into Radio or TV, some type of sports program. Well, he certainly did and had a fine 23-year career in both media.

It all came to a suddenly unexpected end when hearing the heartbreaking news on Saturday July 3, 1993 that Don, at just age 56 and in his sixth season as a Dodger broadcaster, was found dead of a heart attack in his Montreal hotel room during a road trip (the second Dodger Hall of Famer to die in a week—Roy Campanella passed on June 26). Among Don's personal belongings found was a cassette tape with RFK's last victory speech, when he mentioned 'the streak'...that's how much he had meant to him!

I'll NEVER forget that night, hearing Drysdale's broadcast partner Scully having to make the grim announcement during the game. Vin later called it "the toughest broadcast in my life. I am stunned for Ann and the children. Don was not only a Hall of Fame player and a fine broadcaster, but a dear friend and a joy to be with."

And soon after it would be my time to say, "this was the toughest broadcast in my life." I was scheduled as the early Sunday morning (July 4th) sports update guy at Don's old station KMPC and had a few hours to prep for what I was going to say and how I would present it. Still well before any invention of the internet, I found my old album with Scully calling Don's record shutout streak and a few others that I would be able to use the next morning.

As I wrote and produced these 4-5 minute updates, I was too busy to get caught up in the moment. But at 6am sharp, I opened the microphone for my first once-per-hour report of the day with the news that Don Drysdale had died, and it hit me—and very hard. For the first time in my career, I was catching my breath, while on the air. With emotions that were beginning to overwhelm me, I got through that first broadcast (barely) and thought I'd be better in the next one—but it happened again.

I didn't expect it to be easy, but never thought it would be like this? And I was holding back tears at the top of the next hour and then the following. It truly was by far the most difficult thing I ever had to do on the air, until eight days later at Don's funeral services in nearby Glendale, which I strongly requested to cover. Actually, I basically insisted, as in reality who else SHOULD be there? I simply had to be the one, and KMPC management was kind enough to send me.

I was well outside of the church (media covering it live were not allowed inside), when so many familiar faces began to arrive. More than 1,000 friends and family were there to pay tribute to Don, including many former teammates— Koufax, Fairly, Reese, Snider, Podres, Perranoski, Zimmer, Essegian, among others...

Again Vin Scully spoke as only he can in his eulogy "The tragedy of life is in what dies inside a man while he lives...He lived the stuff of dreams—full of accomplishment, inspiration, and love. In God's eyes, Don lived a complete game, and it was a victory." Orel Hershiser read a wonderful letter he wrote for Don's kids. Others who spoke at the service were his former minor league roommate in Montreal and then Dodger manager Tom Lasorda, former Angels and Rams broadcast partner Dick Enberg, co-Dodger broadcaster Ross Porter, Bob Uecker, and even the same Gene Mauch, who so often accused Drysdale of using some foreign substance on the ball. Mauch, with a nice lighthearted touch, said, "The big guy was a giant of a man who walked among giants. Now, if Don heard me say that, he would say, 'Gene, either start over or sit down. I never had anything to do with the (rival) Giants in my life!"

The services ended, and once again, I had to be a pro and not let the moment get to me. I got through a few reports ok, but really had to suck it up! I was also trying to say goodbye to Don (in my own personal way), while telling the listeners what I had witnessed that afternoon.

Life moves on—and so did I. To sum it up, Drysdale lived a fantastic life of which few could ever dream. I got to share it from afar and up close and then later got to know his family some. His wife Annie, who'd worked with my buddy Paul Olden on UCLA basketball broadcasts, gave me a most special day when we were paired to play golf

After golf with Annie

and share a cart during a John Wooden charity event. I told her some of these stories during our day, and it was almost as if Don was sitting there with us.

The first time I met Don's son D.J., it was like saying hello to the same "Big D" whom I saw in pictures during his Brooklyn days, given that their resemblance is that strong. D.J.'s youngest daughter Drew (a very talented singer who was only four months old when we lost Don) really got to me, when I first heard her beautifully sing the National Anthem before a Dodger game. I watched from the pressbox and couldn't help but think how proud Don would be if he could only be there with us. Maybe he was anyway.

With Drew and her 'Uncle' Tommy Lasorda

With the Drysdales including son D.J.

CHAPTER 9

CALLING MY OWN BALLPARK SNEAKS

❏ CALLING MY OWN SNEAK INTO DODGER STADIUM

With Honky Tonk Women constantly blasting on my stereo during the dawning of our Age of Aquarius, 1969 was the 100th anniversary of professional baseball and the first season of MLB's 'Divisional Era,' meaning the first year of a league championship series leading to the World Series. Sunday September 28 was the final weekend game of that season at Dodger Stadium and the finale of a Giant-Dodger series, with a pair of great righthanders on the hill, 20-game winner Juan Marichal vs. Bill Singer who was looking for his 20th win.

Besides my 16-year old self, among the over 32,000 in the house were a couple of legends in HOFer Casey Stengel (who received a rousing ovation) and comedian Jack Benny. Marichal got the last laugh, however, by easily winning his 21st game 8-1 over L.A., prolonging his Giants pennant hopes another day helped by Willie McCovey's career-high 45th homer, while the Dodgers had already been eliminated.

Absolutely nothing about that game matters in this story, it's what happened AFTER everyone went home—except me. Being my final game of the year meant a long off-season ahead, so I was milking my time there, hanging by the Dodgers player's parking lot, getting a few last autographs and basically just saying my goodbye's (like they used to say in Brooklyn, 'wait til next year'). But what lied ahead has me writing about this day over 50 years later.

Just waiting around the parking lot—totally alone—after every car in sight had left, it should've been time for me to leave too. For some reason, I wasn't ready to go home. Standing very close to the outside fence behind the Dodger bullpen, I noticed the gate was slightly open. The first thing I thought of was—how easy it would be to just take a step into the same bullpen that my recently retired idol Don Drysdale used to warm-up in. Furthermore, I could do no harm by doing so (except for possibly trespassing onto the grounds where I wasn't supposed to go).

BUT NOBODY WAS AROUND—ANYWHERE! And it was 1969, no security folk (they were already long gone)…not a soul around anywhere. So, why not just walk over to that mound? With only a slight bit of guilt in my gut, I did just that. I remember picking up some dirt and rubbing it into my hands—feeling what the big leaguers felt. I then stepped on that rubber and looked in towards that huge stadium in front of me. Immediately, I went into my Drysdale sidearm wind-up and pretended to throw a few pitches, before thinking, 'I better get the hell out of here before somebody sees me.'

So, I started to walk out toward that same slightly opened gate and back into the parking lot, when something off to the left quickly caught my eye (giving me an added desire to stay just a bit longer). There was an open door that obviously was the one that the players walked through to enter or leave the bullpen. At that point, my curiosity really peaked, and my mind wandered to the possibility of walking down that runway toward the Dodger clubhouse. I looked past that door, and it was quite dark in there but that didn't stop me from walking a few feet further.

And then the old "one little man on each shoulder" routine occurred. One was telling me to 'go for it,' since you'll NEVER get this opportunity again. The other was saying, "Are you insane? You're not supposed to be here and leave NOW before any trouble lies ahead!" And after a brief self-analysis, I EASILY leaned towards the puny guy, with the 'Just do it' attitude...and off I went.

But now I felt like a kid who had just snuck into a bank vault—with no intention of stealing any money. I just wanted to see something I thought could never be possible. So, I slowly wandered further and further down this long dark walkway with these large blue barrels placed about every 50 feet along the concrete wall. I first passed the old Angels dressing room, which had become just a storage area. The darker it got, the more I felt as if I didn't belong in there. But I just kept going despite the thoughts of turning back getting stronger and stronger. Then suddenly, I heard two voices chatting in the distance and quickly within earshot came their footsteps.

My first thought was to hide behind one of those blue barrels and I did for a few seconds...when realizing that if I was caught this way, I would surely look like a trespasser with bad intent. Being the good, yet curious, kid that I was, I simply surrendered myself by standing up tall in the walkway, until these men could clearly see me in this dimly lit spot.

They both had a look of surprise as they approached me. I could see them well enough to know who they were. The best of buddies on the Dodgers catcher Tom Haller and outfielder Len Gabrielson were leaving the stadium late, seemingly packing up some of their things for the off-season.

—————————— **FUN FACT** ——————————

Gabrielson led the Dodgers in homers with only 10 in 1968 "the year of the pitcher.'

With a very serious look on his face, Haller stared at me and said, "What are YOU doing down here?" Now I knew that I was in real trouble. Being that much more nervous and embarrassed, I sheepishly replied by telling the truth,

"I wandered into the bullpen, and before I knew it, I was walking this way, just hoping that maybe I might get a glimpse of the clubhouse. I knew it was wrong, but I really didn't mean any harm."

Haller then pointed right at me and said, "come with me," while telling his buddy to wait a second. I was SURE he was set to call someone of authority to report my little curious ass. So, I then followed him maybe 100 feet (which seemed like forever), and we approached this large door. There was no security person there to take me away, so now what? He opened it about halfway and with a suddenly welcoming smile stuck his arm out, while pointing ahead and said, "there it is."

Are you bleeping kidding me? It was the Dodger Clubhouse! Is this for real? Tom Haller just walked me through the hallowed halls to the room that I'd always dreamed about seeing with my own eyes. I really was in 'Blue Heaven.' I only took one or two steps inside and with the biggest teenage wide-eyed look you could ever imagine quickly checked the place out and then asked, 'Where was Drysdale's locker?" (Don had just pitched his final game there, before retiring exactly 53 [+2] days earlier.) Haller pointed off to the left. I stared at it for a few seconds and that's all I needed. I got my totally unforeseen fix and thanked him for such a ΓAN-tastic moment.

Then, with a friendly smirk, Haller came back with 'Now get the hell out of here!" Fine with me. As I was now set for one happy off-season, even without any post-season games to look forward to and a great story to tell forever. I just had my own 'Miracle Mets' moment a few weeks before they did. BUT WAIT! There's more...

As Haller told his buddy Gabrielson to walk me out, he headed back into the clubhouse. I thought nothing of it as we continued down the 3rd-base side, below the field level toward the parking lot. About three-fourths of the way there, I suddenly heard the Dodger catcher briskly walking behind us, when he softly spoke up again, "Kid, here you go. It's yours." He just handed me his own personal bat (broken, but I could care less). This guy is phenomenal! He walked back to his locker just for me? I've known him for less than two minutes, and he's treating me like a relative.

Again, I thanked him for being unnecessarily kind and left the ballpark like a kid after his first and best Christmas. I still have that bat. Over the years, I really wanted to ask Tom if he recalled that special moment he gave me? But unfortunately, Haller passed away in 2004, and I never got that chance.

I did reach out to his son Tim recently on Facebook, and we had a wonderful conversation. Tim who's also an ex-pro ballplayer proudly said "Dad was compassionate and loving and knew when to goof around. You got the best of all of that in just those few special minutes together."

The priceless Haller bat—photos by Bridget Silvestri

Tim Haller revealed to me that Joe DiMaggio and his father were very good friends, with some irony given the following story. In February 1968, the Giants traded Tom Haller to the Dodgers for Ron Hunt and Nate Oliver, the first deal between the two rival teams since 1956, before both clubs moved to the west coast. This reunited him with his close friend Gabrielson after playing two years together in San Francisco. They remained very close til Tom passed.

Former Dodger executive Fred Claire once said about Timmy's Dad, "Tom Haller was one of those people who made you feel good about life by simply being in his company." Yes Fred, I couldn't have said it any better, having learned that up close and personal!

❏ JACKIE, CLEMENTE, THE 'SAY HEY KID,' JOLTIN' JOE, AND ME AT THE RAVINE

Exactly six months later (to the day) after my great Dodger clubhouse adventure (March 28, 1970), I was back at Chavez Ravine again. This time, it was not for a real game but for a worthy charity that brought together one of the greatest collections of big leaguers to ever play on the same field. It's also the most little-known about and almost forgotten momentous game in the history of Dodger Stadium (if not ALL of baseball). They called it the East-West Major League Baseball Classic, honoring the late Dr. Martin Luther King, Jr. who was killed just two years earlier.

All-Stars Bench, Santo, and Koufax (L-R) on that special day

His widow Coretta Scott King threw out the first ball to Johnny Bench and joined many other dignitaries on hand including MLB Commissioner Bowie Kuhn, as well as celebrities like Danny Kaye, Anthony Quinn, Greg Morris, and Bill Cosby. Portions of the recording of Dr. King's famous 'I Have a Dream' speech were played before the first pitch at 2 pm. The iconic Jim Murray described this situation as "the greatest baseball players in history will appear in the game in his honor."

Although not that highly promoted, I fortunately had heard about this all-star classic for the ages coming to my own backyard and wouldn't miss it for the world (along with the other 31,000 plus in the house). The rosters, comprised of two players chosen from each of the then 24 big league clubs, were split into squads that totaled 15 future Hall of Famers appearing in this game.

Rose and Joe D yukking it up pregame—photos courtesy of Michael Rayala

How about the following names— Mays, Aaron, Bench, Morgan, Clemente, Banks, Santo, Kaline, Brock, Stargell, Gibson, Seaver, Cepeda, Frank Robinson and Reggie Jackson (and Pete Rose who should be in as a player)? There were also some pretty decent (HOF) coaches involved in the game, including Koufax, Drysdale, Musial, and Satchel Paige, along with managers Joe DiMaggio (East) and Roy Campanella (West).

This was right in the middle of their spring training schedules (a week before the season openers) and before a strong baseball union existed that probably would not have allowed such a benefit game to take place these days. It is also important to remember the times at the start of the 70s. It was a benefit game to honor a Black icon—Dr. Martin Luther King—to help perpetuate his works and teachings. The manager of the West team was a Black individual—Campanella, who was starting a Black pitcher in Houston's Don Wilson. Furthermore, umpiring behind home plate was MLB's first Black umpire Emmett Ashford (a beloved native Angelino). This was absolutely unthinkable not too many years before then, when some of the other notable Black men who coached in this particular game played for real, including Don Newcombe, Larry Doby, Joe Black, and Monte Irvin.

One name that hasn't been mentioned yet is Jackie Robinson, an individual who is easily a top-ten most important figure in our society, ever! It took sports to change the way people viewed life and the different races that shape it. As the years have passed since this game, Jackie wasn't thought to have been in attendance that day, although I swore that I remembered seeing him there (and he's listed as a coach on the West roster in my program). I asked Dodger historian and longtime friend Mark Langill and others but nobody had proof that my memory wasn't deceiving me (despite a few articles that had Robinson there that day). Well after this, Dodger team president Peter O'Malley strongly confirmed to me, "Oh, HE WAS THERE!"

Finally, Langill recently called me to say he'd found a photo proving Robinson was in the house (and that I wasn't losing it). As such, all's well that ends well. Even Ron Fairly didn't recall ever seeing Jackie that day, but I remember him keeping a 'fairly' low profile in the stands, where I had watched him from afar. That's not something easily forgettable. It was also one of the last times Robinson was at Dodger Stadium.

Fairly told me that he didn't know Robinson very well, but they did meet a few times, while fondly recalling sounding like just another fan, "I still have an autographed baseball of his but, I remember a few stories that Duke (Snider) told me about Jackie, and (he was) highly complimentary. And what Jackie had to put up with for those first few years (of playing), in today's world it would be absolutely unheard of."

Any chance to speak with Don Newcombe and gain his wisdom was worth every moment

Ron also revealed a story to me of when he got some great insight from Pee Wee Reese in 1959, and they talked about the famed Reese-Robinson embrace of 1947, when Pee Wee (the popular all-star from nearby Kentucky) silenced Cincinnati's racially charged crowd by leaving his shortstop position to fully support his second baseman. "I had dinner with a bunch of guys and Pee Wee was with us, and the thing came up about Jackie and what happened in Cincinnati—where we don't really know if he put his arm around Jackie or he just stood next to him? There's some argument about that. And someone says, "why did you do that?" Which is a very good question. Pee Wee replied, because it was the right thing to do—and that was it. Because it was the right thing to do! I've never forgotten that."

I was fortunate to also be in attendance at Jackie's final appearance at the Ravine two years later on June 4, 1972 when he was talked into being there (by Newcombe) for his #42 to be retired, along with Koufax's 32 and Campanella's 39. Robinson told us all in the stands that day "This is truly one of the greatest moments of my life" (even though he was openly distressed at the way baseball was treating its Black players after their playing days were over). Seeing that trio stand together for the last time during their pregame ceremony alongside the Dodger dugout that day is a picture that will always be with me.

Robinson and Dr. Martin Luther King were both awarded honorary doctorates of law from Howard University at the same commencement after Jackie retired in 1957. But they didn't always see eye to eye, given that Jackie raised concerns in 1960 that King and some of his followers were claiming that the NAACP (where Robinson was a board member) had outlived its usefulness. And they also clashed on Vietnam, as Robinson strongly disagreed with King's opposition to the war (even challenging his patriotism and that of Muhammad Ali's). But they remained good friends (Jackie attended his iconic 'I Have a Dream' March on Washington where they joined on the speaker's platform) with great mutual respect all the way to the end, while fighting for the same cause, like few ever before or since!

I recently got the awesome opportunity to reminisce about this game with another participant 'Gentleman' Al Downing (he pitched one perfect inning that day), who was then in his first spring with the Oakland A's, and was only added to the West roster as a last-minute replacement, because A's pitching teammate Chuck Dobson's wife had gone into labor.

Having some post golf fun with 'Gentleman' Al

On any doubts about Jackie being at that game, Al vividly recalled, "HE WAS THERE, HE WAS THERE. He went to home plate and what I remember was how white his hair was" (as compared to the previous time he'd seen him). Downing's thoughts on the many complex struggles that Robinson had to live with in being the first individual to break the color barrier in baseball? "He was under a lot of stress, people don't understand it. I know what we went through, to think he went through it a hundred times (worse), because there was nobody backing him up, nobody with him (in his playing days) like we had. It turned out to be one of the most significant events of the twentieth century—not just in baseball, the entire twentieth century!"

Al also added what the game meant to him as a black man, "IT MEANT A LOT, people remembering Martin Luther King and what he meant to society... we all knew the importance of that." Another longtime friend Maury Wills, who led off at shortstop for the West, told me "It was just a total honor to be there!"

Willie Mays traveled the farthest to get here...how about 12,000 miles round trip from his Giants exhibition tour of Japan (just to ground out in his only at bat) and calling this event, "Too important to pass up. At last, baseball players can show their feelings about the late Dr. King and his work through the medium of this game."

Oakland's young star Reggie Jackson was in a six-week holdout from playing with his 'Mustache Gang,' but he showed up for this one, only to ground out twice. His A's teammate (and future Dodger) Jim 'Mudcat' Grant had the most interesting day. He began it by singing a soulful rendition of the National Anthem, standing in deep center field wearing a bright glittery white suit. Later on, he was pitching in his West team uniform and allowed all three runs in the 8th inning to put the game away for DiMaggio's club.

The game itself was of course just an exhibition, but I scored it like it was to be remembered forever. I actually have the scratches and late additions to the rosters that I've never seen elsewhere since. If you ever want to know of ANYONE who participated in that game, just ask to check out my program.

My water-stained MLK game program with Fairly signed ticket

─────── *FUN FACT* ───────

I once shared with Mark Langill my collection of many old Dodger programs and memorabilia, and when I pulled out the one from this game, he was stunned. Saying he'd never seen it before and wasn't aware that any had ever existed—this from a guy who's a walking encyclopedia on this kind of stuff…certainly not one signed by not only Joltin' Joe, but also by the game MVP.

If you're scoring at home, Ron Fairly (then a member of the Expos), who was the leadoff man for the East, went 1-3 and broke a scoreless tie by belting Seattle 'Pilots' righty Lew Krausse's first pitch in the top of the third, just inside the right field foul pole for a home run (as I went nuts in the upper reserve section). Ron Santo then led off the 4th with a homer vs. Lew Krausse. Subsequently, the East got the additional three runs in the 8th, highlighted by a Clemente rbi double (his only at bat) to deep right center.

─────── *DID YOU KNOW?* ───────

Lew Krausse was traded to the Seattle Pilots by Oakland after the '69 season and thought about refusing to report to Seattle. But he wore the Pilots uniform during that spring when the team was suddenly sold to future MLB commish Bud Selig (the move to Milwaukee received final approval less than a week before the start of the '70 season). Lew started the inaugural Brewers game on a cold day in Milwaukee in a more bitter 12-0 defeat.

The Dodgers Willie Davis scored the lone run for the West in the bottom half, as the East won the 'King game' 5-1. Tom Seaver got the win after throwing the first three shutout innings, followed by Bob Gibson's three scoreless. I thought Seaver's reply to the question on if it bothered him to fly 5,000 miles for the game told it all, "Not for a man who interrupted his whole life!"

Of course I loved that Fairly was picked by his peers to be the game's MVP and had to be told after showering to come back onto the field to receive his big trophy from Mrs. King. Ron recently told me, "It was such an honor to play in the game, and I had the chance to meet Mrs. King. We put together pretty good all-star teams, and I was surprised not only to be picked for the game (coming from out of the country in Montreal) but also picked by the guys as the MVP—it was quite an honor."

Some quality time with Fairly on his favorite field—photo courtesy of Jayne Kaymin-Oncea

DID YOU KNOW?

When the redheaded Fairly was traded to the Expos by the Dodgers, he was asked if he expected to become as celebrated a citizen as Rusty Staub who was affectionately known in Montreal as "Le Grande Orange"? Fairly replied, "compared to Rusty, I'm afraid the best they will ever call me is "le petite strawberry!"

❏ OH REALLY, O'MALLEY TAKES OVER FOR HIS DAD

This game was also just 11 days after Peter O'Malley had succeeded his father as the new Dodgers President, and just a week before the end of Spring Training. As such, he obviously had plenty on his plate besides adding this huge event at the Ravine. Peter recently told me that he stayed in L.A. during this time (instead of being with the Dodgers at their spring training site in Vero Beach) to prepare for such a prestigious event and that he couldn't have been more pleased with the outcome. "This went to the top of the list, this was a priority without a doubt. And It went smoothly without any hitches or hiccups at all. Stadium operations director Bob Smith had everything arranged, and it was just a major success."

On who was there, Peter? "The enthusiasm for this game, when you look at who came and supported it, really speaks for itself. For example Joe DiMaggio, I would guess back in those days, Joe hadn't gone much of anywhere for a relatively long time. His enthusiasm and support for the game and for him to be here was amazing!"

O'Malley on putting this game together, "It just caught on. In baseball, ownership, the commissioner's office, everybody had to buy into it; everybody

With Mr. O'Malley at his L.A. office

had to agree to it and support it. We still had to get the talent and the players to come. There were a lot of pieces to it, and once we got the commitment and started seeing the names of the players, we knew we had a winner."

Then Peter thought out loud, "If my math is correct, next March will be the 50th anniversary for that game, Wow, that is truly worthy of something." Subsequently, when I told him how much the game meant to Clemente, he stressed it even more, "My gosh, something's got to be done. And when it might have been the greatest collection of players ever?...that's a big deal."

───── *REALITY CHECK* ─────

I proposed to Dodger upper management and MLB Commish Rob Manfred that this game should somehow be commemmorated at the 2020 All-Star game in of all places, Dodger Stadium. That pandemic thing got in the way, however, before I could get this important anniversary to go viral.

❏ TOUCHING GREATNESS WITH MY PEN

As amazing as it was to see these all-time greats perform on the diamond on the same day, it was what happened after the game that I'll always remember most. I knew these guys were all in a hurry to get out of town and back to their spring training sites, so I quickly headed toward the team bus behind right field that would take many of them back to their hotel. I was definitely in 'autograph heaven,' stopping and chatting with more than 20 of these legends, including Stan Musial, Willie Stargell, Tom Seaver, Johnny Bench [if he only knew that decades later he'd be retrieving my golf balls out of water hazards], Pete Rose, Ernie Banks, Al Kaline, Billy Martin, Bobby Murcer, Ron Santo, umpire Emmett Ashford, and THE Roberto Clemente, who was the last one out.

I will never forget standing right in front of the bus waiting for that last player and hearing the driver say "Is that it? We're leaving!", while still hoping to see a Clemente or a Mays or a Gibson. Literally in the last second, here comes Roberto (dressed in a beautifully pinstriped sport coat), hustling toward me like he's going for an over-the-shoulder running catch. Instead, this was to catch his ride on time. But he ran right past me to get on board and meeting him now seemed impossible. Of course, that didn't stop me from looking up at this speeding blur skipping up the bus steps, all the while asking if he could please sign my book?

Clemente suddenly stopped and while about to head for his seat, looked back at me through the window as if to say 'Oops,' turned around to get back off the bus—smiled and kindly signed his name (in his most unusual artistic style of calligraphy). With his familiar Puerto Rican accent, he said, "You doing good?" I replied, "Yeah, thank you SO much." He winked, friendly-tapped me on the shoulder and then got right back onto the bus. While I then stared at his signature, the door shut, and the bus immediately drove away. Another example of that first (and in this case my only) impression of someone whom you admire giving back something that can stay with you forever. What a wonderful interaction with a person whom I rank as a top very few all-time great in my lifetime, FOR SURE!

───────────────── **FUN FACT** ─────────────────

Years later, I learned that as a great admirer and supporter of Dr. Martin Luther King's philosophy of nonviolence and racial integration, Clemente's concerns for civil rights led him to befriend MLK, and the medallion that he received for playing in this game was one of his most treasured mementos from his illustrious career (it's been on display in a booth, commemorating Clemente in the Texas Rangers museum in Arlington).

❏ MARILYN MONROE WOULD BE ENVIOUS

So, now what? All of the players were gone, and the place was now silent. Instead of walking back to the car, however, for some reason, I headed back inside the stadium on the field level. I looked around at the pristine grounds, thinking about the upcoming opening of a new season and wandered over behind the backstop screen. Of course the last time there, I'd already had my thrill of briefly being inside the Dodger clubhouse, so why not check out that neighborhood again? Just maybe a player or two were leftover stragglers— perhaps a Sandy, Jackie, or even Drysdale?

So, I got up the nerve to walk back down the stairwell to below field level and towards the old visitor's clubhouse on the first-base side, while not sure of my location (since it WAS my first time in that direction). This area was also dimly lit again and very quiet (with no signs of life nearby), as I noticed a door in front of me being only slightly ajar. I slowly walked up to it and caught a glimpse inside (feeling like I was in some James Bond flick, looking for possible hidden baseball royalty), and I remember this like it was NOW.

There was an older man sitting in the middle of the room on a metal folding card table-like chair in a white tank top undershirt and white boxer shorts—all by his lonesome! He was just staring into space, doing absolutely nothing, as I tried to get a better look at him from a side view. It took a few seconds until I realized—it was JOE (Freakin') DIMAGGIO! Here we go again... another incredible one-on-one opportunity with a legend. But do I really walk into his clubhouse un-invited?

You're damn right I do! It's Joe D. The Yankee Clipper. It might as well have been Babe Ruth...but he was long gone. So, I'll gladly settle for 'Mr. Coffee' and can't pass up this once-in-a-lifetime chance. I politely knocked on this metal door as I tip-toed inside and said as I slowly approached him, "Excuse me. Mr. DiMaggio? Could you please sign my program?" He turned to his left (only slightly dumbfounded) and fortunately instead of being the not-so-pleasant

Joe's signature made this kid smile for weeks (and even decades) to come

Mrs. Roxy Campanella gave me this card, while speaking with Roy at the stadium, a special keepsake that any fan enjoyed receiving from the man with the eternal smile.

and moody man whom I'd later heard about, he was in a relaxed state and said, 'Sure kid.' Of course, he also asked how I got into this player's only area? I flat out told him that I had curiously wandered in after getting a bunch of autographs outside, and then here I was.

The unfazed DiMaggio was VERY nice to me and even shared some quality small talk. He not only signed my program (which I had opened to the page with his picture on it) but also my little book. I thanked him, while saying that I wish I was old enough to have seen him play in person. He smiled, and wished me luck. I then walked out of that clubhouse not on 'Cloud 9' but closer to nine trillion—feeling as if I'd just run into one of the all-time ballplayers (which is exactly what happened!). Clemente and DiMaggio back to back? Ruth and Gehrig would be impressed!

I've always told this story as likely being the only person to EVER get Joe DiMagggio's autograph in his underwear (arguably including even Marilyn Monroe!).

Mr. O'Malley recalled for me his feelings when this day was all said and done, "we were very very happy the way everything went. We had it well organized and well planned, and we were very proud of that."

They were calling this event the 'initial charity game.' On the other hand, despite it raising over $30,000 to help construct the MLK, Jr. Memorial Center in Atlanta, it turned out to be the only one of its kind and one of the great days of my youth around a ballfield. O'Malley also remembered that it was supposed to be an annual game, but that it just never happened.

As for my Clemente and DiMaggio stories, Peter youthfully responded, "Just great, those recollections are treasures!" Exactly, why I'm sharing them. After the game, Campanella showed his always positive side by saying, "One heckuva day, even though we didn't score many runs, it was a beautiful day." You can say that again, Campy!

CHAPTER 10

RADIO 101 IN MY DNA

When there was no early April 1972 baseball (thanks to the first player's strike in MLB history), at least we got to watch Jack Nicklaus capture his 4th Masters, as he cashed in for that big $25,000 winner's check. I was following the horses, while making an important personal decision. Should I attend Santa Monica City College for a second year (when it changed names to SMC)? FYI: This was about two decades after the legendary James Dean enrolled there and 20 years before Monica Lewinsky did the same.

This was just a perfectly convenient spot on Pico Blvd. for a nice semi-regular after-school jaunt to the beach (some of us called it Beach Tech), where my grades were very average, but my tan was fantastic! I was a history major, while learning a few things about broadcasting from an actual local sportscaster and department head Lou Riggs—the best part of my brief two semesters at SMCC. Lou was the sports director of their college station KCRW for 16 years, where he also called some Pepperdine and UCLA events. And I would catch him on TV as the host of the Hollywood Park racing replay show.

One class that I took at SMCC, which became extremely influential for the rest of my life and a passion to pass along to all, was a speech class. Not just any speech class, but our teacher actually stuttered. I was thinking exactly what you're probably thinking, how the hell could a stutterer teach a speech class? Very carefully! ONLY ME! (which I thought might be another good name for this book). Of course, she didn't teach us how to speak, but to be comfortable in front of a group which was totally invaluable (our current President is the perfect example of such success). I strongly recommend that everyone also take a similar class. Your personal confidence level should reach new highs, which you'll never regret.

DID YOU KNOW?

I'll bet you didn't know that NFL star receivers Steve Smith and Chad 'Ochocinco' Johnson were once teammates on the SMC Corsairs football team to begin their college careers. I wonder if their teammates even recall that? Somehow, I think so.

Meanwhile KCRW, was an actual FM radio station on campus (now an NPR affiliate), in which we weren't allowed to practice. On the other hand, it really got my future juices flowing even more hopefully about the radio biz. Professor Riggs would give us assignments to call the play-by-play of our football games (with no Smiths or Johnsons out there), which was my first real taste of what it took? We would sit in the small press box or in the stands. Knowing that my athletic days were soon numbered, this seemed like a great way to make a living, if that was ever at all possible?

Riggs doing his show at Hollypark and interviewing 'The Shoe'

I wasn't getting much confidence, however, from those around me. According to too many, this was just a pipe dream for me. Something that someone else might achieve. Why not me? I knew as much about sports as most individuals my age, and there was no reason why I couldn't evolve from there.

What was wonderful was to occasionally connect with Lou over the years (specifically, most recently on Facebook, where he made some nice comments about my career, before he passed away at the age of 81). Well-liked by everyone I'd ever come across, Lou Riggs was not only an inspiration to many, but he left quite a legacy. I'll always appreciate his early guidance.

FUN FACT

For over a quarter of century, SMC had led the nation in transferring students to the University of California system. I wasn't one of them, however. Instead, I would be transferring thanks to my radio DJ idol's recommendation.

❏ MOTOR-MOUTH

That was my well-earned nickname at times, when as a teenager, since I guess I spoke a lot (happily later learning that it was also Elgin Baylor's moniker with his teammates). This was not just talking about anything, but everything! Like many kids, at times, I felt like an introvert, being passive when not prepared to speak up whether in class or just in public. But when I really knew about the subject or felt passionate about something, I was compelled to speak up and wanted my voice heard to let people know I had something to contribute. That's where that speech class really showed its teeth in my future!

I would often hear my mother say things like, "you should be on the radio, or make people laugh on stage." And I would always laugh that off and not take it seriously, responding with "they can laugh just by looking at me." There was also something brewing inside of me that evolved into a passion for wanting to do something with my voice. There's that word 'passion' again (without it, we simply have a hollow existence). I sounded too adolescent and was wondering when complete puberty would finally give me a stronger adult voice that I could share with everyone.

❏ THE HULLABALOOER CHANGED MY LIFE

We could all use a strong mentor, and after high school my thoughts were to somehow get some training, with radio in mind, but I had NO idea on where to start. Fortunately, I had befriended one of the great disc jockeys of all time. Dave Hull was an L.A. radio legend, whom I couldn't wait to come home and listen to when I was in grade school. Every day at 3pm, I would turn on KRLA and listen to 'the Hullabalooer' toot his horn and laugh at the day's events like

no one else I'd ever heard. He'd also talk up to the records that he played and nail the intro (just stopping short of when the vocal starts) in a way that always had me wondering how much fun that might be to do the same some day. As a result, I began practicing doing that in my head.

My high school buddy Larry 'Stats' Kahn used to regularly call into the station (then KFI) with postgame Dodger statistics for Hull to use on his show, which immediately followed the game broadcasts and that's how he got his nickname 'Stats.' He would get a mention of credit at the end of those shows (it was really the early version of postgame Dodger talk, but with music and Dave's personal commentary).

With Hull at KFI when trying to end the 70s Big Red Machine's reign with a Voodoo doll full of pins

Since Larry knew how much I'd admired Dave for years, it wasn't long until we often headed to the station on Vermont Ave (just down the street from my future college), right after leaving Dodger Stadium to watch Hull do his thing. Hanging with my boyhood music radio idol was simply a total personal thrill— even better so when Dave would end his show with 'Stats by Kahn and Sobel.' Now you're talkin'!

In those days, Larry and I would carpool to dozens of Dodger games, and then onto KFI we went. I got to watch the master do his magic in front of that microphone and huge console surrounded by turntables, while being his own board-op. I was in heaven, which solidified any and all my thoughts of doing something in broadcasting one day.

Before long, I asked Dave if he could recommend a school for me? He replied definitely either Pasadena City College or Los Angeles City College. I chose LACC because it was closer and affordable at the time. In all honesty, however, if Dave told me to go to Timbucktu U, I may have, because he knew his stuff, and I couldn't wait to get started. Besides, he's the Hullabalooer!

❏ IT'S ON TO LACC

The first day at my new school was a real eye opener! I had just enrolled as a broadcast major at LACC and entered this large auditorium, which had over 250 others who wanted to get their feet wet in the same radio and TV department, but had no idea of what was ahead of them. The elder statesman of the department Don McCall was about to set the record straight. He was old-school in every way you could imagine and NOT the type to beat around the bush, which he immediately showed.

Mr. McCall greeted us, and then I'll NEVER forget what came next. He looked around the room and then began by stating matter of factly that most of us would not be around after the first few weeks, let alone long enough to graduate two years later. He broke it down that likely more than 50% of us would drop out before the end of the first semester, and 75% would be gone by year two, and if we were lucky, 15% might graduate?

McCall, who had seen it all, definitely knew that many young students were looking for a shortcut in life, loosely thinking that being a DJ seemed like a relatively easy career, which is the main reason I'm detailing this scenario. There are no shortcuts in life—find a passion and follow it! You'd think that getting to talk about your favorite music on the radio couldn't be TOO difficult, right? Wrong again my fellow student-types!

Mr. McCall was right and most of those youngsters we're very soon never seen or heard from again near that department as predicted. NOTHING that he said, however, would deter my path towards what I wanted for my life. And thank God it was a reasonable $7.50 per semester plus books—I wonder if that's gone up yet?

❏ SPORTS WAS AN AFTER-THOUGHT AND SO WAS I

During the first days of our actual classes, I had met several guys who were also into sports and wanted that to be their career focus, just like me (along with my DJ dreams). Unfortunately, our department had no teacher who knew the difference between a ball and a puck, or a park and a golf course. The only time I recall any sports ever brought up in class by the teacher was after the highly publicized 1972 Miami Dolphins perfect 17-0 NFL season. Accordingly, a topical question asked as part of a quiz was "Who's the Coach of the Miami Dolphins?"

Those of us sports guys laughed at such a simple question. Of course it was THE Don Shula (now the winningest NFL coach ever). Other than one assignment to call a few minutes of our school's football game, that was the extent of our sports content ALL semester, which was NOT MUCH to those who wanted it and needed it! So, we were on our own when it came to learning about sportscasting. That's just how it was going to be.

With our LACC mascot Cubby

154

❏ SPORTS TALK FOR LIFE

The first day in class, our new sports group was already arguing about stupid trivial stuff—similar to our 24/7 sports radio of today. This scenario also led to friendships that have wonderfully lasted all these years later, and it was Paul Olden, the first of my classmates, whom I quickly connected with, and we started hanging out together. Paul had the best voice in the group, along with a definite personal commitment to doing this, so I could easily see him advancing faster than most. More importantly, we had fun together.

We were either laughing or arguing, while forming a solid friendship in class, as he quickly became my biggest influence on campus by far! Paul would often talk about how he practiced reading copy and doing play-by-play in front of his TV at home. Which felt quite familiar, given that it was already something I'd been doing. My efforts, however, were more half-ass. Paul's total dedication to regularly doing this to improve his craft was inspiring, which got me to do similar much more consistently.

Meanwhile in classes with my new buddy, we were too often talking sports and might have to be interrupted by the teacher, because we could be too loud and animated (usually more me than him). That was always my personality, but I was much too obvious when not paying the necessary attention, which I would soon pay for awkwardly.

❏ A GOLD MEDAL EDUCATION

Later in my second semester in the department, a teacher and former professional broadcaster named Chuck Edwards stopped dead in his tracks in the middle of his class to get my attention. He was totally pissed-off and tired of my little distractions and really laid it on me, calling me out in front of everyone, while giving me a lecture that I'll never forget. I can still see him now, so mad that his face turned beet red, while pointing directly at me with a purpose. Later, I thought of a famous quote by of all people—my comedic idol Groucho Marx, "If you speak when angry, you'll make the best speech you'll EVER regret."

Mr. Edwards then angrily said to me "SOBEL, you're not paying attention again! In reality, you are wasting my time, your time, and everyone else's time in this class and the entire department. You haven't shown much talent anyway, really don't have the voice and simply, why are you here?"

Are you bleeping kidding me? Maybe he thought he had huge enough balls to say that to me or simply to just let out some steam? He was certainly nothing like my favorite inspirational football coach Vince Lombardi, obviously NOT trying to motivate me, while seemingly hoping I would be one of the weak souls who would quickly drop his class, with deflated beach balls between my legs and never to be heard from again.

WRONG, Mr. Edwards, you were dealing with the wrong kid! So that's what you think of me? Well I'll show your ass what I'm about, and I'm not going anywhere. After being briefly quite embarrassed, you actually motivated me more than I can explain and from then on, I had 'a bit' more of a serious attitude and focus towards my classes (with a chip the size of a boulder on my shoulder). Thanks much to my surrogate Coach Lombardi.

This led to my one time confronting Edwards (showing that my own beach balls were bigger than boulders), "excuse me Sir, but you are a teacher in this school only because you couldn't keep your broadcasting career going! And you are telling ME, that I don't have what it takes to succeed?"

We've never crossed paths since those days, but it sure would be a blast from the past to give him just a few minutes to read this chapter. I'd pay double for front row seats to that. A little verbal payback never hurt anybody, but I guess it's also best to thank him for the backhanded way that he really did motivate me.

TED'S TRUISM

People, please never EVER let anyone try to take away your passion. Some are simply envious because they don't have one, others just want to drag you down to make themselves feel important. But whatever your passion is, make that your personal power to achieve what you want in any phase of your life. And if any of this inspires just one of you, my goals here have been achieved.

My turn to speak to LACC students 46 years later

Back to my deepest passion which was sportscasting, Olden's constant leading by example on how to hone my skills kept me focused on the task at hand. If I was to ever accomplish anything in this very difficult field to get started in, I needed to be more serious. It was feeling just like what Mr. McCall had told us on that first day of class—you're in Fantasyland if you're just looking for an easy career as a DJ or sportscaster. It's NOT easy at all, and if you're in cruise mode this early in your studies, it's probably over before you ever start!

❏ WHO'S GOT THOSE CHEAP ONES?

What really got the ball rolling though was when Paul and I began attending local pro and college games of any sport together to practice our play-by-play in the stands. The rest truly was history. We first met up at the then four-year old Fabulous Forum in Inglewood, but neither of us had a real job yet. Paul had been selling programs at the stadium, while I had just finished stocking the fridges at Danny's Liquor store in West Hollywood. It was time to start saving up some money—specifically after spending most of my summer job cash on a beautiful new top of the line $300 Radio Shack stereo system with a turntable that I just had to have. So, now it was necessary to restock my wallet to have enough to get into the arenas and stadiums.

Obviously we couldn't afford great or even good seats, so it was always about the 'Cheap Ones.' Just get us inside baby, we'd take it from there! Our own fun way of trying to attend sporting events at all of our local venues was by always asking the regular ticket scalpers, if they had any 'cheap ones'?

We mostly dealt with the same ticket guys, just hoping to buy their seats for under $10, and more often under $5, particularly in our earliest days not allowing our lighter wallets to affect our 'onsite training.' Most got to know us as regulars and often when it came down to game time and they were stuck with tickets, we were right there to ask—so do you have any 'cheap ones' NOW? And most of the time they would accept 2-5 dollars per seat, which for them was better than getting stuck with soon-to-be worthless tix. So, into the event we went, many times well after the game had started, but we were in!

In those days most Lakers and certainly Kings hockey games were not sold out, so we would work our way around the arena looking for the best seat location to set up and get our cassette players out to begin our night of 'broadcasting.' After awhile, we started calling ourselves the 'American Sports Network' and did our work as if we were really on the air. Even some of the ushers and stats people in the press area would confuse us with Armed Forces Radio and joke that we were broadcasting these games to many people around the world. In reality, it was really just narrowcasting to anyone within earshot.

An early thrill to have the Dodgers welcome two guys just practicing into our cassette recorders

What stood out most to me was the surprisingly positive feedback from the fans sitting near us. Our biggest concern was bothering those who came to watch the game after paying their hard-earned bucks and us not getting in the way of any of that. Fortunately, most of these individuals were extremely kind (if not even very complimentary). More often than not, they would be listening to our calls instead of our local play-by-play legends who could be on their radios. There was not a better compliment than a fan turning off their radio just to listen to us.

Paul and I remembering the fun years, when calling the action at Dodger Stadium

We would always attempt to sit in the same upper colonnade section 27-28 near the top of the Forum or the last row of the field level at Dodger Stadium in section 105 behind the plate, just close enough for an electrical outlet to let us plug in our recorders and save money on batteries, just part of our regular routine.

❏ SACRIFICING A REAL LIFE

Speaking of a life, I really didn't have much of one at all. Going to these games was almost like a full-time job (without pay) and was a huge personal sacrifice, while not getting to experience what most others my age were. No regrets, as it was my choice, and I loved attending all of the events. But from the age of 19-25, instead of hanging with friends or just doing what normal folk my age were doing, I would be at games—a lot of them. Paul and I were such regulars at these events that it was almost as if we were part of the credentialed media—although DEFINITELY NOT!

But as dedicated as we were with fully honorable intentions, we became quite a nuisance to a few of the teams' media directors, asking them for the actual game notes and stats sheets when arriving, as if we were really there to work. Whether it was at The Forum, Dodger Stadium, the Coliseum or wherever, we were doing exactly what it took to simulate a real broadcast, including finding any used commercial copy from the already departed broadcast teams which would be gold to us.

❏ HOPE IS SUPPOSED TO BE A GOOD THING

One man whom we perturbed more than most was then L.A. Kings public relations boss Mike Hope. He was not very open to us 'student/adults' being in his press area and asking for anything that the 'pros' would expect to receive before and during every game they worked. We noticed that Hope would roll up his game notes and tuck them under his arms like a football, and he wasn't about to EVER fumble them, especially in our direction.

What was the stick up his rear all about? Why treat us like vagrants instead of the highly determined duo that we proved to be on an almost nightly basis? Well, I've recently been back in contact with Mike, and he couldn't have been nicer after all these years. He sent me his version of how he saw the Olden-Sobel era at the Forum, included here to show just what we were dealing with in those days...

> I first met Ted Sobel and Paul Olden when they were broadcasting students at LACC, and I was Director of Public Relations for the Los Angeles Kings Hockey Club. Ted and Paul pestered me to death, occasionally asking for press passes to Kings games so they could practice their broadcasting skills. They were constant "pain in the butts" for their continual requests to be treated like "regular press people," when in reality, they were just local college broadcasting department students. They wanted game notes, locker room passes, interview quotes, etc. They were more demanding than Pulitzer Award–winning columnist Jim Murray of the L.A. Times!!!

(Kings announcer) Bob Miller actually was one of their biggest boosters. He complimented Ted and Paul for their dedication, perseverance, and desire to become the best they could be. When I griped about them wanting game notes and stats, Bob defended their requests, saying these were necessary to prepare for a good broadcast.

They were persistent, hard-working, dedicated craftsmen who regularly sat in the top row of the half-empty Forum during Kings games and honed their broadcasting skills. Each is to be admired for putting in the time to become the best they could be…and they have become respected journalists at the highest rung of their profession.

Today, Ted and Paul are two very successful, nationally known and recognized broadcasters. In retrospect, American Success Stories. They had a dream. They worked long and hard hours at pursuing that dream…and in the end, that dream came true. I couldn't be more proud of them!

Mike, those are wonderfully kind words and all greatly appreciated. And how special for future HOF broadcaster Bob Miller to so positively influence our situation without us knowing. That's the kind of guy he's always been, so no surprises there. As for our actions onsite, we did what we had to do, or get stepped on by a corporate Godzilla and maybe to never be heard from again. No regrets, and we thank everyone who contributed to making our earliest days a learning experience of a lifetime, while getting to attend so many historic events!

With Bob proudly flashing one of his two Stanley Cup rings

❏ NO GAMES—JUST SERIOUS BROADCASTING
(YOUNG HOPEFULS, GET OUT YOUR
HIGHLIGHTERS)

We began formatting our practice broadcasts just as they did on the air. It was starting to feel natural with actual game-break interviews, including a few elite names who were extremely gracious with their time for us. Bryant Gumbel, then a local KNBC TV sports anchor/reporter, would often be at games, along with a former pro goalie and hockey play-by-play guy Stu Nahan (Gumbel's Channel 4 cohort). Bryant was our semi-regular. Both Bryant and Stu would come on with us for their analysis at halftime or between periods, fully aware that this wasn't being broadcast anywhere but just into our own little cassette recorders.

--- **FUN FACT** ---

Gumbel even once helped to break up a stupid fan's skirmish right in front of our location at the Forum, along with Dodger Steve Garvey and his huge forearms that put a clamp on things in a hurry!

We had hit the jackpot whenever they joined us in our utility room just below the press box that we used as a studio, thanks to our friendships with the ushers. During the games, Paul and I would each call a portion and then critique it on our way home. I would then take notes on what needed improvement and what was sounding good to my ears. This is written more for any sportscasting hopefuls than the rest of you—so I truly do hope you're taking notes!

No longer were we just two students sitting in the stands with a recorder, but actual broadcasters who were just waiting for their first real jobs. This went on for the next six years. If that's not dedication, the word doesn't exist! But it was only in the third month at LACC, when my world suddenly changed forever.

❏ THANKS-GIVING?

I had borrowed my Dad's snazzy-looking Electra 225 convertible to drive to the Forum on the night of November 22, 1972, just before one of my favorite days of the year—Thanksgiving. Bring on the turkey, stuffing, and gravy, and I'm a very contented guy.

I called a Kings-Montreal Canadiens matchup into my trusty recorder that night, which wound up a hell of a hockey game, with lots of clean passing and fast skating throughout. It was a nice Wednesday night crowd (for those years) of over 14,000, many of whom, of course, were rooting for the storied Canadiens. The game opened with some heavy hitting and a couple of fights between Montreal defenseman and future Hall of Famer Guy LaPointe and L.A. rookie Don Kozak.

Both future Hall of Fame goalies made some great saves, ex-Canadien Rogie Vachon for the Kings and Ken Dryden for the first place Habs who got a goal from another HOFer-to-be Guy Lafleur. Should be HOFer Butch Goring added two assists, which tied him for 2nd in league scoring behing the great Phil Esposito. L.A. defenseman Harry Howell, another certain HOFer in his last NHL season, scored a rare third-period goal for a 3-3 tie, and the Kings were suddenly tied for first place. What a night of hockey, but what a nightmare ahead...

I remember coming home all hyper, with my father already in bed watching the Tonight Show with Johnny Carson—a very common late-night occurrence in those days. He asked me how the game was, and I said it was fantastic and that I had a particularly good 'broadcast,' which he still didn't seem to take seriously at times. Dad was mostly supportive in what I wanted to do, but also had reservations on if it ever could truly become a reality. He hated the thought of me wasting my time, given that there was a big world to be conquered.

We briefly chatted about that, and then I started watching the show as he dozed off to sleep. It was getting late, so I shut off the TV and went to bed and had no idea that this would be my last time I would ever speak with my father. Soon after, my mother returned home and found Dad had suffered a massive heart attack. After several minutes of working on him with my minimal amount of previous CPR training, I knew that there was nothing more I could do.

So, at the much too young age of just 55, Bernard Sobel was gone. The most devastating moment of my life almost didn't seem real. I was only 19, and this couldn't happen just yet. Then it hit me. It was just a year previous that we had a very deep conversation, because of how much I sometimes tended to overly lean on him for advice and just everyday life stuff. Dad actually said in a serious tone that I might be better off if he was suddenly out of the picture, which would make me have to learn about succeeding in life the hard way, just like he did, when he threw his abusive father out of the house. Hardly my ideal way of moving forward.

Extremely tough words to hear from your father, but he wasn't far from the truth. I was suddenly burdened with truly learning life the very hard way and without the rock who was always there for me! Life goes on for everyone after suffering such losses, but we need to be strong with a full-speed ahead mentality and not get mired in the sadness. As difficult as that was, it's how I tried to look at it, despite little real life experience.

After several hours of sitting at home, consoling my mother and dealing with my own sorrow on this holiday Thursday, I needed some fresh air. First, I had an important football game to watch on TV. Not just any other game on any day, but one that meant something to me and my father—and now for eternity.

Dad will forever be looking over me

❏ DAD'S FINAL WIN CAME SOONER THAN LATER

Well-known media oddsmaker Jimmy 'the Greek' Snyder had written in his column the day before, "Oklahoma is at Nebraska Thursday, and it could be a classic of its kind, with two running backs trying to win the game and the Heisman Trophy—Johnnie Rodgers of the Cornhuskers and Greg Pruitt of the Sooners. I make it Nebraska by 8."

Dad and I had previously talked about the slate of Thanksgiving Day games and he loved the road underdog in this one (the true odds being 7 1/2 points). The game was his top play of the week, and he put his money where his mouth was. That was all I needed to hear to have a strong reason to root for the Sooners. Since he was suddenly gone, I absolutely had to watch this game with the heaviest heart imaginable, while knowing that even with a nice win, we would never see the winning $$.

Oklahoma spotted Nebraska a 14-point lead but roared back in the final quarter for a 17-14 win, which also spoiled the Cornhuskers bid for a fourth straight Big 8 Title in their first home loss in three years. It was the only reason to smile all day—or all week—or even the rest of the year. At least, it momentarily eased the pain. I could never watch those two schools play again without the feelings coming back from that awful Thanksgiving day.

Trying to extend those small gratifying feelings and after much deep inner reflection, I decided it might be best to join my old high school friends in our annual Thanksgiving Day football game on a big grassy lawn across from La Cienega Park. Believe me, I didn't want to leave my mother alone at this time. She totally agreed that it might help just to play and briefly get away from this catastrophic reality.

The toughest part was walking up to the field, being greeted by everyone just like it was another Turkey Day. I had to stop and make the announcement of why it wasn't. I could hardly say the words, but I made it clear that it was important for me to totally put my reality aside for the moment and try to enjoy our little game, before dealing with what lied ahead.

Attempting to ease the situation some (helped very briefly by scoring a touchdown), I told a few of my buddies that the only good news of the day was how my father could leave this world with a smile because he had just won his last EVER bet (that I was aware of). I described the circumstances like I was doing the postgame show. Dad would've loved that too.

❏ BACK TO SCHOOL AND REALITY

Looking forward, I certainly knew that it was best for me to keep focusing on my passion and get the most out of the college experience. In that regard, LACC did have much to offer with some excellent classes, including having one of my favorite local TV newsmen Tom Snyder's wife Mary Ann as a teacher. I took her microphone technique class and then tried to use what I'd learned there and apply it to our campus radio station KBMA, when I was attempting to be a D.J. or newscaster (and throwing in some sports scores and stories whenever possible).

The station's signal could barely be heard a few feet off campus, but it was loud and clear at our little school snack bar, Emma's Galley, where speakers were blaring to our potential audience walking by. What an amazing opportunity to get some very much needed on-air experience, with the backing of professionals who knew their stuff.

I got to spin some records, edit reel-to-reel tape (no digital until decades later), and write/read news reports. I specifically recall one funny moment, when getting razzed about reading copy after referring to our then not too well-respected Vice President with the words 'more on Spiro Agnew coming up.' But it really came out like 'moron Spiro Agnew,' and I immediately realized it, repeated it, and then couldn't stop laughing (on and off the air). No political intent—just a funny on-air flub.

Of course, the biggest disappointment at City College remained that we really had to teach ourselves sportscasting and learn by repetitive practice. Since Olden and I were regularly out doing our play-by-play and by the time I'd reached my third semester, I was getting somewhat bored, while more importantly needing to get a regular job, given that I could no longer afford everyday life after my father had died.

--- ***PROUD FUN FACTS*** ---

I can only imagine how proud he would be to see his son listed as one of the distinguished (and not extinguished) alums of L.A. City College, even though I never did graduate from there. It's such a special personal achievement to join my other fellow radio and TV department alums on that list alongside Olden, longtime USC football voice Pete Arbogast, and joining me in 2018 Cliff Winston, who went on to be a fabulous success on the radio in Southern California.

Cliff may have been the funniest of our LACC classmates. We spent a lot of time together on campus, laughing constantly! He did some great voice imitations, with his best being the longtime TV sports icon Lindsey Nelson. I used to say that he sounded more like Nelson than the man himself, while the Winston smile for the ages would always light up the room.

One of my biggest regrets was not staying in touch with Cliff after our college days, and it was awful to learn of his sudden passing just a few days before Christmas in 2017. I attended his funeral service which was one of the most moving and genuine ever, including a few songs sung by Cliff's good friend and his KJLH Radio owner/boss Stevie Wonder, who sounded as great as ever and was just a total inspiration to a church full of Winston admirers—even more so after singing a customized (for Cliff) version of his hit "As." RIP Cliffy. Sorry we never got to play tennis together, but thanks for leaving us such a wonderful family.

It was great to speak at the 2018 LACC Dean's Honor Tea gathering for their honor students, when I got the chance to praise the school and my classmates for what it meant to me. Then two weeks later, I attended Cliff Winston's banner ceremony. Mine is also now hanging near his and Olden's in the main corridor for one most special class-reunion for the ages.

NO burning desire, NO banner, NO WAY!

LACC has had quite a history, with many notables on their distinguished alum list, which is on their website. The list is remarkable—and it's a huge honor to join them for eternity—including actor and Academy Award winner Alan Arkin; actor and founder of the little people of America Billy Barty; Barbara Billingsley of Leave It To Beaver fame; actor/comedian/director and one of the funniest guys ever Albert Brooks (whose real name is none other than Albert Einstein); actor/producer/director and Oscar winner Clint Eastwood; actor Laurence Fishburne; Academy Award wining actor Morgan Freeman; actor Mark Hamill, AKA Luke Skywalker of 'Star Wars'; actor Jackie Joseph, with whom I was on the board of directors of AFTRA; actor/dancer Ruta Lee (who my mother was often mistaken for); Oscar winner Donna Reed, the co-star of 'It's a Wonderful Life'; Emmy Award winning actor Robert Vaughn who played Napoleon Solo on my personal favorite show 'The Man from U.N.C.L.E.; actor and Emmy Award winner Paul Winfield; actor Joanne Worley of 'Laugh In' fame; composer and Academy Award recipient Jerry Goldsmith; jazz musician Jack Sheldon one of my favorites to watch on the old Merv Griffin show; and composer and Oscar winner John Williams.

Other notable LACC graduates include former L.A. Police Chief and city council member Bernard C. Parks; major league baseball players Don Buford, Larry Demery, Terry Humphrey, Kevin Millar, and Ken Rudolph; LACC's Hall of Fame baseball inductee, sports agent and entrepreneur Dennis Gilbert; NBA player Larry Friend; and NFL players Reggie Haynes, Vince Evans, and Rod Martin.

Evans proudly led our LACC Cubs to the 1973 California JC co-championship, tying Fresno City College 10-10, thanks to a last second 27-yard field goal (in heavy fog) by the Fresno Rams. Evans was the game MVP, despite throwing for only 66 yards on 6 of 17 passing, while rushing for 39 yards on 17 carries. He also got his LACC Cubs to the state championship game, after out-dueling Fullerton JC's Steve DeBerg—another future NFL quarterback. How about those unheralded Champion Cubbies!

Paul and I at the L.A. Coliseum

Great memories with great names that will last as long as the school does. Then again, what the hell am I doing on that list? Too strange after my class debacles there! My bottom line is that I will always be indebted to Paul Olden for his true inspiration from literally day one at LACC, and our friendship remains a close one—even across country, while he continues as the voice of Yankee Stadium.

❑STRIKE THREE—I'M DONE PLAYING BASEBALL!

I knew that I could never be a professional baseball player, but I still loved to play. So, why not give it one last shot by joining a semi-pro team? Finding one was not so easy in those days, along with just making a squad. The one (and only) team that fit my circumstances then played at far away Whittier Narrows fields, but it was worth it for me to put that uniform on again.

So, I went to one or two practices and my shoulder was still killing me with every throw (after a bad high school injury). I didn't care. I still had some decent speed to cover the outfield and run the bases, and was going for one last hurrah, just wanting to milk it as long as possible. Of course I couldn't hide my sore arm from the coach, given that it was very obvious. For some reason, however, (which I think was my small tuition), he kept me on the team.

Finally, it was time for a real game. I was pumped, but also apprehensive. The over an hour drive to Whittier had me remembering times in Little League, Pony League, and even American Legion. Some of these guys whom I'm about to play with and against, had played under pro contracts. As such, I was definitely out of my league. What the hell, you only live once, even if it was on the bench (where I belonged!).

As I was taking in the atmosphere during my first game, this 'comeback' quickly became a disappointment on the scoreboard, as we were getting hammered (something like 9-2). Late in the game, our opponent brought in a fire-balling right hander (and I'm a righty hitter).

I was watching this guy from the dugout thinking, DAMN, who is this? Maybe, some prospect who was immediately piling up the strikeouts, against some of our best hitters? And then someone on the bench began telling us that he'd heard this righty had been previously signed by the Baltimore Orioles and was trying to work his way back to a big league contract.

BALTIMORE ORIOLES??? What the hell am I doing there again??? (Oh yeah, having fun—supposedly). I thought this was semi-pro ball? Well I'm only watching from the dugout anyway, so it really didn't matter. Until the meaningless 9th inning, when our manager from the 3rd-base coach's box looked over into the dugout and through our wire fence and said "Sobel, you're hitting second this inning." So, I found my helmet, grabbed a bat, and grudgingly walked to the on-deck circle.

First, I'm watching these Nolan Ryan-type warmup tosses and was totally sure that I'd never faced a fastball like that in my life! Enough so that I was feeling sorry for the catcher who had to catch this guy, and the sound of the ball hitting the glove was intimidating the crap out of me. Anyway, I joined this team for a reason, and this was my chance to enjoy this game at a level that I'd only dreamed of. So, let's have some fun, right? Not exactly!

I watched our leadoff batter go down in strikes. Each pitch got me thinking that I could leave now, and no one will ever know the difference! But it was my time to attempt the unknown, and I walked up to the plate to face the daunting challenge of my athletic life.

I looked at my third base coach, who just clapped his hands with encouragement. I wasn't about to bunt with one out in the 9th, with my team down a ton of runs (although that crossed my mind). So, I decided to just swing like a man! The pitcher who looked like the size of King Kong on the mound, looked down (probably laughing inside) at all of my NOT terrifying 5-7 150 pound frame, and went to work.

The windup and the first pitch—a fastball (VERY FAST, actually UNBELIEVABLY FAST) was a called strike. It was right down the middle, but the truth is, I barely saw it. I am dead serious. It truly was a total blur. I know it hit the catcher's mitt, because not only did I see it in the strike zone behind me, but my ears were ringing from the loud crashing sound of the ball hitting the leather of his mitt.

My next thought was not what any hitter should ever have—FEAR! If I could hardly see the ball, how the hell am I to ever get out of the way of a wild pitch? I could be instantly killed by a pitcher who must be thinking, who's this Little Leaguer in the batter's box anyway? Is this some charity case reality show (before there were such shows)?

So, I dug in (to a point)...concentrating like I'm flying a plane solo for the first time. The pitcher then goes back to his windup and delivered—another FASTBALL! Boom, I heard it hit the glove again, like somebody had just fired a rifle. The umpired yelled strike again! I'm almost laughing, although the fear of dying kept me from it. I backed out, looked at the ump, and actually asked him how could he call that a strike? If I couldn't see the ball, how the hell could he?

The umpire was not amused, immediately pointing to the ground and said to get back in the damn batter's box. I quickly thought, I'm swinging at the next pitch, I'm getting my money's worth against this guy. I don't care if it's a foot over my head or two feet outside (as long as it's not too far inside, which would have quickly placed me in an ambulance).

Swing and a miss—nobody did it better!—photo courtesy Avery Helm

Now, I'm not sure if the pitcher ever heard any of this meaningless banter with the ump, but he seems to be smirking at me—or maybe that's just his normal look—or at least I was hoping so. Suddenly, it crossed my mind that if he throws me a change-up, I would be so off-balanced that my bat might end up flying over everything towards the parking lot. On the other hand, I'm only thinking fastball against this Bob Gibson wannabee. He just throws tooooooo hard, and there'll be zero chance to adjust. He can't read my mind, so I'm swinging.

The windup and the pitch—FASTBALL, letter high and right down the pipe again. You could feel my swing from Whittier to Chavez Ravine. I tipped it (and I mean just barely) to the backstop screen. It was the greatest foul tip of my life—and I mean it. That was an accomplishment against Mr. Pro Baseball Pitcher. I was thinking, 'THAT WAS FUN'!

Come on baby, throw me one more like that. I just want to hit it anywhere. The windup and the 0-2 pitch—FASTBALL—a swing and a miss! I think my swing started as the ball was already crushing that catcher's mitt again.

As I walked away from home plate, the dimming light bulb went off in my head. I'M DONE! That's it, no more organized ball for me. I can't compete against these guys—not if they throw that hard and I have a chronic sore arm anyway. This is more stupid than it is fun.

On the spur of the moment, I decided to cross paths with our third base coach/skipper before going to the dugout and told him. 'Sorry, but I'm done, I'm out of here but thanks for giving me a chance to play again."

I barely knew the names of my teammates anyway, and after one last game-ending strikeout, I packed up my gear and headed for the parking lot. I wasn't even sad on my long drive home. It gave me a time to reflect on what the game meant to me and how I was fortunate to have just enough talent to play it at 'almost' any level.

OH how I would forever appreciate the big leaguers for what they do. 162 games a year, facing much much much better pitching? NO thanks! I experienced it first hand and don't EVER tell me that hitting a baseball isn't THE most difficult thing to do well in sports. Believe me, I know. I have gladly settled for media and pickup games at the park from then on.

❑ RECOGNITION FELT SO GOOD

So, it was full speed ahead to get to my goal. While working too many odd jobs to mention, my future would entail many many nights at sporting events, trying to improve my play-by-play skills. From 1972 through 1977, Paul and I did our thing at local venues. Fortunately, after a few years, others began to take notice.

In 1976, from out of the blue (or actually a seat close by), a freelance writer named John Boal had seen me in the stands doing my thing a few times and approached me about writing a story on my efforts to get a career started. He sent it to numerous publications and TV stations around the country, and we waited for any responses.

Getting some pub in a local newspaper

Some weeks went by, until we got some nice coverage locally and even a few notices nationally. Although it didn't lead to anything special, it was a great boost to my confidence and gave me more hope that something good was about to happen. The best that came of it was getting some local publicity from TV, putting my name and face out to the public for really the first time. It was at the Forum from where it originated.

One was on a late night show that aired at 11:30pm on KTTV Channel 11 called Metro News Metro News (the title inspired by the other offbeat show that preceded and spawned it 'Mary Hartman Mary Hartman,' an uninhibited spoof of real news programs). Show co-host Chuck Ashman introduced my segment with reporter Bill Smith on the scene from the Forum. It was so great to learn that the station actually sent a reporter to do a story on me while I was simply practicing play-by-play into a tape machine (of course I would've sent a limo for him if I could).

Smith was the perfect reporter to do this story, given that he was one of the best at lighthearted stuff. He came out to a game in Inglewood to record moments of my play-by-play and to get a few comments from me. He did an excellent job with it, and what a kick it was to be able to catch it on their show later that week.

But the first to do a segment on me was then KNXT-TV (now KCBS) Channel 2 sports anchor Ted Dawson. I don't recall the exact circumstances of Ted putting me on his nightly sports report, but he was kind enough to send me his recollection of it soon after his recent retirement from 55 years in the business.

> Because he wanted the stars and the big spenders to sit on the front row, Lakers (and Kings) owner Jack Kent Cooke put Hall of Fame Broadcaster Chick Hearn and the rest of the press about 20 rows up at midcourt. While I was covering a game one night, I noticed this young kid sitting a couple of rows behind Chick, doing his own broadcast.

> After listening for a while, I asked my cameraman to come up to the press box and film him. That night, we broadcast the first story on Ted Sobel. We called it "Little Ted." It was one of the most "talked about" stories I ever covered. Obviously, Ted's career has gone on to far outshine mine, but I can always be proud of the fact that I discovered a great talent early.

Thanks for those extremely kind words Ted Dawson, even if they aren't true, given that you are the one with the long and successful TV career...but I'll graciously take it! My favorite part of Ted's report was showing Hearn do his thing, when calling the game, and me doing the same in the stands, and then comparing us on split screen. Of course there was NO true comparison, but just to see us both on TV together was shear joy. Subsequently, telling Chick about it afterward was just as fun, as he was always so supportive with his advice and encouragement.

I was most fortunate that my story ran twice (so I could see it for myself), once during Dawson's nightly report and later on Channel 2's new Sunday Sports Final show. It was introduced by former NFL defensive back Jim Hill (during his first year of TV in L.A.). Subsequently, some personal momentum began to build, making those many hours spent at the Forum seem worthwhile.

———— *FUN FACT* ————

Hill, who is the longest tenured TV sports anchor in L.A. History (45 years and counting), is the only local electronic media member who's covered more sporting events than I have, Believe me, that's not even close, as Jim truly is the hardest working man in our local sports media—by far!

Calling more hockey high above the eastern sideline at the Forum

—— *A SUPER FUN FACT* ——

I'll always admire Dawson as one of the very few getting to stick his mic in front of Vince Lombardi's face after Super Bowl I at the L.A. Coliseum, as a 23-year old reporter. That's a memory!

❑ PHONING IT IN

To give some insight on how we might do whatever is necessary to get our job done, you've likely heard many live reports from sporting events that of course originate from whatever venue it's being held. Too often, however, I had to do pre-game reports from the Forum and wasn't able to get to the game on time (usually due to my real job). So, prepping while listening to the start of that game's broadcast on my car radio, I would stop at a phone booth and do the preview somewhere in Inglewood and on occasion needing a dime to drop into a payphone, when not using a toll-free 800 number. (To understand that context, Google payphone/phone booth if need be?)

Since I often called from a street corner, my biggest concern was that nobody would honk their horn during my reports when they were driving by, causing it to hardly sound like a live update from any arena or stadium. I WAS supposed to be inside reporting on the game LIVE. Although no one ever complained, and I got my job done, it all worked out, but it definitely always felt strange.

On New Year's Day of '80, when doing a weekly Sports Talk Show on WIBA in Madison, Wisconsin and while he was still in L.A., Paul called in for a live Rose Bowl game report with USC vs. Ohio State. Olden did the reports from his home while watching the game on TV in L.A. It was important for me to hold up some journalistic standards, so I never said that he was live from the Rose Bowl, but live in Southern California. The key point was that my listeners got the detailed report that they tuned in for.

——————— *FLASHBACK FUN FACTS* ———————

The TV announcers for that Rose Bowl game were Dick Enberg, Merlin Olsen, and OJ Simpson, USC running back Charles White was named the game MVP (for a second straight year), after scoring from 1-yard out with just over a minute to play. Coach John Robinson's Trojans won 17-16, while likely denying the previously unbeaten 11-0 Buckeyes a share of the national championship with Alabama. Robinson still smiles from ear to ear when bringing up that game. Now you know the rest of the story.

❑ OUR FIRST HIGH FIVE

One special day on our American Sports Network was the last game of the 1977 Dodgers season. Paul and I were doing our usual play-by-play in section 105 behind home plate, hoping that Dusty Baker could join Ron Cey, Reggie Smith, and Steve Garvey as the first big league quartet to each hit 30 home runs in the same year. This was the final season that we would be doing this together, as I was soon to get my first play-by-play job out of town, and Paul would leave for his first pro baseball gig in Spokane in 1980, just weeks before the immense volcanic eruption of Mount St. Helens had totally assaulted the great Northwest.

After Dusty hit his historic blast heard via our trusty microphone, he crossed home plate and headed to the Dodgers dugout, where he was excitedly greeted by rookie outfielder Glenn Burke, who thrust his right hand into the sky. Dusty spontaneously responded by slapping it back, originating this new 'high five' craze. It's a fun story to recall, and it really did happen that way, something that Dusty has always been candidly happy to give credit to Burke's enthusiasm for this ever occurring.

DID YOU KNOW?

Four years later the term 'high five' entered the dictionary, and celebrations in sports and everyday life would never be the same.

Burke was a fun guy to be around and the first openly gay big league player, which didn't seem to be an issue with his Dodger teammates well before its time. Subsequently, he ended up a tragic footnote in baseball history, as a forgotten young talent, who later died of AIDS, after becoming this unsung pioneer. So, the next time you see others celebrating anything by slapping their hands together high above their heads, think of and thank Glenn Burke for his significant 'high five' *Touching Greatness* moment for the ages.

CHAPTER 11

HANGING WITH
ELGIN BAYLOR

❏ CAPTAIN BAYLOR: THE EARLY DAYS

The summer of '66 had 'Good Vibrations' in the air. It was my first exposure to being around big-time athletes (for more than just a quick meet and greet), when I attended the Elgin Baylor, Rudy LaRusso, Walt Hazzard basketball camp. This was also my first time personally away from home for longer than a night, actually it was a full two-week session. I was in holiday heaven and couldn't wait to feel adult-like. My father knew how much this meant to me, making sure that I got to attend two straight years. Unfortunately, those three Lakers weren't always onsite, as I was hoping to practice each day with or near these NBA stars whom I regularly watched on TV. When they were there, I was listening so much more intently than at 'real' school that if they truly were my actual teachers, I definitely would've been a MUCH better student.

It was the first year when I got to befriend one of the camp's tutors. His name was Kenny Washington, an important sixth man on the first two of John Wooden's ten UCLA National championship teams (1964-65). In 1965, he was named their outstanding team player. You can tell that Kenny and I built up some rapport from his words on the note that he wrote to me on our last full day together. I remember how passionate he was about me needing to be more serious about my game.

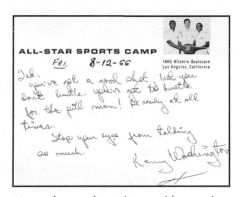

Kenny's words, written with passion

I began shooting 100 free throws a day at Blair Hills Park, after walking home from elementary school—almost every day for months. If I didn't make at least 80%, I wouldn't stop until I did so after another set of 10 shots (a solid recommendation to those hoops players who are struggling from the charity stripe—NOTE: it's much too late for you Shaq!). I got good enough to feel comfortable with entering a free-throw contest through a local Culver City car dealership, and advanced as one of a very few in my 12-13 year old age-group to shoot before a Lakers game at the Sports Arena. There, I made 7 of 10 missing one of them (in-and-out), which cost me from going to the finals at halftime in front of the crowd and my father that night. Needless to say, Kenny Washington was a big influence in the rest of my days as a participating athlete, which I've always appreciated.

In my second year at Elgin Baylor's camp, Dodgers World Series hero Lou Johnson's sons were also on campus, and I befriended them. Lou visited on parent's day and couldn't have been nicer. We spoke for a bit, and he said anytime we wanted tickets to a Dodger game (during his final season in L.A.) to please contact him. Subsequently, the next time I was at the Ravine, I called him over from stands, and he came through, just as promised.

We lost 'Sweet' Lou just months before this printing, and I'll never forget his pure kindness over the decades

Just a great caring guy with whom I've interacted many times over the years, while he worked in the Dodgers community relations department. Mostly a career minor leaguer, 'Sweet' Lou had one special season in the bigs ('65), and the Dodgers rewarded him with what turned into a lifetime deal of working in their organization (after some unfortunate years of drug and alcohol abuse)—a factor that he's always openly talked about and how grateful he's been since.

❏ BEATLE-MANIA IN 90069

In late summer of '68, the Steppenwolf song 'Born To Be Wild' was heard constantly on the radio. My father did what he knew best, finding a way to upgrade his family's lifestyle (whether affordable or not). Somehow, he got us a new house high in the hills above Beverly up Doheny Drive, about a mile and a half north of a very busy Sunset Strip (just down the street from the renowned

'Whisky a Go Go' music venue). Doheny truly was a 'long and winding road,' like the Beatles song suggests. Speaking of those boys from Liverpool—one of the first things I had heard when moving to our new house was that George Harrison could be living somewhere very close by when he was in town.

Well that turned out to be totally false. In fact he never lived in that neighborhood at all. But he did (at least once) briefly stay in the 'Bird Streets' section of our town which featured roads only named after species of birds. As a curious 15-year old Beatles fan, I needed to know where and why this was a supposed story. As a result, the newskid came out in me.

Some time later, I'd learned that Harrison was staying in a rented house on the nearby but very well hidden Blue Jay Way, about a five-minute drive away from my street Nightingale Drive. To be exact, he was there on August 1, 1967, one summer before we moved into that neighborhood, while waiting much too long for his friend and ex-Beatles publicist Derek Taylor (then with The Byrds and Beach Boys), who had gotten lost driving there on another very foggy night up that hill.

To keep himself awake and as a joke to pass the time, George wrote the song 'Blue Jay Way,' while messing with a Hammond Organ in that house. It included the lyrics 'There's a fog upon L.A. and my friends have lost their way.' This song was later recorded for the 'Magical Mystery Tour' film and soundtrack album. I thought it was so awesome that as a 'neighbor,' George could contribute to a Beatles album just down the street from our house.

FUN FACT

Paul Simon partially wrote the song 'Cecilia,' as well as the first two verses of 'Bridge Over Troubled Water,' while staying in that same house on Blue Jay Way in the summer of '69 (when we were living right up the street). Not surprisingly, he never stopped by my place to say hello.

I only lived on Nightingale for two years, but vividly remember some of those densely foggy periods, when it really could be dangerous driving up there. Of course, I never did see Harrison or Simon in the neighborhood (even on clear days), but I did have some great interactions with others whom you just may've heard of...

FUN FACT

Harrison's story got so public that the City of L.A. eventually had to spray paint 'Blue Jay Way' on the sidewalk curb because of that street sign being stolen too many times.

George last returned to L.A. to die of cancer in November of 2001, in the home of his friend Paul McCartney (which he had reportedly bought from singer Courtney Love, who had previously purchased it from comedian Ellen DeGeneres). This home was located on the very hidden in the hills Heather Road (off of Coldwater Canyon), just a few minute drive from my family's last house before my father died. George Harrison was cremated at Hollywood Forever, where my grandparents Fannie and Izzy Foreman are interred. This scenario means even more to me, since Grandma is the person who first stressed to have music in my life.

❏ FEELING STOOGE-LIKE

It would be quite often that driving up or down that hilly Doheny Drive, we would see a very familiar 'bowl' haircut on an aging gentleman, who regularly walked briskly on its most steepest sections. That always impressed my father specifically knowing that he couldn't do close to the same, even though he was about 30 years younger. The man was the inimitable Moe Howard of the Three Stooges. He looked like the guy we saw in the movies, but just a much older white haired version. Feeling Stooge-like, I one time rolled down the window to say something to this comedic icon "HEY MOE?," and he simply smiled/waved and continued on his serious daily exercise.

Moe's penned legacy to me was soitenly better than a poke in the eye!

Seeing him always made me think of when I was five or six, when my dad took me downtown to a Three Stooges book signing, and I shook the hands of all three Moe, Larry, and the last of the Curly Joe's (Joe DeRita). Moe spoke the most with me that day and was very friendly. I couldn't believe Larry's funny fluffed-up hair was just the same in person as it was in the movies.

Sometimes, as a kid I would sit in front of the tube and just watch a Stooges marathon non-stop, so to meet them was a bit surreal. It was Moe who signed the little picture card that they gave to me, which I've kept all of these years. A fun piece to look at now for sure! One suggestion should you be having a bad day, just turn on a Stooges flick, and they will NEVER let you down. No matter how ridiculous it might be, if you're not smiling in the end, something's drastically wrong!

❏ TOUCHED BY AN ANGEL HITCHHIKING

Then, there was my daily routine of hitchhiking from Sunset Blvd up Doheny on my way home from school. I didn't have a car yet (moving there before the age of 16). All in all, it was very common in those years to stick your thumb out for a ride. I never knew when I might get picked up by any random neighbor, but one who was consistently gracious was the multi-talented entertainer Della Reese.

Ms. Reese was just like she appeared on TV, always friendly and with that very familiar huge smile and gravelly voice. She was quite popular in that era and became the first Black woman to guest host the 'Tonight Show.' She was also the first Black woman with her own variety-talk show 'Della' in 1969. I thoroughly enjoyed her company, with mostly just friendly small talk during my semi-regular rides to a bit more than halfway up the hill. Ending at my usual drop-off point, I would say thanks, and she would peel away toward her house. I always looked forward to seeing her and that smile, which I'll never forget!

To give you an idea of some of our neighbors who lived in the same Doheny Estates neighborhood at that time (mostly on or near the Bird Streets) that I knew about were good friends Dionne Warwick (Grammy Hall of Famer) and Leslie Uggams (award winning actress/singer); 'Mr. Universe' Mickey Hargitay and his then 5-year old daughter and future actress Mariska (daughter of Jayne Mansfield); model/Bond Girl Britt Ekland ; actor Ricardo Montalban; Elton John's brilliant songwriting partner Bernie Taupin; NFL all-time great Jim Brown; singer Nancy Wilson; comedian Paul Lynde (of Hollywood Squares fame); singer Eartha Kitt; actress Elke Sommer (who was in my uncle Carl's film 'The Victors,' more from her later); and the one and only Englebert Humperdink. Bon the other hand, with all of that 'star power' nearby, only one name EVER mattered to me.

❏ 'STALKING' THE CAPTAIN OF THE LAKERS

When playing on the 'C' basketball team in 10th grade at Fairfax High, a teammate told me that I had moved into the same neighborhood as the future Hall of Famer, whom I had long admired on the court. Ever since the early 60s no NBA player had moved me like the man who revolutionized the game (above the rim), and I would get chills when Lakers P.A. announcer John Ramsay introduced him, "Number 22 from Seattle, the Captain of the Lakers, Elgin Baylor."

Elgin played like no other, with a combination of grace and power and could hang in the air, defying gravity, like a glider. The best basketball announcer EVER, Chick Hearn used to say, "Elgin's still on the mezzanine, while his defender is already back on the ground floor." On and off the court, Baylor always had my special attention (including at his camp). Now, I needed to find out if he really did live nearby?

Of course, I use the term 'stalking' most facetiously, as this was all in fun, I really just wanted to find out where he lived, and if at all possible, just shake his hand as a friendly neighbor and hopefully get a ride up the hill from him some day. Too many months went by and with Doheny being the lone major street to get anywhere up there, there was no Baylor sighting, which had me wondering if he really did stay close by?

FINALLY, one day as I was walking the last few blocks near home, a large brown Buick Skylark with a black top was approaching. I instinctively looked over my left shoulder, and there HE was. I didn't even try to get a ride (no thumb in the air) but wanted to confirm it was him and watched closely as the car drove on. It was definitely HIM. Now, my number one job in life was to find that car parked somewhere in the neighborhood.

Some days, after returning home from school, I'd wander throughout nearby streets like a private investigator. Where could that car be? There were several directions I could check out but no luck yet. Then, some weeks later, while walking two blocks up the hill from our house, I found a small cul-de-sac, and suddenly THERE IT WAS! That elusive beautiful car was parked in a garage driveway at the end of the street, I had found my pot of gold. NOW WHAT?

I'm not going to be some kind of intruder or trespasser, I just wanted to personally meet and greet my basketball idol one on one. I remember running home immediately and telling my mother and how excited she was for me in her own way. I then told her that I needed to go back and introduce myself. She said that there would be no harm in trying, but to, of course, just be respectful of their privacy.

So, the next day after school (without telling anyone yet), I anxiously walked back up the street, as one extremely nervous teenager—which was far from my nature. I was just incredibly excited at what might happen but wondering if this was the right thing to do (yet still with doubts about pulling this off). As I headed onto Marcheeta Place and saw that house again, my heart began pounding. I remember thinking if I was an old man, they'd have to call an ambulance to take me away.

Even approaching the front door, I was last-minute thinking that this is a stupid idea. The teachings of my father, however, to always go for things in life pulled me through the most stressful moment of my short existence. I got just enough courage to actually knock on the door, but I was also now more scared than if the Frankenstein monster himself was on the other side.

The door opened, and there was the lovely Mrs. Ruby Baylor, who thank God couldn't have been more pleasant. I introduced myself as a neighbor who was a huge fan of her husband and just wanted to shake his hand and say hello. Fortunately, she made me feel at ease by her kind reply of, "he's taking a nap right now, but if you'd like to come back at about this same time tomorrow, he'd be happy to meet you."

Are you bleeping kidding me??? This was the greatest day of my life! Can you imagine that happening today? Try walking up to Kobe Bryant or LeBron James' house with the same intent and with the alligators in the moat and a security team ready to pounce on you alongside their version of the old Berlin Wall between you and your sports idol. At the time, Elgin was considered by most as 'pound per pound' the greatest player ever. It was my time to get this one shining moment with him!

I thanked Mrs. Baylor and said I'd be there 'on time.' When I got out of range of their house, I sprinted home in a state of true euphoria. I ran inside and quickly told my mother again. She laughed saying something like, "just like your father. I'm proud of you going for it."

FUN FACT

I really did come up with the term 'Just Do It' LONG before Nike coined that slogan in 1988 but can't prove it. As a result, I'll have to leave the millions of bucks owed to me to my cash-less imagination.

The next day came, and it was hard to be in class, knowing what my after-school plans were. But the clock continued to tick until sometime after 4:30pm, when it was time to hike back to the Baylor compound. At this point, I was a different kind of nervous—knowing that this time meeting Elgin Baylor should become a reality. That couldn't keep my heart from pounding like a Gene Krupa or John Bonham pair of drumsticks, however (look them up—if necessary).

I approached the door again, took a very deep breath, and then knocked on it to be sure somebody had heard it. In a brief moment it opened and again it was Mrs. Baylor, with a very nice greeting, as I unnecessarily re-introduced myself. She said, "please give me a minute, and I'll get Elgin." She then politely closed the door. It was maybe a minute but felt like infinity, and my mind was going faster than a speeding bullet, knowing that I was about to share a private moment with the man who was able to leap tall buildings (or power forwards) in a single bound. He wasn't Superman, but he was more than close enough for me.

I couldn't catch my breath, when suddenly the door re-opened and there he was standing VERY tall (at 6'-5") in front of my face. He reached out to me with his scoring hand and said, "Hi, I'm Elgin (as if I didn't know), nice to meet you." I then introduced myself, and then the best part occurred. Instead of just saying it's nice to meet you, he actually invited me in. Wow, I really hit the jackpot. I then quickly looked around as if it was the first time I had ever been inside a Hall of Famer's house, which it was. This, however, as I tried to remind myself was just a neighbor's house. Elgin Baylor walked me down the hall and into his trophy room. He explained what some of his shiny 'stuff' was from and then told me to enjoy checking out the rest of what was on display.

I will NEVER forget the first thing I noticed was his beautiful NBA All-Star game MVP award in this huge armoire, filled with so much shininess. I had such a brief time, but what I really needed was all day to study each piece which included some of his special Lakers and Seattle U mementos. This was better than seeing the Mona Lisa for the first time by far. It also went by SO QUICKLY. As all good things must come to an end, after maybe 10-12 minutes of pleasant small talk, he thanked me for stopping by, and Ruby walked us back to the front door.

For one last time, I shook Elgin's incredibly large hand. As my little one sunk into it like quicksand, I profusely thanked him and was led out the door. Mrs. Baylor being very neighborly thanked me. Of course, I was more thanking her, and I remember turning my body to begin the short gleeful walk home. BUT WAIT! THIS CAN'T BE ALL THERE IS? It was like a sudden addiction, I needed more ASAP. Subsequently, I decided to not get greedy either as I already took up enough of the greatest basketball player on the planet's time.

So, as Elgin's wife was kindly saying her parting words and closing the door behind me, an enormous light bulb instantaneously went off in my head. And JUST before the door was shut, I very quickly turned around and asked, "Excuse me Mrs. Baylor, but would it ever be possible to go to a game with you, since I don't drive yet?"

You talk about 'Beach Balls' growing into the size of a Mt. Everest avalanche! Where the hell did I come up with that line? It certainly wasn't premeditated. I guess it was that 'Just Do It' mentality, and then whatever happens, happens?

I'll never forget the baffled look on her face. Mrs. Baylor thought for a second and then calmly said, "I don't know, I'd have to ask Elgin about that? Maybe, if you stop by another time I could let you know?" Well that's ALL I needed to hear. I have been invited back (sort of), and if I get a yes answer from Elgin, I would be joining the game's late inventor James Naismith in basketball heaven.

I again thanked Mrs. Baylor and hustled home to tell my parents. They couldn't be happier for me, as I began anticipating a 'chance' to be taken to a game with the Baylors. The next day at basketball practice, I couldn't wait to tell my teammates and friends, while also not wanting to sound like some braggart. Some didn't believe me, thinking that it was too amazing to be true, while others congratulated me. It really didn't matter, I was having such a great time enjoying the possibilities.

After a few weeks of being on a different high than any of my drug-using friends (it was the 60s), I thought it was time before the Baylors forgot who I was to get the answer to the most crucial question in my life. So, I got up the nerve to walk back up that hill and knock on their door again, hoping that the third time there would be the ultimate charm!

Now, I was a totally different kind of nervous hoping for a YES that could change my life. Mrs. Baylor answered the door again and seemed to almost not recall what I had previously asked about. Instead of stalling me or just kindly saying no, she said "hold on a second, and I'll ask Elgin now." The door was almost shut, when I could barely hear her muffled voice from afar, as she called for him. My heart was pounding again, would this be my last time at the Baylor household? It took a LONG minute until Ruby returned and to my huge surprise, he had told her "Sure, Why not?"

I could've died right there, but then I would have never experienced a Laker game with the Baylors. My time in front of their house easily lasted less than five minutes, but I got my winning lotto number. I said a quick 'THANK YOU SO MUCH' to Mrs. Baylor who then told me to get back in touch and that we'd work out the best night for our schedules to make it happen.

I ran home again, wanting to scream to the whole world—WE DID IT! I will always remember telling my mother, who replied with, "YOU are amazing... How did you pull that off?" After sharing some extremely happy laughter, my life really did change forever.

The first time I went to a game with the Baylors (enjoying their fantastic seats behind the basket), it was also with their son, Alan, and daughter, Alison, whom I'd never met before. Both were much younger than me. We all got acquainted, chatting away in the back seat (of that same wonderful car I remember so well) and throughout the game. We really hit it off, feeling like true friends by the end of the night.

Alan was only about 9 at the time, so it was nice of him (with his mother's consent) to occasionally invite me back to the house to hang out and shoot some hoops in the backyard. As a big bonus, they had a glass backboard set up which was like found gold in those days. It was totally unreal when Elgin joined us a few times to practice his free throws (which I could mimic, like he was seeing himself in the mirror).

FUN FACT

The funniest moment ever spent on the way to a game in the car with the Baylors was when Ruby asked me "So, what would you like to do when you grow up?" type question. I quickly responded sort of seriously "Be an NBA player, of course." They both laughed very hard (as I'm probably 5'-6"—125 pounds at the time and can't jump!). I told Elgin that I had a hell of an outside shot. He tried to be as diplomatic as possible by telling me "that my body type probably wouldn't get me to that level, so what else might you like to do?" I replied, "well if I can't be a player, maybe a broadcaster?"...and the rest is history! That's when it was really cemented in my mind.

The Baylors took me to the Forum somewhere over a dozen games during those two years as a neighbor. I remember it like it was yesterday listening to Elgin singing to the R&B songs on the radio, such as 'Didn't I Blow Your Mind (this time)' by the Delphonics; "What Does It Take (to win your love) by Junior Walker and the Allstars; "Love or Let Me Be Lonely" by the The Friends of Distinction; and an obvious favorite of his "O-o-h Child" by The Five Stairsteps. Everytime I hear any of those songs since, I'm right back there in the backseat, enjoying every second to and from a Lakers game.

❏ BAYLOR NIGHT AND ONE

Of course, every experience with Baylor was extremely special, but the absolute capper came on the night of March 21, 1969. Imagine today, a pro sports franchise holding a night honoring their star player's career a few years BEFORE his retirement (and not to retire his jersey number). That was the case on this historic 'Elgin Baylor Night.'

L.A. Times sportswriter Mal Florence wrote in the paper that day " A man is going to be honored tonight at the Forum. This man happens to be one of the greatest basketball players who ever lived. But this is just one reason why an expected capacity crowd of 17,500 will salute Elgin Baylor in ceremonies preceding the game with the Atlanta Hawks.

This program still looks perfect after all those years.

Few athletes in any sport have conducted themselves with more dignity or leadership than the captain of the Lakers. Elgin has a quality that sets him apart from most men. In a word, it's class. It's something you can't buy or have bestowed upon you. Either you have it or you don't."

Without question, Elgin has always exuded class and what a night of which to be a part. And just the fact that the Baylors included yours truly, driving me to that game was as unforgettable as anything I'd ever experienced. Think of yourself being in the car with your favorite all-time superstar athlete on the way to the biggest night of their professional career...I was pinching myself every minute of that day.

Everyone was dressed up for this special occasion, and I'll never forget us driving into the Forum parking lot, where the usual player's entrance attendant welcomed Elgin like never before. Then, another with a greeting like "Enjoy your special night Mr. Baylor." This was not just any night, but all about him, which was quite obvious with TV trucks parked in front of the Forum Club entrance, awaiting #22's arrival.

Someone from the media walked up to us as Elgin parked the car, and while getting out, he was suddenly asked questions like who was with him? He mentioned that it was his family and a neighbor friend (me), who just happened to be climbing out of the backseat and right into history. I totally remember this guy glancing over at me as if thinking, "who's the white kid in the car?" How about THE proudest teenager on the planet that night?

Chick's Baylor stories would've made for an all-time book, with more of his in a future volume of Touching Greatness!

So, we were faced with an 8pm pregame ceremony, lasting 40 minutes (unheard of today), and I can't believe this whole night is real. Elgin's mother and father were in attendance from Washington, D.C., along with several dignitaries, including NBA Commish Walter Kennedy, with whom I later met and briefly spoke.

Lakers eventual HOF broadcaster Chick Hearn (then in his 8th season with the club) emceed the ceremonies and introduced those on hand, including team owner Jack Kent Cooke. Elgin was given some great gifts, which included a lifetime NBA pass, a car, and a 100-year old regal chair once owned by the president of Mexico (to relax in at his advanced basketball age of 34), presented by his good friend and teammate Tommy Hawkins. 'Hawk' later told me that was one of the special moments of his Lakers days.

Meanwhile, there was an actual game to be played, as we approached 9 o'clock. 'Old man' Baylor then did his usual by responding with a team high of 21 points in an easy win over the visiting Hawks.

My times with the Baylors were once in many lifetimes experiences that will last with me forever. Following the remainder of Elgin's playing days became a personal thing as I could see his many injuries taking its toll on his body. It all ended on November 4, 1971. After just nine games into the '71-'72 season,

Elgin suddenly announced his retirement at the age of 37, which was much later than most had ever expected.

——— LIFE-CHANGING FUN FACT ———

A year later, before my family moved to another area and when I was getting the bug about a possible broadcasting career, Elgin gave me my first one-on-one interview (with anyone in any field) in that same trophy room in his house—the most nervous I've EVER been for any interview. Not exactly with Howard Cosell's precision, but my first interview was unthinkably with the person who most considered then as the greatest NBA player of all time. The situation was a most memorable personal feat that still boggles my mind! Imagine any kid getting to interview Babe Ruth, Jim Brown, Gordie Howe, or Jack Nicklaus as their first, and in their house? C'mon, that just doesn't happen! But it really did for this lucky dude!

Lakers team doctor and orthopedic surgeon Robert Kerlan removed part of Baylor's knee cap in 1966 and said before his 'Baylor Night,' "at the time, I thought the operation would enable Elgin to become a part-time player...stretch out his career a bit longer. The fact that he's playing full-time and so effectively amazes me."

I never heard the end of it, when Baylor respectfully walked away to give the kid Jim McMillian a chance to start—and the Lakers immediately (as in the next game) reeled off 33 straight Ws, still the longest winning streak in pro sports history on their way to a first NBA

Sharing some time with McMillian at our Lakers 40th anniversary dinner, celebrating their first NBA title

title in L.A. Jimmy Mac later told me, "it just showed the class of the man how he went out." Forty years later, I got to co-emcee with Bill Walton, the Lakers first championship anniversary charity dinner and more on that special night in a later tome.

❏ BAYLOR FACT CHECK

If you didn't get the point by now or just never saw him play, I want to stress Elgin's greatness on the court and how overlooked he's been when most people rate basketball history nowadays. Celtic great Bob Cousy on Baylor's 61 point game in the 1962 Finals, talking to the then best defensive forward in the league Tom 'Satch' Sanders after that game, "Tom, I think you did a hell of a defensive job. Elgin was just that spectacular, where he became the first player who literally couldn't be stopped!" Adding to that, the incomparable L.A. Times columnist Jim Murray once said about Baylor, " He's as unstoppable as a woman's tears."

It was that series that changed the course of NBA history forever, when L.A.'s Frank Selvy missed a last second title-winning shot, and the Lakers would go on to lose Game 7 in overtime...and then fall five more times in the next seven years to the Celtics, which became the Boston 'Dynasty/Mystique,' as well as the Laker's personal hell for a few more decades to come...until the Magic Johnson baby hook shot in Boston changed the newer era's course of history.

I've kept this old school ball since being a teenager, and Elgin was kind enough to personalize it years ago.

❏ A SORE SUBJECT TO ALL LAKERS AND THEIR FANS WHO REMEMBER

The key matchup problem for the Lakers in the 60s was never having a center who could deal with Bill Russell during a center-dominated era, which would affect how the world would forever see Baylor. Instead of Elgin going down in history as one of the winningest superstars ever, he never won a ring, until he was voted one after the Lakers great 1972 championship run (the year he retired). If you judge greatness by only titles, you're missing reality. The last time I checked, basketball is a TEAM sport!

Dr. J proudly talked about patterning a lot of his on-the-court moves after watching the greatness of Baylor many times on TV saying, "he did things no one else could do, just like ballet in basketball." Elgin revolutionized the game, he was the one who brought one-on-one basketball to the NBA, like no one had ever seen before. Chick Hearn didn't tell me just once but several times how Baylor saved the Lakers from either bankruptcy in Minneapolis or possibly moving out of L.A. during the early 60s. Their owner, Bob Short at the time, said it all to the *L.A. Times* in 1971, when asked about signing Baylor out of Seattle U (after a 19-53 season in Minny) and convincing him to pass up his senior season, "If he had turned me down then, I would have been out of business. The club would have gone bankrupt." BINGO, enough said!

So, NEVER EVER FORGET Laker and NBA fans, that means without Baylor, most likely NO eventual Laker dynasties (at least not in L.A.), NO Fabulous Forum, NO Showtime, and NO Staples Center.

DID YOU KNOW? ———

Baylor led his Seattle U Chieftains to the 1958 NCAA championship game—Seattle U, the perennial college basketball power? Established in 1946, Seattle got past the 'Sweet 16' one time in their school's history. Now you know which time that was, when Elgin was named the tournament's most outstanding player (on the runner-up's team,) before going #1 in the NBA draft.

It took too many years for the L.A. Coliseum Court of Honor to finally award plaques in 2009 to Baylor and West (still one of the great 1-2 punches in NBA history), with Tommy Hawkins serving as the emcee. It was special to be there. That day, I had one of my favorite private chats ever with Elgin in the parking lot, as I bumped into him on the way to our cars. He was talking to an old friend, and I got involved in their discussion which had to be close to 30 minutes of chatting about times in the past where he'd suffered indiscretions due to race. It was fascinating to hear some inside stories that I was never aware of (scary to learn about now, and I couldn't imagine having to live through at the time). Elgin was at his chattiest best that day, with also plenty of laughs, which was the same as how Hearn used to describe him to me on their years of road trips together.

Elgin joins me in front of his (and West's) long overdue plaque.

To watch L.A.'s first NBA super-duo get their due with this honor was fantastic. Just as special was my chance to ask Jerry how important Baylor was to a young West, who had moved to the big city as a raw collegian after spending his life in West Virginia? West responded, "In my rookie year to have the opportunity to be with him was really special for me. I watched him, I grew from watching him. I watched him closely to see how he conducted himself and I had an incredible desire to try to at least play somewhat on his level—and I think (it was) watching him enough that encouraged me a lot."

❏ FINALLY ETERNAL GREATNESS

In early 2011, the Lakers announced that Jerry West would be honored with the fifth statue during NBA All-Star weekend in front of Staples Center, which of course was as well deserved as any. Jerry was not only one of the most flawless pure shooters who has ever played the game, but just a great all-around player and as successful a front office career as accomplished in any sport. He's also running out of fingers for the nine total championship rings he's earned during his illustrious career.

As much as West's fantastic looking statue was long overdue (I still have an issue making such an observation, given that the statue is getting a bit gaudy outside of the arena). What's fair is fair, however. An obvious void remained to be addressed. Jerry was running the L.A. Open PGA event at Riviera. Then, at their media day, he sat down at my table for breakfast, and we had quite an in-depth emotional chat about how he was getting a statue before the Lakers first true superstar would. Jerry was dead serious when he said that he almost didn't want to be a part of that ceremony, because he was embarrassed and went on talking about the importance of Elgin to the Lakers, to this city, and to the NBA and how under-appreciated he's been. The unfortunate reality was that Baylor never won a championship. Furthermore, his years with the Clippers' historically poor franchise may have (but should not have) negatively affected his legacy.

I had already been the unofficial president of the 'Get Elgin his damned statue already Fan Club' and was running out of ways to try and get those involved in that decision to wake up and see that the man who invented 'hangtime' won't live forever. A considerable amount of effort went into opening the eyes of the upper management at AEG and the Lakers owners—the Buss's. I had the very strong backing of Tommy Hawkins and Bill Sharman (then after he passed Bill's wife, Mrs. Joyce Sharman). While they were wonderful, hope was wearing thin. Who knew what Jerry West may have said behind the scenes to the aforementioned?

It was easy to relish being the lettuce in this prime sandwich with the Lakers first great one-two punch of Jerry and Elgin.

During West's awesome ceremony, West was flanked by his close friend Baylor, as well as other HOF greats, including Kareem, Magic, Pat Riley, and the ultimate 'Hated' Celtic himself Bill Russell (who has always stayed close to the Lakers he'd regularly beaten in the past). 'Mr. Clutch' was as humbled as we knew he would be. Afterward, he was gracious with his time—because that's who he is. Jerry is one of the most unassuming and self-less people (let alone Superstars) I've ever known. He was more tough on himself than anybody should ever be, but he made it work for him, which is all that matters!

Jerry West is everything good about sports and humanity. How he subsequently spent his semi-retirement time, giving back to the city by running the PGA event at Riviera is another example of why his adopted L.A. has always embraced him as one its own. If only others that weren't all about ME were paying attention to 'The Logo' and his honest approach to life? Most will never know just how special it is to interact with someone as admirable as Jerry.

❏ WATCHING IT ALL HAPPEN LIKE A HAWK

Immediately after the Shaq O'Neal statue ceremony in March of 2017, I chatted with Elgin and his second wife, Elaine, and told them I will NEVER EVER stop my efforts in anyway possible to help make a statue of him a reality. I made more phone calls, and sent a few more emails but still nothing. I also sat down with Hawkins (who was also strongly pushing this same agenda in his new book that had yet to be released). Hawk and I got together on Wednesday August 9 to mostly speak about how I might possibly self-publish this book, since he had advice to share his previous experiences by doing the same.

It was an extra special three hours together, sitting in front of Gelson's Market. When after about 30 minutes of picking his brain on the publishing aspects, I suddenly asked to record a few-minute interview about his book and any other subject of note (including of course our co-passion, the void of no Baylor statue). It was very fortunate that I did. With no notes in front of me, I started my recorder, and our chat went on and on and on. Before we knew it, almost 90 minutes had gone by, and I needed to wrap it up.

The last thing I asked Tommy was to describe to the masses who should know from those who were there, why we rave about Elgin as a player? "Because he was the great innovator, he was the Godfather of improvised basketball, because he brought a new dimension to offensive basketball every night, and because pound for pound in terms of rebounding, ballhandling, passing, scoring—he's the greatest player ever to play the game."

My last moments with 'Hawk'

I interjected, "To this day?" Tommy looked me right in the eye, and with the strongest conviction, replied, "NOBODY did everything that Elgin did (and) AT six-five!"

We finally finished, and as I soaked in this very special insight to history, it was if Tommy had wanted to tell me his life story (or anything that wasn't already fully covered in his new book), including about being the first Black Notre Dame All-American, the first Black to host a radio talk show (not sports-related), what Jackie Robinson meant to him, and so much more. So, after concluding this session for then, we promised to connect the following week to further discuss our books (he also wanted to include three of my personal pictures in his).

─────── **FUN FACT** ───────

At the end of our chat, Hawk then signed a piece of the recently demolished Sports Arena (the Lakers first home in L.A.) that I had acquired to remember this building for so many reasons, including seeing the earlier Lakers there several times and later doing my own basketball and hockey broadcasts out of it. It's since been signed by the co-original L.A. Lakers Baylor and West.

Jerry proudly completed this special piece of history for all to enjoy at our SoCal Sportcasters luncheon— photo by Martin Leon.

Exactly seven days later, I sat stunned when getting word that Hawk had died in his sleep at his Malibu home. He had looked and acted so healthy and spry at the age of 80, just the previous week which made the situation more difficult to take. I did take some solace that we had recorded this very in-depth, long interview for people to hear forever. On the other hand, it still seemed impossible that he was gone so suddenly.

It was seven weeks later at his family memorial service in downtown L.A. that I got to share this story with so many who were in attendance, including Elgin himself. He was also in disbelief that his friend, who seemed so healthy, had died like this. Elgin was still his usual poised self.

When the service concluded, and as ironic as at all possible, I ran into Lakers owner Jeanie Buss and told her about my last conversation with 'The Hawk' and how we've continued the fight for years (each in our own ways) to get Elgin recognized with a statue. To my total astonishment, as I was beginning to plead my case for the umpteenth time, Jeanie calmly stopped me and said, "Ted, Elgin IS getting a statue, and it will be before the end of this season."

I truly was totally floored. Likely due to the emotion of just completing Tommy's services, I began to weep for a few seconds. I felt a bit embarrassed, caught my breath, and gave Jeanie a huge hug and thanked her. She said, "You don't have to cry." I replied, "You have no idea how hard I've tried to help in any way to finally get this to become a reality. Thank God this is actually happening!"

Jeanie then asked that I not tell others, as it was yet to be formally announced. I of course did the 'old school' thing and kept my promise instead of 'tweeting' it out immediately, because I knew something that nobody else did. Now my biggest personal dilemma was keeping it to myself for a few months (although regularly giving multiple hints and teases on my Facebook posts until the official announcement came).

DID YOU KNOW?

Hawkins loved telling how he and Baylor took the same cab to Elgin's 71-point game in New York, when the driver looked in the mirror and said "You guys look like athletes." Elgin replied, "Yeah, we're boxers, and we're boxing at Madison Square Garden. And, it's Tommy's turn to win (followed by huge laughter)." The driver then realized this was a joke and that they were both basketball players. After Elgin introduced themselves, the driver quickly asked, "how many points are you going to score tonight?" And Elgin casually and jokingly said, "ABOUT 70!" Hawk then seriously added this comment to me about that night, "You can take the best game that Michael Jordan has ever played, it would NOT COMPARE with the variety of shots and the amazing feats of legerdemain that Elgin exhibited that night. He was absolutely incredible!"

I caught this special moment with Russell, Elgin, and Jerry at West's 2011 statue unveiling.

❑   A MASTERFUL SCHEDULING BLUNDER

Finally, when the rest of the world knew about it, I checked the scheduled date of the ceremony. It was on Friday April 6. NO, NOT THAT NIGHT! That's on Masters weekend and I was already credentialed for a fifth straight year at Augusta National (the most difficult credential in all of sports to obtain). I waited all those years for Elgin to be so honored and now I'm out of town? NO bleepin' way! Normally, it would take a family emergency for me to have to leave the Masters early, but not on this, the ultimate Elgin Baylor Night—the most momentous of his post-playing life. I still got my work done at the Masters, so no harm no foul. I then flew home after round one to be at Staples on time.

What a ceremony! On stage with Elgin were Magic Johnson, Kareem Abdul Jabbar, Shaq O'Neal, singer/friend Bill Withers, and, of course, the other half of the great Lakers 60s duo Jerry West, who showed his true admiration for a man who was an early mentor to the kid from Cabin Creek, West Virginia. The great Bill Russell was also in attendance, along with several former Laker players and dignitaries. Longtime team broadcaster Stu Lantz wonderfully hosting it all. I was hoping to find Kobe there after the many compliments he had given to Elgin over the years, but at least Bryant recorded a video, with some very honoring words towards the first captain of the storied Lakers franchise.

The All-World lineup (L-R) of Jerry, Elgin, Magic, Kareem, Withers, and Shaq—a group only missing Chick and 'Hawk.'

Then, FINALLY, the unveiling of a wonderful statue with Elgin's famous hanging in the air pose (although the ball should've been in his right hand). I looked over at Chick's statue to see if he was checking this out and could almost see him perpetually winking, as the ceremony continued. At the conclusion it was hugs for the Baylor family, several high fives, and a special private moment with Elgin next to his eternal likeness for a picture that I'll forever cherish.

It was terrific to get the special invitation from Jeanie and the Baylor family to not only Elgin's statue ceremony, but also a personal VIP ticket to the after-party which was just outstanding. Of course, there were several ex-players in attendance at the festivities, including my one-time radio color analyst Jamaal Wilkes, as well as Shaq, milling around. There were also a few individuals in attendance whom I'd never met, including Rock and Roll Hall of Famer Bill Withers and longtime radio and TV personality and Philadelphia Sports Hall of Famer Sonny Hill, who's been a forever advocate of Baylor getting the full respect he'd so well earned.

I spent much of that night sharing stories with Sonny. The highlight though was reconnecting with Elgin's daughter, Alison. I hadn't seen her since she was a pre-teen, and we got caught up on our lives. Unfortunately, her brother Alan couldn't be there but it was like old home week for us. All in all, the party couldn't have been better.

Bill Withers, who was a longtime friend of Elgin and his company was in charge of the statue ceremony production, was someone I'd 'sort of' met previously. While at my first job working in the liquor store, I once delivered some booze to his house for a big party (soon after his first huge album hit it big in 1971), with his then girlfriend actress Denise Nicholas. I reminded him almost 50 years later, that I didn't recall him tipping me much that night, which got a little chuckle out of him. Withers also performed at the 1974 Zaire Music Festival that preceded the classic Ali-Foreman 'Rumble in the Jungle' fight, along with other greats, like James Brown, B.B. King, and the Spinners.

FINALLY a reality…if only Chick and Hawkins could've been up there with us.

❑ THE ULTIMATE BAYLOR FILES

So, finally at the age of 83, Elgin Baylor got his statue (so fortunate while he's still here to enjoy it). We all could revel in his accomplishments which would take another book to mention. It should not be overlooked that he averaged a double-double at 6'-5" during 11 of his 14 injury-plagued NBA seasons, including back-to-back years with 34.8 points & 19.8 rebounds followed by 38.3 & 18.6. I'll never forget his unbelievable '61-'62 season of 38, 19, & 5, when playing only when he could get a weekend pass (with very little practice time) due to his military service. Without question, Elgin is the greatest unappreciated NBA superstar ever!

Forget what I say, easily the co-most unappreciated star Oscar Robertson can tell you much better when asked who tops his greatest all-time player list? "Elgin Baylor. He did so many great things. Nobody could guard him, playing in the forward spot. I'd love to see some of today's greats playing against Elgin. They couldn't guard him. Nobody could." Jerry West's comment on Elgin was equally complementary, "he was one of the most spectacular shooters the game has ever known, who made shots that would just defy you!"

I had a wonderful chat with Celtics legend Tommy Heinsohn right on his team's bench before Game 5 of the 2010 NBA Finals in Boston—after kindly introducing myself as an L.A. guy who despised him as a kid (fortunately he responded with his patented belly laugh). We talked about the great rivalry with the Lakers over the decades. Then, I wrapped it up by asking what it was like facing Baylor with championships on the line. I also asked about the statue issue, with so many others honored ahead of him? Heinsohn's body language totally changed, and he got very serious and matter of factly. "It's a shame that the Lakers don't recognize him for as great as he really was. In my way of thinking, and I've been watching this since 1946. Elgin Baylor to me is still the best quick forward who ever played the game. Alright? Better than Dr. J, better than Bird, better than anybody else you could name." That's right, the ultimate Celtic homer saying that Elgin was better than Larry Bird stunned even me—although, in reality, it didn't!

Baylor's teammate for his final five seasons with the Lakers Keith Erickson stressed the ultimate praise like it was etched in stone, "Elgin has NEVER, EVER received the recognition that he deserved. He should be the ALL-TIME forward on any Lakers team or ANY NBA team. During Elgin's three best scoring years, he averaged more points a game than Michael Jordan did in his three best scoring years. Elgin was unstoppable, he was a man amongst boys before his time. Before Lebron James came along and took that honor. Nobody could stop him. He was THE BEST."

Keith continued, "I joined the team in '68 when Wilt did, during Elgin's last years in the league, and he was kind of on his way down. I guarded him in practice, and we are the same height. IT JUST WASN'T FAIR! He was too good, He was too strong. He could do so many things. There was no way to guard him. NO WAY! It was just ridiculous. And to watch Elgin and Jerry play every night, they were so outstanding and so effortless in what they did, it was just unbelievable."

As to what to tell those younger folk who never saw Baylor play, Erickson remarked, "Elgin's greatest seasons were even better than Michael's. Everybody thinks that Michael Jordan's the greatest ever. He's no better than Elgin was. ELGIN WAS THE GREATEST IN THE GAME WITH THAT BALL, WITH ONE HAND, AND JUMPING AND WHAT HE COULD DO WITH THAT BALL. IT WAS CRAZY HOW GOOD HE WAS!"

And as Lakers HOF teammate Gail Goodrich once told me, "Elgin Baylor and Chick Hearn sold Los Angeles professional basketball. Without Elgin, Los Angeles would not've been an NBA city, and for him to not have a statue, it's sad and it's just not right! Elgin was just so spectacular, he was ahead of his time, just a tremendous impact player so maybe one of these days the Lakers organization will wake up a little bit." So yes, Baylor's statue should've been the first one. At least the suits finally woke up from a long self-induced coma and righted their wrong!

FUN FACT

My longtime friend and sportscasting colleague the late Dave Stone may've been the only guy who was an even bigger fan of Elgin's. Dave once told me, after being hospitalized, that he got a surprise call from Baylor, wishing him well, which meant more to him than anything outside of his family possibly could. Dave used to call him (among MANY other things), "The greatest gentleman I ever met." Dave also used to call me with long rants on how it was a travesty that Elgin didn't have a statue. Well, you can truly finally rest in peace Dave, if only you were here to share this.

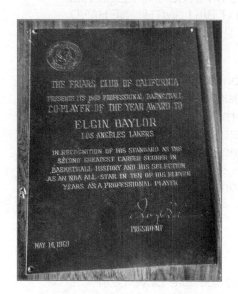

One of the special pictures of my life, randomly taken when I introduced Elgin to my father at his Friars Club roast. Look at Dad's smile. A priceless moment

To think that after five decades since we first met, Elgin and I have our first books released within such a short time span. It was another very special night, spending a few hours with Elgin at his 2018 book signing on the westside of L.A. in Brentwood for *Hang Time: My Life in Basketball*. It was so much fun sharing my collection of old pictures, programs, and other Baylor paraphernalia with Elgin and his wife Elaine during some private time. Specifically, the items included ones that they had never seen before, like a picture of Elgin with Jackie Robinson. I was surprised to learn that Elgin not only didn't recall ever seeing it, but also that he'd only met Jackie that one time.

The most special moment was showing Elgin a picture from when I introduced my dad to him at a Lakers Friars Club luncheon. Furthermore, to tell Elgin and his wife that I now own the plaque (pictured below) he received that day in 1969, thanks to Paul Olden getting it as a gift for me from the Baylor auction—one of the classic gestures I could ever receive. My father died just a few years after that picture was taken, but he's eternally smiling even larger than in this picture, knowing that Elgin enjoyed my story about this.

Elgin then lit up like a Christmas tree, after I showed him a picture of him scoring over Bill Russell (who's a good friend of his). He got even more giddy when telling me that he recently found an old video, without knowing what was on it. To his extreme enjoyment, it was of him dunking directly over the head of Russell. Even at 83 years young, Elgin's competitive passion was showing like a neon sign, which we were both loving every second of it.

Baylor also explained to me how when he asked for number 22 early with the Minneapolis Lakers, they gave him a few numbers (including number 14 which I showed him a picture of), until the guy who had 22 was no longer around the following season. Elgin was also given a scrapbook by one of his fans, who came in to buy his book *Hang Time* and we were going over all the pages of the aging yellowed newspaper clippings, I was amazed that at his age, Elgin could read even the small printed box scores without reading glasses or contact lenses. He smiled and said, "I guess it's hereditary." He then asked, "when ARE you supposed to lose your good reading sight?" I replied, "in your case, probably at a hundred and thirty, so you don't have anything to worry about!" That explains his all-time amazing court vision that Chick used to love to describe.

After this LONG, but fitting, detailed tribute to the man and his legend, I'll conclude this section with one last Tommy Hawkins definitive description of the guy he played with, when Elgin was at his healthiest peak, "Pound for pound Elgin Baylor was the most exciting, and competent basketball player I've ever played with—and please include this addendum, THE GREATEST OF ALL-TIME! Thank you Muhammad Ali. Simply the greatest all around player who ever lived. Greater than Lebron James, greater than Magic, Dr. J., and YES, greater than Michael Jordan. Nobody did what Elgin did. I want the world to know if you missed Elgin Baylor play, YOU MISSED IT! I then added, it was like a combo of Jordan on offense, Dennis Rodman on the boards, Magic Johnson's passing, and Baryshnikov's footwork—ALL in one body. Tommy then smiled and quickly replied with, "YEP, that was Elgin!"

Oh and some guy named Kobe once responded to my question of what he saw when studying old video of Elgin, "INCREDIBLE MAN. He started all of this. SHIIIIT! If I had his 'hang time,' MICHAEL WHO?"...followed by a sarcastic belly laugh that any Bryant fan would appreciate.

The moral to this fabulous Hollywood ending is you don't need a statue of yourself to prove your greatness. Elgin Baylor is the perfect example of that. I know he'll always be underappreciated. I've tried to share what I know (and most importantly what his most esteemed colleagues know) and what I have seen with my own eyes to those who didn't have that opportunity. At least now he has it all and can fully enjoy the rest of his journey on this planet, with an honor bestowed upon him as deserved as any athlete who ever lived! Whether or not I contributed even an ounce to the efforts of helping make that Baylor statue a reality, I am eternally grateful for its outcome and for being allowed to play a small particle in the successful conclusion of that journey.

Elgin got to enjoy the fairways and greens of life down the homestretch—it doesn't get much better than that, specifically for this kid who once shared a cart and round of golf to never be forgotten.

❏ ONE FINAL REVERSE SPIN SHOT

HUMBLE, CLASSY, DIGNIFIED, KIND are all words that the greats of the game have used to describe Elgin Baylor.

Sadly, on the expected last day of my final edits for this book, we learned of Elgin's passing at the age of 86. I remain so grateful that he was still with us to finally receive the ultimate respect statue, putting the exclamation point on his place in history! But it's difficult not to get to share all of these words with him which I so longed to do—leaving a huge void in my being.

May the generations ahead continue to appreciate his greatness—and not just via an almost 17-foot tall piece of bronze. Because if we all elevated our potential the way Elgin elevated others around him on and off the court, that might just help us to remember where 'Hang Time' comes from.

Elgin Baylor and Jerry West made up the greatest one-two punch of their generation, with Jerry sentimentally saying that he loved his buddy and teammate like a brother. He kindly sent me the following note as a final memorial to Elgin, which perfectly speaks for the both of us: "I will cherish the time we spent together. A great man!"

Thanks Jerry and Elgin—they truly don't make 'em like you guys anymore!

CHAPTER 12

HOOPING IT UP IN L.A.

❏ WOODEN IT BE NICE!

"WINNING TAKES TALENT, TO REPEAT TAKES CHARACTER." Legendary coach John Wooden had a wealth of great sayings that anyone breathing can learn from for infinity. At the time, the guy I grew up with, who began winning all of those national titles at UCLA, was always referred to as Johnny Wooden. I vividly remember the first few times being around him was while attending some Bruins games at his new Pauley Pavilion during its greatest era.

YOU SHOULD KNOW!

If you're not familiar with Coach Wooden's greatness, after no national titles during his first 16 seasons at UCLA, he then won 10 in the next 12 years—including an amazing SEVEN IN A ROW, while once winning 88 straight games.

My first private moment with Coach was at the Fabulous Forum after a Lakers game, when he was strongly being rumored to being wooed away from the college game by the Lakers as their next head coach (and Jerry Tarkanian was also once very close to getting that job). I was about 16 at the time. While having him sign my autograph book, the always inquisitive me asked Coach if he was seriously thinking about joining his greatest student/hoopsters Lew Alcindor (before his name change to Kareem Abdul-Jabbar), Walt Hazzard, Gail Goodrich, Lucius Allen, and other Bruins in the NBA? He had always balked at leaving his teaching roots for the pro game. He then kindly responded with, "OH NO, I don't think so. I'm VERY happy with where I am. But they're trying."

Nowadays, that would be something to IMMEDIATELY tweet out, if a person were so inclined. But I was just happy to get the inside scoop from a humble man, who was having some big bucks being thrown at him. I guess his inner values won out. He never left for the larger fortune and a different type of fame—no matter how tempting that must've been?

Coach was extra nice to everyone whenever they were around him. He was certainly no different with yours truly. I didn't get as much private time with him, as I had hoped over the years but when it did happen, it felt as if I was speaking with a best buddy on Mount Rushmore. To pick his brain was like getting to ask Socrates what he thought of the full-court press and how it came to be? Without question, he was the elite of the elite folks. As such, any time I got to spend with the man was cherished—even as a teen.

Right there at the top of my favorite moments with Coach Wooden was being alone with him (and his ex-player/close friend Mike Warren) in late December of 2003. This was the 40th anniversary of his first NCAA championship team. During pregame ceremonies of the UCLA-Michigan State basketball game, he was being honored with the naming dedication of his storied Pauley Pavilion basketball floor to be forever known as 'Nell and John Wooden Court.' Although press releases had gone out some months earlier written as 'John and Nell Wooden Court,' Coach pretty much said, this won't happen unless his late wife of 53 years was placed first, which is how it went. He matter of factly said to me that day, "Oh, my Nellie ALWAYS comes first!"

Coach Wooden, surrounded by most of his storied UCLANs on his special night, just a few feet in front of me

— DID YOU KNOW? —

Keith Erickson was on that first Bruins title team in '64 and was only 6'-5" the same height as center Fred Slaughter. They were the two tallest players in the starting five. Keith proudly added, "Walt Hazzard and Gail Goodrich were the leaders of that team, and I think they are the best pair of guards who EVER played college basketball. And because we were a running, pressing team, it was really fun to watch. One of the guys who really enjoyed watching us play was this tall kid from New York who ended up coming to UCLA, Lew Alcindor."

With Coach on the Bruins bench, after his pregame court naming ceremony— photo by Steve Grayson

Coach Wooden was introduced as 'the greatest teacher, coach, and the finest man in UCLA and intercollegiate history.' Wow, while that's a lot to live up to, it was also hard to argue against, despite the dark cloud of big bucks Bruins booster businessman 'Papa Sam' Gilbert's money constantly hanging over the program during its heyday (but that's a longer story for a different book).

Wooden's star pupil Kareem Abdul Jabbar (whom he used to call Lewis) was also present, gingerly walking his elderly coach off the floor during this celebration event. The duo were the perfect symmetry of greatness which was the most memorable picture of the night for this reporter. A somewhat fatigued Wooden then took a seat on the Bruins bench, when I then had the opportunity to walk by and congratulate him. As perfect timing would have it, my photographer friend Steve Grayson was standing right there and kindly asked Coach if he could capture this moment for me—unforgettable!

As the game with the visitors neared the midway point of the first half, with Spartans alum Magic Johnson on hand, I headed down to the interview room early enough to get my wish—spending some real quality alone time (at least 15 minutes) with the then 93-year old Coach on his special night. We watched the rest of the half on the TV monitors together and discussed almost every play and how he may have reacted on the bench differently? It was like a private coaching clinic from Wooden himself (always sitting next to Warren). We also reminisced some about his glory days, since 63 of his former players were with him on this historic night. It was all off-the-record, friendly chatter that sticks in my mind to this day. Personally, I was hoping that halftime would never come.

When it did, Abdul Jabbar and Bill Walton joined us for an informal presser. It was like winding back the clock to the greatest era in UCLA and all of college hoops history. Kareem stressed how he always appreciates the man and that we'd taken it for granted, somehow expecting him to be around forever. Big Bill calling Coach, "a timeless treasure, with the perfect soul."

It was simply a perfect night to friendly banter together with Coach inside his own shrine, while getting to see his true reactions behind the scenes. He was his always humble self and truly honored by the occasion, mostly enjoying being around the players/students who put him and his storied program on the eternal map, as well as grateful for every second of it. As he told me a few times, "I consider myself a teacher much more so than a coach, we never stop learning."

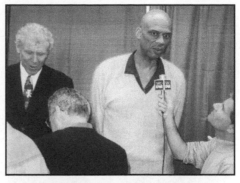

Interviewing (as usual on my toes) Kareem and Bill at halftime

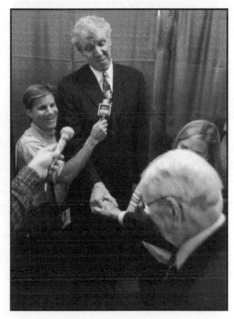

Perfect timing, when Coach was leaving the room, he stopped to shake Walton's hand and got us all to laugh with, "I see you're still talking Bill, you guys will probably be here awhile longer!"

Nine years later, Kareem got his statue put up in front of Staples, ironically only two weeks after Coach Wooden's statue went up in front of Pauley. I had to ask the ex-Bruin center about the timing of that? And with a huge smile he gladly added, "YEAH, I like the way that worked out!" I also had mentioned after his ceremony that I once got to meet his father at a game and now wondered what he and his coach might think if they could be at his statue unveiling? "My dad would be really happy to be here, but it's ok. He's looking down, he's up there with Coach Wooden, and I'm sure they're smiling!" NO doubt!

Nine years later, with coach Wooden's daughter Nan who said at the statue unveiling at Pauley Pavilion, "to our family, this was the biggest honor ever bestowed to Dad."

Now years after his passing, I am still a proud John R. Wooden Award voter (college basketball's top player). I can only hope that each and every winner of that honor takes the time to learn about the man who's name will forever live in their trophy case. And still, when his birthday comes along each year, my first instinct is to pick up the phone and call Coach (my last annual one being on his 98th).

I would always joke that despite screening his calls, via his old answering machine, he would still take my call anyway, even after hearing my greeting. In one of my last calls, I asked, "so what's it like to be 97 and John Wooden?" After a moment of hesitation—he humorously replied, "Well it's better than being 98—let's not rush this!" Fun memories to last forever with the greatest coach and person of values anyone could ever imagine and simply the ultimate in touching greatness.

DID YOU KNOW?

Wooden was the first player ever to be named a basketball All-American three times, and the first to be honored by the Basketball Hall of Fame as a player and a coach.

❏ FRICK & FRACK

There's only one Batman and one Robin, and NBA execs tell us that you can't have two Batmans on the same team. Anyway, Adam West is the only real Batman, and George Reeves is the only real Superman. In L.A., super G.M. Jerry West had to recreate a hoops version of the dynamic duo to start the Shaq and Kobe era with the Lakers in 1996. He truly was genius in acquiring them both.

DID YOU KNOW?

The very likeable Lakers center Vlade Divac, who was traded for the 13th pick in the '96 draft (which turned into a high schooler named Kobe), almost quit the game, preferring not to play in Charlotte. Fortunately, he changed his mind or else that trade would've been nixed and much of this chapter would've never existed. Thanks Vlade!

I was double-dipping that season only covering some of the Laker's games and practices, when available for KFWB while calling Long Beach Ice Dogs IHL hockey games. It was playoff time for each of us in May of '97, with my Ice Dogs just having clinched their first round series at Utah. I had an extra night off in Salt Lake City, with the Lakers facing elimination at the same Delta Center, where we had just put away Coach Butch Goring's IHL Grizzlies. For a nice personal change of pace, I called for a credential for what turned out to be the nightmare game of rookie Kobe Bryant's young career. He suffered through shooting four airballs in crunch-time, including the last one which became an award winner—but not for him!

My job was to do live KFWB reports twice an hour. As such, the timing was impeccably fortunate, when waiting on hold for the next Joe Cala :15 & :45 sports update. As if it had been scripted, the Lakers were ready to take the ball out of bounds, down by three points with just 14 seconds left in overtime, when Cala came on and said, "let's head out to Utah where our Ted Sobel awaits a big inbounds play with the Lakers' season on the line."

Kobe, who was an18-year old bench player then, took a pass and worked his way to an open 3-pt. shot and fired a 26-footer that was a foot short. I could almost hear Chick scream out his own invented term 'ANOTHER AIRBALL.' The Lakers season was over with the kid facing the heat (4-14 from the floor), while I was being praised for a nice play-by-play call (just skirting league rules-I hope) of the last shot of Kobe's first pro season.

It was weird telling Bryant some years later that my call of his miss, got me my second Golden Mike award for 'Best Sports News Reporting' in 1997, while he only got crap from everyone on what should've been only an off-day during my hockey team's playoffs. Of course, he more than made up for it over the next 19 seasons, which I covered them all. At least, I got to timely cash in on his rookie-ness (Zelig-style), when there were just too many mistakes by Salt Lake in his infamous 'Airball Game.'

❏ GETTING OUR PHIL OF CHAMPIONSHIPS

The underperforming Lakers brought in the almost mythical Phil Jackson to replace the departed duo of Del Harris and Kurt Rambis as head coach in 1999, and he immediately added to his eventual career record total of 13 championship rings (11 as a coach) by later leading them to a three-peat. I wondered more about the man behind the Jordan-led Bulls titles, after watching him play with the championship Knicks teams as a gangly lefty forward whom I'd remembered on the court at the Forum. During his introductory news conference, I asked the man who used his earlier mentor (and mine) fellow HOFer Tex Winter's triangle offense to perfection, "can you see yourself as ever being an L.A. guy?"

Causing some loud laughter in the room, Jackson replied, "I've been practicing singing 'I Love L.A.,' maybe that would help? But I do like the beach, and I'm looking forward to warm weather. I've spent a lot of my career in New York and Chicago, so it's about time I got to the west…I feel VERY lucky to be a part of this."

I also inquired about his feelings on that 'Zen Master' nickname? "Well, I don't like it, but I'll accept it because I think there is some ring about it that is kind of unique. It does say that things are going to be done a little bit differently than square. We're gonna look at this life a little bit obtuse and see what can come out of changing reality, and that's kind of the thing I like to do with basketball. Keep it fresh, keep it lively, and, hopefully, make it fun!" SAY WHAT? I think I got SOME of his growing up in the 60s lingo? These next few years were definitely going to be some form of obtuse, whatever that is?

I certainly can't speak for the fun part, although it looked like it was for year one anyway. The Lakers incredible run of titles then began. And OH, did it get LIVELY after that including enough stress in the locker room to kill an EKG machine. I was there for it all. It was like regularly visiting a disgruntled family that didn't want to ever have dinner together. In this instance, I was invited to join them at the table (with my recorder in hand), while uncomfortably ruining my appetite, which wasn't fun!

I have never been around such a tension-filled room of jocks before or since. We spent almost every single day dealing with who didn't like who, which of course was headlined by the two megastars, starting in 2000, when Shaquille O'Neal came into training camp out of shape. Which bent Kobe out of shape, given that he wasn't mature enough to handle such things well yet. His approach looked petty to the public, while Shaq wasn't serious enough to overcome his own issues, including the obvious fitness and work-ethic questions.

Despite his obsessive nature, it was hard to fault Bryant's attitude at the time, as he couldn't understand why others (specifically, 'The Big Aristotle') didn't work their asses off daily like he did? He once intensely told me, "I'll pass it into him when he works for it." If not for Derek Fisher and Rick Fox in that incredibly dysfunctional room (two of my absolute favorites to ever deal with), there may have been a literal 'War on the Floor'! Yet the rings kept coming (thanks in large part to Coach Phil's calm demeanor). The league couldn't stop this runaway championship (but too often teetering) freight train.

❏ UNDERACHIEVING NO MORE

After being around for many of the team's 67 regular season wins under new coach Jackson, what a time to cover the greatest NBA playoff comeback I'd ever seen, when the Lakers returned from the dead in Game 7 of the 2000 Western Conference Finals to Portland, down 15 points with 10:28 to play. The crowd was as quiet as a morgue. Their team had blown a 3-1 series lead, and the situation appeared grim.

Kobe, Shaq, and Brian Shaw came through down the stretch, however, like the eventual champions they were. Then, an unforgettable crowd eruption when Bryant's high lob pass from heaven (almost as high as the stress level in the building) was slammed in by O'Neal to seal the deal with 40 seconds left. That slam opened the door to the Lakers first of three straight titles, although I missed the first one, having my pre-scheduled vacation set to visit the highest waterfalls in the world, the breathtaking Angel Falls in Venezuela.

Rick Fox, who was a chippy player and had a whatever-it-takes-to-win attitude, called that Portland series a "borderline wrestling match," which sounded similar to a typical day in the unsettled Lakers locker room. Oh the expectations of that squad who didn't want their legacy labeled as just another underacheiving team. The unlikely Game 7 comeback win over the Blazers, however, changed the course of NBA history. After a few blinks of the eye, the Lakers won five more titles in the next 11 years, which made my job a lot easier and a hell of a lot more enjoyable, for sure.

Kobe showed himself as simply one of those rare athletes, or just people in general who's selfish cockiness actually matched his greatness. It could be said (and I just did) that he needed this attitude to achieve what he was able to. While winning three of his four NBA championships in L.A., Shaquille called his pairing with Bryant the most talked about, the most enigmatic, the most controversial duo, and the best one-two punch in the history of the game! His observations were well after the fact, however. Of course if he had that same outlook in the early 2000s, the Lakers likely would've added a few more O'Brien Trophys, which he admits now. They were simply that great to overcome such constant inner feuding, which of course regularly affected us media folk's jobs immensely.

Covering the 2002 championship parade with my KFWB colleague John Brooks, while Kobe speaks to the hords of fans

The aforementioned proves something I've often said that you don't always have to get along to be great teammates, but if you don't have respect for the other person or their approach to the game, then you have very little shot to reach a common goal. Their time together simply hit a brick wall. Considering Shaq's goal was to win one NBA title and that he finished with four rings, he's told me that he's extremely content with that! But, oh how it could have and should have been so much more.

❏ GETTING WILT CHAMBERNEAZY UNDER
    OUR TREE

After losing the '04 Finals to Detroit and Phil Jackson temporarily gone off into the sunset, the Lakers broke up their historically great dynamic duo. This was during a tumultuous period, when Bryant was strongly contemplating changing uniforms with his hallway neighbors the Clippers and while Shaq was holding his owner in monetary hostage. Something had to give.

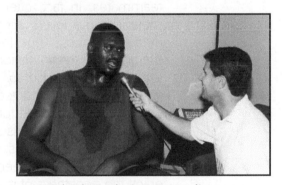

With Shaq during an earlier zany story, for another volume of Touching Greatness—*photo by Avery Helm*

Frick and Frack, with their universal-sized egos, continued to point fingers at each other's flaws (including morally and legally). Personally, I wasn't into covering this petty soap opera which had become all a part of their on-going story. Unlike too many of my colleagues, I preferred great basketball over trivial adolescence in the room. Not coincidentally, Kobe stayed a Laker signing a seven-year deal on the day after Shaq was shipped out of town to Miami. As such, tension was immediately eased in the building, although with huge future uncertainties. Then Clippers G.M. Baylor later told me, "We thought we had him (Kobe), but he changed his mind the last day." Oh, how history would've been SO different!

I was there on that most anticipated (and insanely hyped) Christmas Day game in NBA history in 2004, when Shaquille, the new Heat center, came back to face his old team for the first time since being traded after eight long wonderfully arduous seasons in L.A. It was like going to the Super Bowl. He and his ex-good buddy Kobe hadn't spoken a word since the deal, and there was a different type of sports-tension cloud hovering inside the arena.

The BIG and LITTLE brothers shared only a cold forearm bump to open the game. It was then fierce competition the rest of the way. Shaq even swatted away Kobe's first shot of the game—perfectly setting the tempo! This battle of drama kings came down to the wire with, of course, Kobe going for the winner in overtime, missing a three-pointer that clanked off the front of the rim. The Heat won it by just two, despite Bryant's 42 points (on 30 shots, with nine turnovers in 50 minutes). Now we could all move on—or could we?

Shaq was pretty even-kealed with me after the game about getting booed throughout, "it's a sign of respect, I've been booed before. I could walk anywhere in the city by myself, people are going to say hi and ask for autographs, so it's a sign of respect. That's what they're supposed to do, when you come into the opposing arena you're supposed to boo. I don't take it personally." Taking it in stride on the feud with Kobe, "I'm over it, it's old news now." Bryant was also low-keyed afterwards, "Hopefully this is all behind us now."

The following season, it was much more cordial between the ex-teammates. In fact, after their MLK Day game at Staples, the tension was more like old lovers accepting their new lives shaking hands and hugging during warmups. Kobe then softened about his big buddy, "He came up to me and said congratulations on my daughter Natalia and the fact that we were expecting another kid so." Were you surprised? "Very surprised, you know it's good man. I think it's good for the city of Los Angeles and for the NBA, as well as especially good for our youth on MLK Day. It's good for all the African Americans who idolize us and look up to us, seeing that we can be mature and put everything behind us. It's a lot bigger than the sport itself. It made me feel good because we've been through so many wars together and to be able to enjoy the sweetness of it. Now, it's best for the city and the organization just to move on and to wish him the best in his new city in South Beach."

❏ SHAQ CREDITS THE ULTIMATE CHAMP FOR HIS NEW OUTLOOK

When covering the 2007 NBA All-Star game in Vegas, I met up with the great Bill Russell during a marketing newser for Wheaties. He was praising Shaquille O'Neal bigtime. So, I then asked Shaq what kind of a mentor the winningest center of all-time had become to him? "A LOT! He was the ONLY great big man who has actually initiated a conversation with me. Like a lot of the guys, I tried to initiate conversations with them, but for some reason, they never wanted to talk to me. Kareem, Wilt, Walton." Why so? "I don't know? But, with Mr. Russell, 'how you doing Sir?' He sat me down told me a million stories. Told me, 'Oh you think you had it hard? One time I went to bla-bla-bla, and they wouldn't let us eat because of my color. Red Auerbach then came in and took everybody out.' We could actually sit there and have a conversation."

Russell deserves another ring just for getting Shaq to co-exist with Kobe. "Actually he was the one who said 'I think you and Kobe need to make up!' If it wasn't for him saying that, then we'd probably still be having problems. But he just told me to suck it up and just shake his hand, be a man, and let bygones be bygones. And that's what I did." Years later, a more mature Bryant added, "Shaq and I have a really good relationship now—and I think it's a good lesson for all of us!" YOU GOT THAT RIGHT! As a radio geek, it's gratifying to equate the ever-evolving Howard Stern to the likes of Kobe and Shaq and even that Tiger Woods guy, who've all nicely grown into their eliteness!

After chatting with Russell, being posted up by THE greatest team champion (even a Celtic) was a kick

❏ DEALT A NATURAL BLACKJACK BY KOBE IN VEGAS

I've always said that Kobe Bryant has cussed me out more than any other athlete. It's not even close—a record of which even 'the Mamba' would likely be proud. He's also shown his exceptional sense of decency in return on numerous occasions, which aided my earliest mindset of never taking any of this crap from an elite athlete personally.

A great example came in 2008, when visiting family in Las Vegas. I very much wanted to cover Team USA's final practice before they headed to China for the Beijing Olympics. I contacted a few folk to get a media credential but struck out, being told I needed to connect with the Olympic officials in charge, whom I didn't know. It looked bleak, until the night before their last day in town, when I randomly walked into the Palms casino where I headed to the food court. I got in a long line with of all people on this planet, Kobe's lead security guy standing right there, who recognized me immediately. What are those odds? Like a billion to one? Where was the sportsbook for that bet? Actually, just over my shoulder!

I told him of my dilemma, and he gave me the Olympic contact name to ask for at the team's hotel. Then I went to see him in the morning on the final day before Team USA was scheduled to fly to China. I was led over to the practice site at a local school, where I finally found my man. Cordially, he said that this needed to be done in advance to receive a credential and he apologized for turning me away. I could hear basketballs being bounced on the other side of the wall and decided to go to my biggest and last hope double-down card in Vegas. KOBE!

I asked this gentleman to get Bryant to confirm who I was, should there be any doubt on his part? He laughed (as in, yeah sure, whatever!). At that point, I said with stronger conviction, "I'm dead serious. Please get Kobe over here and let's clear this up now. I'd like to get some work done here, before you guys leave the country." Still looking at me funny, he then grudgingly walked through the door to enter the gym as I waited, giving me some hope.

A minute later the door opened, and this guy came back with Bryant alongside, and Kobe smiled at me, "HEY, WHAT'S UP? You need to get in here?" Then, I heard beautiful music to my ears (even greater than Viva Las Vegas), as Bryant looked at his team's media guy and said, "GET HIM HIS DAMN CREDENTIAL! We've got work to do, see you inside." God had spoken, and all was good.

Kobe saved my ass, and I'll never forget that comment and that look. I went into the 'Redeem Team's' practice and interviewed Bryant, D. Wade, and their head coach Mike Krzyzewski. I was a happy guy. This situation was easily my most favorite non-cash related win in Vegas EVER!

Meanwhile in Coach Jackson's book he'd questioned whether Kobe was truly coachable earlier on? So, I asked that question of our national team's bench boss, and Coach 'K' never flinched, "The guy has an incredible work ethic and will do ANYTHING to win. You can't ever ask for anything more than that! If only I could've had him on my Duke teams for a few seasons." Or even a few weeks! For the many who reasonably couldn't stand Bryant's antics, they all had to admit that he was evolving. Ever since Team USA won Olympic gold with Kobe in 2008, and 2012, he's been duly credited with reshaping the culture of our national team for the foreseeable future.

During that last practice before leaving for the Far East, I asked Bryant if he was starting to feel a little old, since the average age on his Olympic squad was 26, and he was just turning 30? "Ya know, surprisingly, I'm actually feeling a little younger than I did even last summer?" Why is that? "I have no damn idea, I don't know. I guess ya hit 30, I'm like fine wine. FINE WINE BABY!" That wine didn't begin to stale for another several years, squeezing every bit out those grapes, literally to the last drop!

With Kobe after the 2008 Team USA practice that he made sure I'll never forget

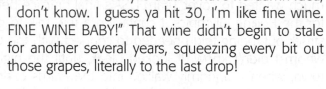

FUN FACT

It wasn't until five years later that a friend nicknamed Bryant 'Vino,' which he really loved. But I was right there first when his favorite Italiano Cabernet fruits were still ripening.

❑ TWO MORE RINGS WITHOUT 'THE DIESEL'

The Lakers saved Kobe's prime years and my sanity with the acquisition of Pao Gasol on the first day of February 2008, as he made life easier for us media hacks. Pao was the easiest guy to deal with and just a true pleasure to be around. Thank God, he changed Bryant's outlook, since KB was then like dealing with a bitter uncle. This resulted in three straight trips to the finals, with back-to-back titles in the rebirth of the old Lakers-Celtics rivalry, just as good as it gets!

But not for L.A. fans in this first finals matchup of the bitter rivals in 21 years. Time flies when you're not having fun and it was great to cover that series until a Celtics 39-point championship clinching win (the largest in NBA history). An embarrassment for sure for the locals, who went out and beat Orlando the following season for the franchise's 15th title and a Kobe 'I-told-you-so' moment that he didn't need Shaq to get it done.

KOBE & TED FUN FACT

In the year of the 2020 virus, our old NBA Finals video went viral when the Lakers were heading for their first title with LeBron James. Before winning their 2009 championship and right after taking a 2-0 series lead over Orlando, we got the too often 'Moody Mamba' in his postgame presser. So I took the mic, wondering why Bryant's surly look by saying, "Still waiting for a big smile out of you, you're up 2-0. What's the story? Are you NOT happy?" Kobe stared back with his now infamous reply, "What's there to be happy about? JOB'S NOT FINISHED! Job finished? I DON'T think so." And you just might know the rest...

SHAQ FUN FACT

It was always a bright spot in our day, when hanging with Shaquille in front of his locker. He made it obvious that if he ever wanted to get into broadcasting after his playing days, it would be an easy transition. And now O'Neal is just like he was with us—open, glib, and funny. To now observe his success as a broadcaster has just been so totally cool to watch. The guy you see on your TV, is who he is—and that's a good thing!

❏ SMILE, YOU'RE ON NATIONAL TV

In the 2010 finals, it was redemption time for the Lakers in my first and only chance to cover all of the games in Beantown around that incredible atmosphere. I remember in my live reports telling the folks back home that it was the loudest arena I'd ever witnessed a basketball game in. Bostonian's hated anything related to L.A. (although they were really great to me, not knowing I briefly used to be a New Englander). There were BEAT L.A. signs and t-shirts and a lot worse everywhere, in a time when sports dominated the headlines. I loved every second of it.

The Lakers also loved the situation, when they took a 2-1 series lead at the new GAH-den, making my life easier with a nice positive story to tell for our KFWB listeners. It was just after Game 4 that made national news, although I didn't have a clue about it. Early the next morning, I got a call that there was an entire segment on the Jimmy Kimmel Show dedicated to me. WHAT THE HELL DID I DO TO DESERVE SUCH A FATE? He doesn't even know who I am or why I was there—as just another schmuck reporter on the scene?

It turned out that their network camera caught me close up interviewing Lakers guard Derek Fisher at his locker, with my usual smiling at the subject, trying to make him feel as if he's the only human who matters. Kimmel, however, zoomed in on me while showing a continuous smile that even creeped me out— believe me, I wasn't THAT happy at all. He laughed at me (and not with me), as the reporter who couldn't stop smiling. I then soon got texts galore from those who saw it. Thanks for the national pub Jimmy, but not exactly how I would've preferred it. I did get to see it one time (which was more than enough). I think it's since been taken down from online due to lack of interest?

Watching Fisher and Laker teammate Sasha Vujacic celebrate their 2010 NBA title, seconds after being handed the trophy

——— **FUN FACT** ———

Derek Fisher began his legend in Lakerland with some well chronicled big shots, including in the Orlando finals, before being anointed as the club's modern Mr. Clutch. To me, however, he'll always be the fantastic go-to-guy in the locker room who ALWAYS made himself available, while being the ONLY NBA player of his era to make the effort to regularly call me by my first name, which tells a lot about the man.

The Lakers returned home to win Game 6. Although they were down 13 in the third quarter, they then completed back-to-back titles with their first Game 7 win against the C's in five tries. Kobe won his fifth and final ring (despite struggling mightily on just 6-of-24 shooting, but with 15 huge rebounds) in a very disappointing performance by both sides. It meant a great deal for this kid who grew up in L.A. (me) to be in that environment, while satisfying to feel the home crowd relish in the joy of the players beating Boston for only the third time in a dozen tries, while almost feeling the deep exhale of Baylor and West. (the thought of Elgin telling me decades earlier in his trophy room how much it hurt to never beat the Celtics seemed fresh all over again). I then headed down to the victorious locker room, which included Bryant as the finals MVP for a second straight year.

❏ KOBE PASSED ME THE BALL!!!

While the champagne continued to flow in the Lakers championship locker room celebration, the excitement wasn't as much about 'The Mamba' but the volatile Ron Artest (and soon to be known as the loving Metta World Peace). I had always liked dealing with Artest, given that he showed his honest emotions, although they were sometimes off the deep end! With 1:01 to play in this Game 7, which was still very much up for grabs and with only a 3-point lead, Artest took a pass from a double-teamed Bryant, where he was wide open (for a reason) for a three. Artest then coolly shot that jumper that not only had his coaching staff collectively biting their tongues and holding their breaths, but the entire Laker nation's hearts stopped.

You could almost hear them all yelling out, NOOOOOOOOO as the ball flew threw the air. Until SWISH! Then the loudest crowd eruption of this tense game occurred. It was 20 points for Ron, who could always shoot, but that wasn't his role on this team (and certainly not with an entire season on-the-line). After making the shot of his life, he then threw the crowd a big two-handed kiss, leading to an unforgettable championship moment and his first and deeply cherished only NBA ring.

The place went wild and so did Ron, who was then labeled as the Game 7 MVP by his Coach Jackson. As we crowded around the new local hero in his triumphant locker room (before his podium gathering), we asked about what had just happened? Talking into my mic, while gathering steam with each word, "Kobe passed me the ball! KOBE PASSED ME THE BALL. The BLACK MAMBA, he NEVER passes the ball, and he passed ME the ball."

There was no way I couldn't start laughing at this unexpected yet true emotion. Respectfully, we got some, which heightened this passionate moment in time even more. Ron's family enjoyed every moment of this while standing right behind us. Catching some of his exuberant fever, I quickly screamed out, "How the hell did he pass YOU the ball?" Ron looked back over to his left at me and screamed even louder, "I KNOW, HE NEVER DOES THAT!" Then, seemingly running out of gas and vocal cords, he softened his final words, by stating again, "Kobe passed me the ball."

Believe me, everyone was as stunned as he was. Almost feeling stressed out, I got what I had needed and finally walked away, while Artest put on his next postgame show for the ages joined by his entire family at the podium for the rest of the waiting media. The all too often rage in his eyes was gone, and this crazy sequence of events became even more gratifying, seeing the evolving Ronald Artest, Jr. enjoy something that he'd worked so damn hard for. He was just a total joy to be around, and I just couldn't be happier for him—the person.

But those decades of feeling the pain of the Celtics domination of the Lakers still hung in the back of my mind—not just because I was a big Lakers fan as a kid. My feelings were also a byproduct of what Elgin had told me in my first one-on-one with him just after his retirement in 1972. He stated that he was 'VERY HAPPY' with his career BUT, "Naturally I had many disappointing years, I've gotten very close just a matter of a few lucky bounces with the ball (vs. Boston)." His expression had told me much more than those words on how devastating the years as a runner-up were and how it took a toll on Baylor and his teammates.

The classically humble Jerry West (who took losses harder than any athlete I've ever known) was more demonstrative when conveying his feelings to me on this subject. "I played in nine NBA Finals and won once (never against the

Celtics). It makes me feel like I failed as a player, because at that point in time, I was as good as ANYONE who played. ANYONE! I was a defender at both ends of the court, and offensively, I could just score, it was a gift. But the losing was the thing that always wore on me." Jerry long ago also told me that he owned nothing in his wardrobe close to Celtic green that he could ever wear, which says it all.

Winning is serious business in all sports, but never like it was in those days when they didn't play for the big bucks—and when prideful championships was like finding gold. Lombardi's 'winning isn't everything, it's the only thing' was how many of those greats lived and breathed. You could feel their pain after failing as if they were throwing you jabs to the jaw.

❏ 60 AT 37 FOR KB'S FAREWELL

Kobe doing his thing one last time in front of his family—taken from my upper hockey pressbox seats

The goodbye game for Kobe Bean Bryant in April of 2016 wasn't really about the winning, with his team being simply awful, but rather to complete his two-decade career with some flair. I fully expected to see him gun it for 30-40 points, until his arm fell off. This was a Super Hero version of that. At the end, it actually looked like it was his legs that were falling off in a storybook finish to hardly be believed. Kobe scored 23 fourth quarter points and led a comeback from 14 down to the star-struck Utah Jazz for his final win, which was from another universe with a going away 60 point night!

With the last ounce of energy left in his 20th-season, hardwood torn-up body, Kobe grabbed his final rebound, threw a long pass for his final assist for a Jordan Clarkson slam dunk, and that was the game—with a Hollywood ending. That was it for Bryant who literally had NO MORE TO GIVE. He was spent! It felt almost surreal to be standing there on the court level in the tunnel, just behind Kobe, when he threw that last pass. I'm thinking I can't believe he just hit for 60 points on 50 shots (the most taken in at least three decades). But 60? REALLY? In his final game—EVER?

It was then a matter of taking in the extra-long still on-the-court celebration, until declaring himself 'Mamba out.' KB was out of there for good. It was time to go into the interview room and do what I've done hundreds of times—but never like this. The arena was very surreal, with the sky full of purple and gold confetti being shot from the rafters, but to end the worst season in franchise history? Just too strange. Of course, what made the entire night so special was the buzz in the building from the second the doors opened until the last person had left. Maybe, they all just wanted to get their money's worth, with ticket prices to the game like in the NBA finals. Or maybe, it was the entire atmosphere of the city saying goodbye to their hoops hero and needing to let that soak into their nostalgic memory banks.

Kobe admitted during his pregame presser that he didn't prepare any speech for his number retirement ceremony. Although this was a very emotional time due to the circumstances, he himself was not very sentimental. I even heard some people giving odds on whether he would cry during it, and I would have put a ton of money on the NO and would have been a winner. He's always been polarizing, but you can't ever say that he's not fascinating.

I took this picture, when walking up to Chick Hearn Court & Figueroa, before Kobe's last game—it was a street party.

I'd never seen the media so out of their minds in awe of what they had just witnessed. With Kobe entering his final postgame media session and with his jersey still on (I don't think he was ready to put it into eternal storage just yet), he told us, "It's a weird year. Go from villain to now being a type of hero. And go from everybody saying, 'Pass the ball!' To saying, 'Shoot the ball!'" The basketball world had strangely turned upside down, with Kobe taking in the moment in a most refreshingly tranquil way.

The whole area around Staples was littered with #ThankYouKobe signs everywhere. I wondered how much of that did number 24 see for himself and how he was able to dig deep and grab that big SIX-O after such a long emotional night? "Seeing everything that was taking place before, I was enjoying, it and I was very appreciative of it…and I quickly got right back to…ok, you GOT TO get out there and perform. And so, I was able to focus and try not to get too emotional, not to take away from my performance. Despite my best efforts, I had to settle down." My follow-up comment was, "You were dragging pretty good in that fourth quarter!" KB: "I WAS TIRED MAN…SAVE IT FOR WHAT? I was just hoping I didn't hurt something!"

That was Kobe Bryant for the past 20 years—save it for what? Could you imagine how much greater sports would be with more playing like that? What an end of an era (just the team's 17th win in their crappiest season ever, and nobody cared)—a truly bizarre event that will be impossible to replicate. Furthermore, it was in front of about 25 of his stunned ex-teammates, including Lamar Odom, Robert Horry, Derek Fisher, and Rick Fox, and that guy named Shaq, who had a smile that extended from downtown L.A. to South Beach. It was great to mingle some with a bunch of the now older stars who once were all nice regulars to shoot the bull with, after getting my required 10-15 second sound bites.

Kobe's finale program, with media notes, my credential, and #24 confetti

The bickering was long gone, and it was just part of a certain Hall of Fame ending, which got me looking back again on how Kobe had told me on several occasions that he was just born too damn late. How he would have loved to have played in the very physical era of the NBA. Not for the ridiculous fights and taunting, but just the hard-nosed play that got his juices flowing on any playground or court at anytime. As he put it, "if you drove down the middle of the lane and you got an elbow to the neck (especially in the playoffs)—tough shit!" The now mild-mannered Dad then walked off into the sunset with the perfect storybook ending, except for perhaps beating the Celtics for one last ring!

❏ KOBE, TIGER AND PLENTY OF GROWLS

Kobe stopped to greet my wife Elisa after his final Christmas Day game and graciously spoke in her native Spanish. Finally meeting her favorite athlete was the ultimate gift.

In the middle of a typical Kobe media day madness scrum—courtesy Jayne Kamin-Oncea

Several weeks after the Tiger Woods personal incidents that derailed his life and career in 2010, I was in just another postgame scrum, with Kobe in front of his locker. As it broke up, I walked over and privately asked if he had a comment on the Tiger situation, since he was the only man alive I could think of, who could truly relate to Woods after his own previous legal and family issues from seven years earlier in Colorado? He glared down at me with that infamous 'Kobe death stare' (for hardly the first time) and said, "ARE YOU FUCKING KIDDING ME? You expect me to answer THAT? C'MON MAN! No fucking way!" I took the hint, but at least I tried!

Laker P.R. guy John Black standing just a few feet away and hearing every word of this then walks up to me, "I can't believe you asked him that? I CANNOT BELIEVE that you had the balls to ask him that?" I explained why he was the ONLY relevant human on the planet to ask about Tiger. John then quickly said, "You're on his shit list FOREVER!" Good luck ever getting anything from him again!" Whatever…I have a job to do, and I did it respectfully and had no regrets for doing so.

Turning to walk out of the Lakers locker room, I suddenly felt a long arm wrap around my shoulder. I looked up and it was Kobe? With a huge welcoming grin he said, 'It's ALL good man, but there was no fucking way I was going to answer THAT question…but good try anyways!" We then walked out together like buds, chuckling as if nothing had ever happened.

That's Kobe and my relationship with him during his 20 years on the court—never knowing when we'd get the most competitive maniac or your happy relative who's willing to go out of his way to help you. Who knows? Maybe, I'll get cussed out one more time just for writing this? Man I hope so!

As difficult as this is to write while still feeling numb, I left the previous sentence in as it was originally intended, well before Kobe's tragic death (which occurred as I was completing this book), to show just how I truly felt then. Now, I'll never get that chance to share these stories with KB, despite just a brief mention to him. I never got close to the Bryant family, which is the way I usually roll, not attempting to combine private and professional lives with those whom I cover. I did enjoy, however, the many times greeting Kobe's wife Vanessa and their first two kids since they were infants, as they patiently sat waiting postgame for Dad just outside the Lakers locker room.

It was adorable to see how their little Gianna was always 'Daddy's Girl.' Her loss in the January 2020 helicopter accident makes it so much more difficult to accept and comprehend. 'Gigi' had an amazing smile, with a great aura about her. She was a true chip off the ol' block, with an obviously proud father watching her grow into a quality young woman, who also just happened to passionately love to play the game he loved. Oh how he enjoyed watching 'Mambacita' do her thing, with long-term hopes of her possibly playing at the University of Connecticut (the preeminent school for women's hoops) and beyond.

The sudden catastrophic loss of the two Bryants and the other seven lives that day is another life lesson that Kobe would certainly be stressing today. Life's too short to waste a moment (which he perfected like few others); our purpose here is much greater than our time spent. After a slow start in the public eye (and remember he came here as a 17-year old), and then being a dad to four girls, he became a great example for fathers everywhere, while doing his best to get the world to recognize the importance of women achieving whatever they wish to in sports and in all of life.

To sum up Kobe as best as I can, he was far from perfect but learned how to be a successful human in ways from which we can all learn. The man was simply unafraid to fail. That airball game as a teenage rookie being the perfect example. Do you realize that he holds the record for the most missed shots in NBA history (check out that list of all-time greats sometime), but could care less, given that he lived by "You can't score if you don't shoot," on and off the court. He wanted everyone to do the same in whatever their chosen field.

Kobe's purpose was first to always win each play, and then every game, and then again in every facet of life. The guy actually won an Oscar early in retirement! THAT'S JUST NOT NORMAL! After his playing days he wanted to pass on his knowledge to the next generation, like he'd received from those who had preceded him. He subsequently went on to become a revered inspirational humanitarian through all of his work. I loved how he, unlike most of his generation, would express his appreciation for the playing days of Elgin and Jerry, and he wasn't even born yet. West would later express his grief, saying that the loss of Kobe was like losing a son—there was just an eternal bond that went far beyond basketball.

Kobe and Gianna's breathtakingly emotional public Celebration of Life brought us a moving and courageous Vanessa Bryant tribute speech for the ages, with even more fervor than watching her husband limp to the free throw line with a torn achilles tendon. Imagine, if only Gigi could've had the chance to someday surpass family friend Diana Taurasi's all-time WNBA scoring record, it's a heavenly thought for sure.

Interviewing Kobe at his shoe appearance, with wife Vanessa, then pregnant with Gigi—photo by Mario Villegas

Michael Jordan's eulogy for Kobe was simple perfection, an awe-inspiring few minutes more graceful than any switch-hands layup he could ever muster up on the floor. It reminded me some of a younger Michael, who was usually open with us, who stood in front of his Forum visitor's locker for postgame reactions during his Bulls dynasty run—when he was in the mood to really speak his mind. This was an ultimate from-the-heart display for a friend that we should all be so lucky to receive when it's our time.

Kobe had turned himself from a student of the game into a student of life. I believe much of that was influenced by the insights offered in Phil Jackson's books, as well as his soul-deep talks with Phil and Tex Winter. Whatever anyone's outlook on Kobe Bryant the man, his combination of passion, skills, and intensity left a legacy that will last as long as the game itself, while his worldly impact transcends into so many other facets of life. For me, it was just tons of personal memories that will stick to my soul forever. Thanks for letting me touch greatness with you Kobe—until the next time you cuss me out...and I can't wait!

CHAPTER 13

PASSION FOR PIGSKIN

I grew up in a time when baseball was the national pastime, and no other sport was ever in the conversation. We NEVER discussed any other sport during the baseball season, and the game's stats meant everything compared to all others without competition. To a large degree, sports remain the elevator music of this country. But The Babe, The Mick, and The Duke are long gone, and that talk has totally flipped to football—most recently, TB12, Beast Mode, and Honey Badger rule, as it's just a different world. The gridiron is now what dominates the minds of fans year-round.

People want more action than baseball provides, and I can't blame them. As much as I love the game, if I didn't grow up playing on the diamonds daily, while gaining the passion for the sport that I did, I likely wouldn't watch today's slower game much either—besides I'm running out of a random four hours to kill!

Today's football is also not the same to those of us over 40. It's gradually turning into glamorized flag football, with the lack of big hits and quality tackling (which is great for the player's health, but not for the viewer). Vince Lombardi's Packers' power sweep that swept the nation is totally unfathomable today. It's all about slinging the ball around—pass, pass, and RPO again. One of the great winning quarterbacks of all time Bart Starr (my boyhood football idol) once told me, while laughing, that Brett Favre "could throw a ball farther on his knees than I could standing still" and that he would have a hard time making any team these days. As I always say, it's a waste of time and effort to try and compare eras with only one sure truism—if you were great in your era, you were great, PERIOD! Yet even with all the rules changes, this game is still GREAT!

Roaming the sidelines during a Sports USA broadcast in Cleveland, the best part was wandering past the playfully frothing at the mouth 'Dawg Pound'

❏ RODGERS' DODGERS

Speaking of great, my life in football has been around some of the all-time names and places, including 'The Fearsome Foursome' and 'The Bus' in L.A., 'The Black Hole' in Oakland, 'World' AKA Rice—the San Francisco treat, the 'Dawg Pound' in Cleveland, and the greatest place to experience a pro football game, 'The Frozen Tundra' of Lambeau Field. The one player who I've dealt with and has lived in Green Bay since he was knee-high to a Favre is Aaron Rodgers.

Aaron had a prolific chip on his shoulder the size of a boulder since his days at Cal. And certainly right after the 2005 NFL draft, when many expected him to be taken by his favorite team the S.F. 49ers #1 overall, before his disappointing fall to 24th, when he was chosen by Green Bay. In our first long interview a few years later, I asked my fellow California native if he could've ever imagined where he wound up? "THE PACKERS? I had to look it up on a map where Green Bay was." He then had the infamous wait behind Favre, which was always the norm in the NFL, sitting behind the #1 guy and learning your craft until it's your time to play. In 2006, it wasn't Aaron's time yet. It was my time, however, to incidentally meet and greet after the Packers first preseason game in San Diego.

Standing about 20 feet away from Rodgers' locker, while waiting for Favre to finally get out of the shower for a brief interview, I overheard Aaron and a few writers talking baseball. BASEBALL? I wandered over first listening in and then joined their discussion, first asking a few Packers questions and then getting Rodgers to myself with a quick introduction. "I'm from L.A. and with the Dodgers flagship station KFWB and heard you guys talking baseball." Aaron's eyes opened like a kid's on Christmas morning, "DODGERS BABY!"

I thought he was F'ing with me. Dodgers? Rodgers is a northern Cali guy, he couldn't be interested in the Dodgers, or could he? He then explained that he had become friendly with then new Dodgers third-base coach Rich Donnelly, whom he knew previously from the Milwaukee Brewers. Donnelly invited Aaron down to Vero Beach and he immediately became a big Dodgers fan. He said to me, "I can't tell you how excited I am about the 11-game winning streak, I think we've got 13 out of the last 14 now—and they beat the Giants. DODGER BLUE THROUGH AND THROUGH!"

WE??? "I hope that once we win the World Series, that Rich and some of the guys will be able to come out to watch us play. I'm a big sports fan, and I know I've become a traitor in Northern California." I responded with "but what about the hated Giants?" Aaron quickly replied, "I'm not a big fan of one of their players (gee, I wonder who that could be? #25?) I can't say I was ever a Giants fan, more of an A's fan. I loved it when they had Zito, Mulder, and Hudson."

Aaron told me that Nomar Garciaparra was his favorite player on the Dodgers. "Not only because my roommate calls me Nomar sometimes thinking I look like him, but I've just always been a fan of his, the way he plays shortstop. I used to play shortstop, and so did he." I then asked how long he'd been a Dodger fan? "Uh, this year! But I'm behind them 100%."

This guy really knew his baseball too. I was very impressed. He was even more interesting to me, knowing EVERYTHING about the Dodgers. So, I thought it would be fun to have him come on the radio with me and be my NFL baseball 'analyst' during my KFWB Dodgers coverage. He loved the idea. Rodgers then joined me when the Dodgers clinched the Wild Card and again the week they got swept into the off-season by the Mets. He was excellent and quick-witted (which is what made me very open to this), while also talking a little Packers football, but not much! And some damn good on-air practice 15 years in advance of hosting 'Jeopardy!'

We continued this baseball radio relationship until the Favre retirement fiasco, when Rodgers would eventually take over as the Packers' starter to begin 2008. That sparked a thought to possibly cover his first NFL start (on a Monday night vs. rival Minnesota). So, we spoke during that training camp, and I said I'd fly to Green Bay, IF he promised to give me a one-on-one after the game. After hearing, "You got it!" I was off to storied Lambeau, my favorite place to watch a game on this planet!

Catching Aaron running onto the field for the first time as a starter

Although then in N.Y. Jet's green and white, the Brett Favre era was not over for a large percentage of fans in Green Bay. I ate at Favre's steakhouse that weekend, and they weren't easily accepting that their beloved gunslinger didn't live there anymore. I wandered the stadium. The faithful almost had a defiant attitude that Favre was no longer a Packer that night. There were thousands of #4 jerseys in the crowd, while I could count the number of Aaron's #12 shirts on both hands. It was a wait-and-see attitude, but it wouldn't be very long until the always sold out Lambeau would turn into Mister Rodgers' neighborhood.

This Packers locker room tunnel plaque is what Touching Greatness is all about

The Packers won that game, with Rodgers throwing for one touchdown and a one yard T.D. run that 'vaulted' him into his first 'Lambeau Leap,' which was not pretty. Actually, Aaron barely got over the railing, but we had a good time laughing that off later, after I'd waited for him to finish his first postgame media scrum of his starting era. Biding my time, Rodgers finally came walking into the Packers locker room looking for me. To my surprise, he was wearing a Brooklyn Dodgers warmup jacket.

So, of course, I immediately asked about the jacket he was wearing, which, he said brought him "good luck." Since I was working for an L.A. station, I tried to make this chat as much SoCal-related as possible. Linking Aaron Rodgers to the Dodgers was exactly that. This was also his future favorite receiver Jordy Nelson's first NFL game (no catches and just one target that night). We subsequently got to speak again, after I had interviewed him the day he was drafted by the Pack. It was quite a successful start to the Rodgers era in Green Bay—really for both of us. I felt right at home again in Wisconsin.

❏ AARON AND 'THE BART'

In a 2016 phone interview with Rodgers, it was tremendous to share experiences about the legendary Packers quarterback Bart Starr. We talked about Bart coming back to Lambeau Field for Favre's jersey retirement day,

Rodgers and I have connected several times on the golf course at Pebble Beach, where I got these pictures of the 3X NFL MVP teeing off and throwing a spiral on its scenic 18th fairway.

after Starr's grueling rehab from so many difficult health issues. I asked if Rodgers got a few private moments with Starr that day? " I did, we had a lot of time actually. We took what I think will turn into a fairly iconic picture of the three of us—Bart, Brett, and myself. It is one that I'm looking forward to getting up in my house as well. So, it's really fun to see that come out, and Bart has been such a great supporter of mine, he and his wife (Cherry), since I took over and really since I got to the team in 2005. And he's a great mentor for anybody out there looking for (not only) what it looks like to do it incredibly well on the field, but also conducting yourself as a gentleman with humility off the field. I'm just fortunate enough to be able to have gotten to know him, and I love any chance I get to spend time with him."

I then asked Aaron to explain to any football fan who hasn't experienced it, what it's like to attend a game at Lambeau Field? "I'm just going to encourage anybody who hasn't been here to come here, whether you're a Packer fan or not. I think it's an incredible venue to watch a game, so much history here. The team has done a great job of making some incredible tourist attractions, (like) our Hall of Fame, our tour we put on, the atrium, it's an incredible game-day experience. Then you talk about the tailgating to see the welcome attitude that our fans have. They love meeting people, helping to serve brats to people and cracking open some cold beverages. It's a special place to play and watch, and it's fun to have my friends come out for the first time to take it all in, because it's a really special experience. I think it's got to be on the bucket list for EVERY football fan." Amen to that Aaron.

❏ FEELING SUPER

Of course, on everyone's bucket list is going to (or playing in) a Super Bowl. Rodgers gave me first dibs on all of his interviews in late January 2011, two days after beating Chicago to get the Packers to Dallas, when they beat the Steelers in S.B. XLV. I interviewed every key player in the champion's locker room that day. That audio collage can still be heard at my website Sobelsports.com. I was also in New Orleans when Favre and the Pack beat New England, so it was a kick to be around each of their two titles after the Lombardi era.

Aaron has continued to be great to me, granting an interview during most of my years hosting the Sports USA network NFL pregame shows (a rarity to get a quarterback at anytime). It's greatly appreciated that he remembers the guy who was there with him almost from the start—although now it's BUCK'S BABY, with Rodgers a minority owner in Milwaukee's NBA franchise.

❏ LIVING THE TITLETOWN DREAM

Growing up a Packers fan in L.A. was strange in the '60s, but the Rams owners then somehow turned me off to their team. In contrast, the early mystique of Lombardi, Starr, Nitschke, and company in green and gold seen regularly on my TV, with the great HOF voice of the late Ray Scott, got me hooked. I only wanted to one day see Lambeau Field for my own eyes and just shake Bart Starr's hand (which I did once after a game in L.A.). In reality, I got to experience so much more than I could've ever imagined. And, there was ONE GAME that has fascinated me to this day.

Standing at the corner of Lombardi and Starr is like waiting for your team bus in football heaven, maybe Rodgers Road will end up a Hail Mary away from Lambeau Field?

❏ THE ICE BOWL AT THE BEACH

It was New Year's Eve day 1967, and I'll never forget sitting in my Culver City living room on a typical beautiful day rooting for the Packers against the Cowboys, amazed at how cold it looked at Lambeau, with smoke flowing out of people's scarf protected mouths and noses. The heavy layers of clothes that everyone was wearing, with so little skin exposed, and the players trying to find any warmth they could on the sidelines had me intrigued to no end. This game was more about survival until the final gun than any game in memory. The slipping and sliding on the frozen turf and dirt made this a must see 35th NFL Championship Game for the right to play in Super Bowl II.

As the fourth quarter rolled along, it seemed more unlikely by each play that the Packers would find a way to win, as their offense had completely stalled throughout much of the second half. I so wanted to ask Bart Starr to his face what was going through his mind at any point in this game, but you can't do that even now with the best interactive TV. But, 47 years later, I finally got that chance and how good of a week it is to fulfill two of your top sports bucket list entries, covering the Masters and meeting your childhood football idol back-to-back? Exhilarating to say the least!

While Bart Starr and I had spoken on the phone several times over the years, he lives and works on the other side of the country from me in Birmingham, close to where he once played at the University of Alabama. The previous time we had spoken, he said that if I was ever in the area to please call him. Augusta, Georgia was close enough for me (checking online, it was ONLY a four and a half hour drive away). Fortunately his schedule was open to meet on that Tuesday after the 2014 Masters.

Bart is a true gentleman in every sense of the word. He was so gracious to allow me a few hours of his time to finally meet for some quality time together.

I was immediately welcomed at the front door of his office, we then shook hands, and I said, "Mr. Starr, it's so nice to finally meet you in person"…before I could say another word he quickly replied to call him Bart, and the rest of our afternoon was something I'll never forget.

FUN FACT

I once read that Bart Starr was a big tennis fan, so after learning he'd be coming to SoCal for business, I invited him to our L.A. Open at UCLA. He absolutely wanted to attend, but his travel schedule wouldn't allow it. He did get excited, when I told him that I worked for Hall of Famer Jack Kramer's son Bob. Bart then explained how Jack was his hero as a kid, and I passed along mutual greetings, when Mr. Kramer said that he admired Starr, too. The best thing from that was Jack Kramer signing one of his signature wooden rackets to Bart, which I hand delivered to him some years later and Starr was a like a kid when receiving it. He then gave it to his wife Cherry, who was an even greater tennis lover than Bart. He really made my day bigtime!

Bart kindly signed this Masters pin flag as a special keepsake of our afternoon together

It was deja vu sitting in the back seat of Bart Starr's car on our way to get some pizza and chatting away, just like I had done with my basketball hero Elgin Baylor decades earlier. This time, however, I was 61 and not 16. Although it was a much different experience, it was quite ok to feel like a kid again.

After lunch with his most welcoming son, Bart, Jr., and three of their nice officemates, including his wonderful assistant Leigh Ann Nelson, I sat down with the MVP of Super Bowl I and II, and we talked for about an hour (wishing it was all day) covering some of his career highlights, mainly focusing on the Ice Bowl, as well as Super Bowl I (which was most special to me as it was played in my hometown of L.A.), and his relationship with Coach Vince Lombardi and how he had forever changed the lives of almost every Green Bay Packer who ever played for him.

Every second of our sit-down interview was very special. There was a different type of focus, however, when I brought up the Packers falling behind in the Ice Bowl and what Starr's mindset was at the time? He admitted that it was very difficult to move the ball, even more so in the debilitating bitter cold second half. Their final drive really was one of the all-time greats in the history of the game, specifically considering it was for the NFL Championship and in such impossible conditions. Dallas Hall of Famer Bob Lilly said his team was stunned by the worsening frigid second half, saying it had gotten to 69 below zero, with the wind chill (which seems a bit exaggerated—at least I would hope so!).

ICE BOWL FUN FACT

I once got the opportunity to ask Cowboys legendary coach Tom Landry about that game, which he called after chuckling under his breath, "the most devastating and disappointing loss of his career." I told him, "Sorry Coach, but I was rooting against you bigtime!" and he just laughed— with a friendly twinge of displeasure.

What I loved the most, however, was how Bart described to me what I had wondered about as a kid watching this unfold on TV during this nervous time for any Packers fan. It came down to almost perfect execution in the most imperfect minus 16-degree conditions, as the Packers began that fateful final drive with potentially 4:50 left in the season at their own 32-yard line. Starr used a heavy dose of his backfield running mates Chuck Mercein and Donny Anderson to pick up chunks of yards on a thin sheet of ice and through that arctic air.

Trailing 17-14 Green Bay got it down to the Dallas one-yard line with 16 seconds left, but could they score after trying a pair of slippery but ineffective dive plays or lose in the worst way with S.B. II just inches away? Bart called his final timeout and hustled to the sideline to speak to his legendary coach, before requesting to sneak it in himself, due to the poor footing for his running backs.

It was THE most precious moment (even though I'd heard it numerous times before) to have Bart Starr look me in the eye and tell me exactly how he convinced Lombardi to take it himself, "Coach, I'm standing upright, I can just kind of shuffle my feet and lunge in. So help me, this is exactly what he said, 'well then run it and LET'S GET THE HELL OUT OF HERE!'" I start cracking up every time I hear those words, and I asked Bart, "how did you keep from laughing at that moment?" Starr admitted to me that he had to hold back his laughter as he ran back onto the field, not wanting to show any emotions to his desperate opponent at the time.

Starr took the snap and dove into the end zone behind that most famous Jerry Kramer block, with 13 seconds showing on the clock, and the rest is history. 'The Sneak' was consummated, and the Packers were NFL Champs for a third straight year, thanks to their 21-17 win over the Cowboys.

I was in such a great mood immediately after the game that I thought how awesome it would be to celebrate on a sunny beach, while thinking of all those frozen fans in the stands at Lambeau. What a way to enjoy our very nice wintry day in L.A. (which was in the mid 70s), so I hopped a bus to Santa Monica and just sat on the sand smiling until sunset, because my Packers were going to the Super Bowl following Lombardi's final game in Green Bay.

It feels like yesterday, when sitting on the Santa Monica sand rocking out to my psychedelic transistor radio's current greatest hits, like Summer in the City by the Lovin' Spoonful, Daydream Believer (The Monkees), I Second That Emotion (Smokey Robinson & the Miracles), Hello Goodbye (The Beatles), Incense and Peppermints (Strawberry Alarm Clock), Summer Rain (Johnny Rivers), and Different Drum (The Stone Poneys featuring Linda Ronstadt). Great songs before hustling home to hear the Lakers open their new Fabulous Forum with a win over the San Diego Rockets, while waiting to see the video of Evel Knievel's failed 141-foot motorcycle jump over the Caesars Palace fountains in Las Vegas—all just hours before the start of the turbulent 1968.

During this special Touching Greatness moment, I said to Bart, "This is as close I'll ever get to hanging with you and Lombardi."

Starr signed Lombardi/Green Bay first day cover—from the Sobel collection

Oh how Bart enjoyed hearing about my day of watching his most famous game and then winding up on the beach (sunning it) while he had to deal with frostbite issues after his long work day. But not a tenth as much as I did sharing it with him. That's a feeling that's indescribable, and I hope my description of that day gives you just a little taste of this little kid living out his dream. A day in the huddle with Bart Starr—beats any Super Bowl EVER PLAYED!

❏ A STARR SHINES FOR ETERNITY

I sadly finish this story, awakened on Sunday morning May 26, 2019, with a text from Alabama and appropriately from the longtime voice of 'Bama football Eli Gold. "I just got a call that Bart Starr has passed away." It was a message that I had dreaded for too long, with Bart experiencing so many life-threatening health concerns over the previous five years since we got together. Now, all of those wonderful Sundays watching #15 play on my TV, as well as once in person at the L.A. Coliseum, and seeing him a few times as the Packers head coach roaming the sidelines came back to me. Our phone conversations and finally the 2014 meeting seemed like yesterday in my mind and heart. I wanted to just feel and taste every moment of it one more time.

This was not only a loss of possibly the greatest field leader in NFL history—winning five Championships with a 9-1 postseason record and the only QB to lead his team to three straight NFL titles (including the first two Super Bowls)—

but also one of the kindest gentlemen I ever met. We had shared a nice laugh talking about him being the 200th pick in the 1956 draft and how his perseverance and tutelage under Coach Lombardi (which began three years later) set up so much success for the rest of his life.

It was an emotional Sunday (without football), watching the many reactions via social media, etc. come in about arguably the most popular player in Packers history. To a man, they all mentioned the man, more than about his football playing days. Starr was a giver, like few others ever and just a good person. His favorite term came from being part of a team and not just out for yourself. In our half hour interview Bart repeated again and again what T.E.A.M. means to him, which says it all, "Together, Everybody Achieves More." That's in all phases of life.

Starr would be smiling, knowing that his compelling definition of team is out there for all to read and comprehend here. It is the perfect descriptive slogan, used by as great a TEAM leader as any in the history of sports. It was almost as perfect as his name Bart Starr, which easily could've been the name of your favorite cinematic football hero, except he was more real and humble than any other on the field or off. I was privileged to have spent some personal time with him. Thank you for your 85 wonderful years Bart, and please say hello to McGee and Fuzzy for me.

❏ ANOTHER LAMBEAU-L.A. CONNECTION

The Ice Bowl will always be known as the signature event in Green Bay's storied history, but few would know that it was refereed by the SoCal duo of Los Angeles High School principal Norm Schachter, who was a friend, and a close colleague of my Fairfax High principal (two years later) Jim Tunney. Mr. Tunney was an alternate ref that day for Schachter, who later talked about how his whistle froze even before opening kickoff and that ignoring an unofficial league rule that officials not wear earmuffs, "was the best call I made all day."

Schachter was not only a very bright man but had a great sense of humor, which he used wisely during his multi-career years. Norm also got to stay home and referee Super Bowl I at the Coliseum between those Packers and Kansas City Chiefs. Quite a Southern California connection to this historic inaugural game!

─────────── **FUN FACT** ───────────

If you don't know the name Norm Schachter look it up, as your kids might be reading one of his English books in class right now? As a prodigious writer, he wrote many of them that are highly acclaimed to this day (12 English and vocabulary textbooks and a few more about coaching and football).

I've always had a fascination with Super Bowl I, which, of course, was played in my own backyard at the L.A. Coliseum on January 15, 1967. I was under the impression that I would be going to the game as my father had gotten tickets through a friend. Since he decided it wouldn't be much of a game, however, with the Packers almost a two touchdown favorite over the lesser AFL franchise from Kansas City, he backed out. As a result, I was stuck trying to watch it, while holding our TV's rabbit ears antenna (only intermittently picking up a fuzzy San Diego station).

FUN FACTS

Many rip Los Angeles for not selling out Super Bowl I, with about 32,000 unsold seats for a game considered to be a total mismatch. It was a local TV blackout, as per NFL rules. Rarely spoken of after a year of hype, were the reports out of Miami the night before Super Bowl II that read 'a sellout crowd is expected'! A forgotten fact is that they were hyping seats for that game during the 'Ice Bowl's' TV postgame, with "still tickets available" comments for the coming matchup at the Orange Bowl (where the third man in that telecast was my Fairfax High co-alum Jack Kemp).

I'd always wanted to interview the very outgoing and personable Packers team HOFer Max McGee, who spent a very legendary night on the eve of the inaugural big game out on the town, hitting his favorite L.A. hot spots, after breaking curfew, while never expecting to play—and I mean NOT at all. How was I to ever sit down with one of the most successful post-football businessmen when we lived in completely different worlds?

Well in 2004, I had scheduled myself to cover a Packers game in Green Bay and called the team in advance to hopefully set up an interview with McGee (their former longtime radio colorman). I was told that he then irregularly showed up on a whim to Lambeau, and that they didn't know his schedule. So, it was up to random luck. And did I have the rub of the green (and gold) on the day of my flights.

We first stopped in Minneapolis to change planes for Green Bay, and as they called for first class on my connecting flight (which did NOT include me), this man who looked amazingly like McGee walked towards me with his wife and then boarded. IT WAS Max! What would those odds be in Vegas???

When us regular folk boarded the plane, I fortunately saw McGee sitting in an aisle seat on my way to mine and stopped to quickly introduce myself. "I've been wanting to meet and interview you forever and can't believe you're on my flight!" He was like an old friend, immediately inviting me to meet at his hotel (walking distance to Lambeau Field) the next morning for breakfast.

On this same trip and I took a drive to Fuzzy's #63 restaurant/bar, hoping the Packers legendary O-lineman Fuzzy Thurston might be there. I lucked out, as he was in the back billiards room chatting with a few friends. I briefly waited, while staring at all the Packers memorabilia on the walls like I was a 10-year old again. I then walked up to him..."Mr. Thurston, I traveled 2,000 miles hoping to shake your hand." He grabbed me with a bear hug that literally took the breath out of me (as if we'd been friends forever), and we

Fuzzy was simply an old skool football classic!

spoke for about 15 minutes. On my next trip to Green Bay, Fuzzy and I chatted at the same pregame dinner table at Lambeau, where he became only one of three players in pro football history to play on six NFL Championship teams. He was an even better guy! Damn that was GREAT!

McGee (who at one time was a partner in a restaurant with Thurston) and I spent about three hours shooting the bull. We hit it off more than I could've ever imagined, while recording about a 20-minute interview where we talked about my favorite Packer subjects: Super Bowl I, the Ice Bowl, and Lombardi. As for that Super Bowl eve night out, carousing in my hometown? Max was enjoying recalling such a fun time with plenty of laughter throughout our chat, "It was hard to sneak out during the curfew time, because it was too far to get back to L.A. before morning." But Max left his hotel a second time "took a little trip to see what was going on at the bars" (at he and his longtime roomy Paul Hornung's favorite hang out, a very famous bar, which he just couldn't recall its name). "I actually got in at 5 or 6 in the morning...I was feeling OK! I sure as hell wasn't planning on playing football, but I was feeling pretty good."

FUN FACT

McGee told me that this was the most important game in Lombardi's career. "Vince was the immortal God at getting teams ready to play football and not having letdowns. It was the perfect situation for Vince Lombardi, when you're that big a favorite, and you have so much pride in the NFL vs. this upshot bunch of dummies from the AFL (although not K.C.), which is the way Vince looked at it. He probably worked harder that week than he worked in his entire career to make sure we didn't have a letdown and embarrass the NFL."

So, the first Super Bowl kicks off, and on the third play of the game, Packers starting flanker Boyd Dowler re-injured his right shoulder. His coach looked around for his favorite partyer/receiver...and Max described to me Lombardi's call for him on the sidelines "McGEE! McGEE! Where the hell is he??" Max said he was sitting all the way at the end of the bench, hanging with his buddy Paul Hornung, talking about Paul's honeymoon and bachelor party plans (he got married in Beverly Hills three days later). McGee was barely paying attention to the start of the game.

Hornung says to Max, without knowing that Dowler got hurt "He's gonna fine you in front of 90,000 people for getting out last night!" [more laughter]. Remember that this was DURING the game! Max continued," So, I ran up to him (Lombardi), and he said, 'GET IN THERE!' Of course, the rest was history." McGee said it happened so quickly that he had no idea where his helmet was and played with another teammate's lid for much of the first half.

Starr threw one to Max on his first pass attempt which was incomplete. In a scoreless tie on their next possession and in McGee's words on the first TD in Super Bowl history and longest play of the game, "Bart threw me a little quick post, and—TOUCHDOWN! I ended up having a kind a banner day for an old guy who was 35-years old, and didn't have any sleep." [More laughter] And on this TD pass that was thrown well behind him? "I loved kidding Bart, now, for making me look good here, because it's my last game. So, he did. He threw it WAY behind me, and I just reached back, and it actually stuck in my hand! I was gonna make sure the guy didn't get an interception. The damn thing stuck, and I went over the goal line." McGee was so excited, while telling me this story that he almost tipped over his hot coffee.

"I will admit I was a bit surprised, number one to be in the game. And number two to get this opportunity. It turned out to be a heck of a day." Yes, it did Max, you led the game with 7 catches for 138 yards and two touchdowns and one huge hangover!

On not being named MVP of Super Bowl I, when he easily could've won that honor? "Ya know Hornung and I are sitting on the bench (nearing the end of the game), and he says, 'Jesus Christ McGee, you're gonna be MVP of this game.' I said, you're kidding me? And here's exactly what I said, 'No, they'll give it to "The Bart," he's the quarterback.' Bart was the main man behind that offense all year, and I think it's only fair. If I'd played all year, I would've probably got MVP. But who wants an MVP from a guy who walked off the bench and hadn't played all year?"

Max humbly continued, "After the game, a reporter said to Lombardi, 'What a great job you did putting McGee into the game the way you did!" Max on Vince, "I know he was telling a lie, Vince was a great coach and everything, but he liked the publicity. And he said something like, 'well we had a lot of confidence in McGee, and I thought this was a good spot for him.' I was sitting over there laughing like hell. Vince was a great friend of mine. I know you read the stories about him jumping on me and Hornung for curfews, but I think that's the (kind of) guy he really liked, because he depended on you (us). When the pressure's on, you can play!"

Then McGee praised the man whose name is on the Super Bowl trophy, "That was an amazing era. Vince Lombardi changed football. Him and the Packers, beating the New York Giants and the San Francisco 49ers. Beating these big town teams, I think that's what really brought Pro Football where it is today."

DID YOU KNOW?

Proving their excellent relationship, Lombardi talked McGee into playing one more year with the Packers, which culminated in the last of the Green Bay dynasty wins in Super Bowl II. They went out together.

Max wrapped up our chat with, "I like Vince Lombardi's line about as good as any ever, 'Winning isn't everything, it's the ONLY thing!'" That summed up the Packers of the 60s, one of the great dynasties in the history of sport. I'll never forget my time together, reminiscing with some of the key men who made it happen.

McGee gave me his phone number to stay in touch, but I only called him one time after that day, which I totally regret. On my return from a European trip in the summer of 2007, I had a message that Max had died in a fall at his home. Such a sad ending to a wonderful life. Knowing McGee, however, he's smiling down as you read his story. Just a gregarious guy, whom you'd love to spend time with, particularly if you were a 60s Packers fan. Thankfully, I got that chance one perfect morning right down the street from Lambeau Field!

Max laughed, when signing his first Super Bowl TD-catch picture to me after an unforgettable few hours together with lots of coffee.

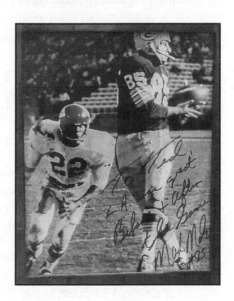

❏ SUPER ELI AND THE PROP BET FOR THE AGES

I've covered several Super Bowls, but none stands out as when the Giants stopped the Patriots perfect season in Glendale, Arizona in early 2008. The actual game itself, however, became secondary to me than the stories that I found myself in the middle of that week. Everyone remembers the 'HELMET CATCH' by David Tyree, who was the most unlikely of any receiver to be involved in one of the all-time historic plays. He was this virtual unknown, a huge part of my story.

Almost everyone, including bettors, did not know that Tyree had ONLY four catches in 12 games that entire season (because few were aware of who he was), while starting in just five games during his six-year career. An even more obscure number was the Las Vegas Super Bowl proposition bet of over-under a 1/2 catch for Tyree, which was one that my friend Ron Marmalefsky and I were mulling over that week. Why not surprise them by throwing it to a guy who's not normally involved in the offense? That made sense to us, as the Pats' defense certainly wouldn't be focusing on him—EVER!

Future HOFer Strahan, speaking into my KFWB mic before his final game ahead of launching himself into a network broadcasting career

When I got to Phoenix on Thursday, it was the final day for player access to the media. I decided to go to the Giants location, since the whole world was all over the Patriots probable perfect season. Besides, there were several Giants players with SoCal ties and that was the angle I chose for my pregame reports. After speaking to many of them (including stars Eli Manning and Michael Strahan) and about ready to leave, I noticed one player still sitting by his lonesome at the receivers' table with the name tag that read David Tyree. I follow the game closely, but only barely knew of him, outside of his 'prop' bet, and I just had to tell him about it.

With the room now about empty, he was quite approachable, "David, do you know what a proposition bet is?" He had no idea, which was totally expected. Of course I just had to explain it to him. "Yours is if you get one catch or more, then you'll be over 1/2 catch. If you don't get any catches, you'll go under 1/2. People put their hard earned money on those types of bets in Vegas."

Tyree suddenly got very animated with me, "Then, you tell them to put their money on ME!" And I said, "But it's over or under, which one should they choose?" David then replied with conviction, "You tell them OVER! I'm going to make a BIG catch in this game—MARK THAT DOWN!" He was a great sport. I thoroughly enjoyed our brief exchange, as I wished him good luck on my way out the door. After finishing my work, I immediately called Ron to tell him of our chat and it not only made our day with extreme belly laughs, but of course, we now just HAD TO play the overs on Tyree.

We all know what happened in the game with the Giants stunningly ending a Patriots' possibly perfect 19-0 season, as 14-point underdogs. What you wouldn't EVER remember was that Tyree had already covered the over play with a 6-yard reception of an Eli Manning pass early in the second quarter. That was worth a call to Ron (more laughs). We put that one in the win column! But wait, there's more!

I was very impressed with Tyree the person when we met. He would then show me how he's a man of his word! He said he would make a 'big catch'… and with 11:05 left in the game, it was Manning to 'the man' Tyree 5 yards and a touchdown for the Giants first lead, since being up 3-0 early. What he didn't tell me was that he would make multiple 'big catches'…hence, that classic against his helmet on the Giants' winning drive.

❏ ELI'S A COMING—AND WAS HE SUPER!

With a late plane to catch that night, I hustled down to the locker-room level and saw many media types lined up by the Giants door, which wasn't open yet. Around the corner was the tunnel walkway to the field, but my credential would not allow me to enter. So, I patiently waited for when the players would rush off the field in elation after celebrating their big upset win over the stunned Pats to get the next best reaction sound possible.

Here came Plaxico Burress (after his game winning TD catch), Amani Toomer, fellow Angeleno Antonio Pierce, and the rest of the newly crowned champion Giants, each of whom gave me quality emotionally charged audio after the biggest upset in Super Bowl history. I brought up an expected book called, "19-0," to some of them that was written about a perfect New England season—THAT NEVER WAS.

LB Kawika Mitchell: (in his only NYG season) told me, "And it NEVER will be! It's nice just to get a ring. We got a ring and we're champions, NOBODY'S better than us!"

LB Antonio Pierce: "I heard it's on eBay already, going right back. They can't even get the author of the book to give him his money back. It don't matter what they did in the past, we didn't give them those records. We just wanted one." On the Fantastic finish? "Yeah man, that had to be one of the best Super Bowls of ALL TIME."

Kicker Lawrence Tynes on the book that needs a re-write, "I would love to see the Final Chapter!" On the last Drive: "there's another Manning in town. Our two-minute offense has been great all year, I think some people forget about that. When we got the ball back, I started kicking it into the net, people were kind of looking at me, what the hell are you doing? I said we're going to score! We got two and a half minutes, two timeouts, Eli's at his best with two minutes!"

Defensive end Osi Umenyiora: on the incredible win, "Stupid, is the word I describe it. NOBODY gave us a chance. We went out there and dominated a great football team, sent them home with a loss."

The Giants defense that gave up a league-leading 80 points in the first two weeks of the season, shut down the Tom Brady-led Patriots, who were the highest-scoring offense in NFL history going into that Super Bowl.

Guard Rich Seubert, "We shocked the world, but we didn't shock each other. We knew we were going to win this game from the get-go. 13-and whatever-point underdogs. We've been that all season. I like being the spoiler. They can keep on writing their books about being 19-0, meanwhile we're writing about being Super Bowl champs!"

All great postgame comments from an ecstatic group, but I wanted Manning (the game's MVP). OF COURSE, so did every other media member foolish to think that could ever be possible? I waited and waited. Just so you should know, the Super Bowl MVP is NEVER, EVER, EVER available for one-on-ones after the game unless you're on the podium with him or you are THE network covering the game. Certainly NOT with some local radio schmuck from L.A.

Understandably, Eli was the last player off the field. While constantly staring at my watch (hoping to not miss my flight), Eli finally started walking down the tunnel towards me, surrounded by a few men in suits while wearing his clean new Super Bowl championship hat and t-shirt. I was the lone media member in his sight, with the other few hundred waiting around the bend at the entrance to the Giants locker room. NO ONE else but two security guys and a familiar face from the New York Football Giants recent past (who was off in the distance) were in the vicinity. There was NO WAY I could get a comment from Mr. MVP, right? WRONG!

I cordially stood directly in Eli's path. His unusually quick elusiveness from the Patriots' pass rushers (and almost sackers) on the 'Helmet Catch' play was not nearly as effective against me and my KFWB microphone, which I eagerly used for a quick comment from the star of the moment by asking, "It must be an amazing feeling to be the SB MVP of this incredible win just one year after your brother earned the same honor?" Manning was totally into it for a handful of special words, while getting very animated and even a bit emotional, UNTIL SUDDENLY and in mid-sentence from over my right shoulder, I was RUDELY interrupted by a guy named Tiki Barber (the Giants all-time leading rusher).

Yes, the same freshly retired Barber who was on the Giants' shit list after earlier ripping the fourth-year Manning in the media as someone who couldn't lead his team to the big game, saying his ex-QB lacked "strong leadership!" Barber was there on his new gig covering for the Today Show and thought he owned the moment, but it was MY MOMENT with the game's MVP. He screwed it up, while half-ass apologizing to me. I'm talking about a once-in-several-lifetimes opportunity that was gone, JUST LIKE THAT!

As I understood it to be their first personal encounter since the public criticism, Barber and Manning 'most uncomfortably' renewed acquaintances, as they walked away from the suddenly gathering large contingent of mostly New York media. One by one, they were fascinated by this strange reunion story of these two ex-teammates. ALL AT MY EXPENSE, OF COURSE. I was seething, but it was too late to change things, and I stood in the far corner and just watched this very upsetting moment unfold, as a few dozen media members then began milling around.

A few short minutes later, their interview ended. The security was now everywhere, telling the media to open a lane for the MVP (who was sought after, like Elvis), so he could head to his locker room to join his guys' celebration. As the seas parted and Eli began to leave the scene, I noticed him abruptly looking around, as if he had just misplaced a friend and somehow found me standing well off to the side like I was his wide open target in the end zone. This guy amazed me forever by walking well out of his way, straight over to me in the far corner and putting his arm around me with that familiar aw-shucks smile, "C'mon, let's finish what we were doing!"

As we slowly approached his locker room and in amazement (an understatement), I began with my original question again while thinking, this CAN'T be happening!! The Super Bowl MVP sought ME out to finish my one-on-one? I'd never met Manning in my life, and he had the class to do that?...that's NUMBER ONE on my all-time list of special postgame interview moments. Nothing comes close, as he got back into answering my question, "It's not about individual awards—it's about us finding a way, and finding the desire and the fight to win these last four games ON THE ROAD, and to make this happen. There's not a BETTER feeling in the world!"

I followed up with, "And that final drive was UNBELIEVABLE!," Eli then replied like a kid radiating an even larger championship smile, "YEAH, YOU CAN SAY THAT AGAIN! DAVID TYREE, that's all you gotta say. David Tyree, Plaxico, Steve Smith, EVERYBODY having catches, everybody making plays—ya know it's just an UNBELIEVABLE way to finish a game." How proud was his dad Archie? "VERY PROUD, I got to hug him a second ago, and he couldn't be more excited."

Neither could I, and the great finale was approaching Eli's locker room like we were old buddies, still with his arm around me and with tons of media just staring at us—knowing that each and every one of them had to be thinking, "WHO THE HELL IS THAT GUY" (with Manning)? I guess they'll just have to get this book to find out!

I thanked Eli, and then he cordially un-embraced me, while saying he was glad to help me out. He then walked into his championship room, with everyone still gawking at us (I felt a little like that kid in the old TV spot sharing his soft drink with 'Mean' Joe Greene). Soon after, we were all allowed into the room where everyone was engaged in championship celebration bedlam, enjoying their ultimate upset.

After a few minutes of casing out the joint, here comes who else but Tyree, with a smile to light up the Grand Canyon. After speaking to several reporters, he began walking towards me, when I stopped him and said, "You remember me? You did it, David. Just like you said, you won for those who bet the 'over' proposition in Las Vegas—and your last catch was INCREDIBLE!"

Tyree came right back at me with a very proud, "I TOLD YOU!!! I TOLD YOU! I told you I would do it. Don't be surprised if I mess around and get MVP or something crazy. It wasn't MVP, but it was just a big game and ya know, ENJOY IT VEGAS! You really spurred me on with that one! " We shared high-fives and laughter for that brief moment that I'll never forget! What are the chances of that happening??? Zelig would be envious and not believe this storybook ending! David Tyree never had another NFL catch (that was his final game). He'll always be remembered, however, for 'The Helmet Catch'— even more by me than ANY diehard Giants fan!

❏ MANNINGS' REACTION

Before leaving the Giants locker room party, I almost literally ran into Eli's big brother Peyton, whose smile was large enough to cover his entire Manning family. I then asked him, "If I had to told you when you were 15 that you and your brother would be back-to-back Super Bowl MVPs someday, would you have said that I'm out of my mind?" The laughing Peyton nodded and agreed after praising the N.Y. defense, "Yeah, I really would have, probably something STRONGER than that! It's been really special, and I certainly have an appreciation for what these guys (Giants) are feeling right now. As his brother, I couldn't be any happier and prouder." And how about the way he did it on that winning drive, which I described as THE instant classic play? "THAT DRIVE, and the play to Tyree, the scramble, will go down as one of the greatest plays of ALL TIME. It was fun to say you were here to witness it, and the fact that I'm related to the quarterback who threw it makes it pretty neat as well." Ya think?

Interviewing Peyton at Pebble Beach, when he reacted without any surprise of his brother's super response to my dilemma with, "That's who Eli is!"

Then, almost exactly a dozen years later and just two weeks after announcing his retirement from the Giants, I got to speak with Eli for the first time since, right after his Pro-Am round (with Peyton) at Pebble Beach. Initially, he first gave me his reaction to Tiki in our story, "he said some things, he didn't know if I'd be able to be a leader and lead the Giants and, of course, that year we go and win the championship. I don't hold grudges, and so Tiki and I are still buddies and still talk. I was happy to do an interview with him at that time. That's just New York media, right? That's the only way to kind of get ahead is to say some things, and that's just part of it."

When I reminded Eli that he walked totally out of his way right after talking with Barber to complete our interview, he giggled and humbly replied, "There you go, you better be a good guy in good times, and obviously, I was trying to be good to a teammate of mine who was good to me, and obviously finish off what I started (with you)." It was great to get to thank him again after all those years, while sharing some laughs about a very special Super Bowl experience and definitely my MVP (Most Venerable Player) and a SUPER touching greatness moment!

❏ MY SUPER RUN TO THE AIRPORT

It was also a very memorable time for me, just hoping to catch my plane. I packed up like there was no tomorrow and hustled to the street corner to grab a taxi, which should be no sweat, right? WRONG AGAIN! There were several organized LONG LONG lines of people waiting, as if they were giving out free tickets to the next Super Bowl. I asked a policeman on the street, how long of a wait should I expect? Of all the things he could've replied with that I didn't want to hear he said, "I just hope you don't have a plane to catch!" SAY WHAT? That's exactly what I had to do, and I had NO CHANCE to make that happen now?

There was only one slim hope, if someone could get me to the front of the line, without those several hundred others not charging after me like I was the Frankenstein monster. While desperately flashing my game credential, I asked another officer if there was ANY WAY I could get a cab sent my way since I had to get my work done at home before the next morning, or the radio station would've sent me to Arizona for nothing? He looked around and said, "There are hundreds here who want to leave just as badly as you do, but I can see how anxious you are. So hang on a second."

This newly revered all-time officer suddenly stopped traffic and frantically called someone saying, "I've got a VIP who needs a cab to the airport and RIGHT NOW!" VIP? Maybe Eli and Tyree's super aura rubbed off on me just enough? Thank God he didn't know me—VIP? HaHa, but I took what I could get at that moment. And then here comes my favorite cabbie of a lifetime who drove me through traffic like a robbery getaway car, first stopping at my hotel to pickup my locked up luggage, while begging the valet to immediately help me. I then ran through that Phoenix airport in a manner that would make O.J. jealous from his old rent-a-car commercials from the 70s.

Stuck in another line at security, I finally made it through, while hearing the announcements in the background all along that my flight was about to end its boarding. I made it by less than 60 seconds and was schvitzing (look it up) like I had just played in Super Bowl XLII. I was headed home, however, to tell stories to last until the next football season and for perpetuity. The Giants beat THE GIANT to kill the perfect season, and it was my perfect super weekend to never forget!

CHAPTER 14

TIGER TRACKING

❏ HELLO WORLD!

Being around the SoCal golf scene as I have, this kid named 'Tiger' from nearby Cypress was of course someone I'd heard about, going all the way back to seeing him as a two-year old hitting balls in front of Bob Hope and Jimmy Stewart on the old Mike Douglas TV show. Then in 1992, the huge hype had become a reality, when 16-year old Eldrick Woods was entered as a sponsor's invitee into our L.A. Open at Riviera Country Club. Everyone wanted to see just how special this Western High School sophomore was on the course (the second youngest to ever compete in an official PGA Tour event). They followed him around like the Pied Piper—and I mean in swarms, like bees! WHO REALLY WAS THIS GUY?

I first met Tiger at that week's media day, when he was there with defending champ Ted Schulz to help promote the event. Schulz told us with Woods in mind, "when I was 15, I was working in my dad's grocery store. I (just) wanted to be a baseball player." It was that same day that we were introduced to Tiger's dad Earl, who was an extremely confident straightforward military man and obviously very proud of his son and what he was about to show us.

I vividly remember Earl boasting how Tiger was about to change the game—and not just become an important figure in sports, but in the world in general. All of that sounded great, but we were talking about a teenager so, of course, he had a lot to prove to overcome plenty of skepticism by us all.

After covering so many L.A. Opens at Riviera, my first in 1976 when Hale Irwin rallied to beat Tom Watson (I also covered Irwin's U.S. Senior Open win there 22 years later), there was a totally different buzz around this tourney. Yet, we were only getting a small taste of what was to lie ahead. I loved interviewing the almost 80-year old legendary tournament honoree Sam Snead in his familiar straw coconut fedora during the week, and getting his reaction to this kid Woods.

Snead was his usual low-keyed, yet cocky, self when saying that he was "impressed" with Tiger after watching him in the pro-am, while cautiously adding in his folksy twang, "You don't know how much better he can get or if he's at his top right now? You'll have to wait and see. He looks like he's going to be a force on the tour." YA THINK?

Snead also enjoyed being back in LA where he had his own earlier successes at this event, with two titles and an incredible close second at age 61. He laughed when recalling winning at Riviera in 1945, using the same ball for all four rounds due to the World War II shortages. Not exactly the quality of balls like they have today!

I wasn't on the grounds just because of Woods debut, like so many of the other media types on hand. It was simply my regular yearly local event to cover. So, it was much more cluttered with the wandering about of the not-so-usual 'golf reporters,' who got caught up in the latest Hollywood-hype, which turned into the start of a HOF-career documentary.

I totally recall hustling to the iconic first tee high above the entire course for the kid's first PGA Tour shot, as Tiger smacked it down the middle with a 3-wood and then two putt for birdie (his only one of the day). I watched a few of his holes with an extremely excited and loud gallery following him throughout, which seemed to amaze Woods. Of course, he'd never had a real gallery around him before, and they were cheering everything their new local favorite did! I had never experienced anything like it either, including when Arnie was playing in town.

Then, after Tiger's opening round, it was quite an aerobic walk having to join the media zoo who were followed him back and forth to the scorers area and subsequently, to the driving range to get his youthful yet fearless and poised first post-round comments. Meanwhile, I had to dodge this frenzied horde of reporters with their cameras, microphones, and note pads in my face, along with the newbies who weren't very cordial. It was like trying to fight your way in line for Beatles tickets as 'Tiger-mania' on its first day was now upon us. I also got a quick response from an emotional Earl, who said (of course) he expected his son to make the cut.

After his somewhat disappointing second round, Tiger assessed his pro debut to those of us who were athletic enough to catch up with him, 'It was a learning experience, and I learned that I'm not that good...yet." He called it "the best two days of my life," despite, not surprisingly, missing the cut by six strokes with rounds of 72 & 75. But, I didn't miss the start of one of the great careers in all of sport. Everyone would soon learn just how amazing this guy's game truly was.

Who would've thought all these years after our chat in '92, that Slammin' Sammy's all time official PGA Tour record 82 wins (although he said it was really closer to 125) would eventually be approached by Tiger, who as of this writing at age 44 has tied Snead's 82. I also got to witness Sam follow this wonderkid, while connecting with both that week, simply a remarkable journey! As great as Snead was, 1968 Masters champ Bob Goalby told me that he could have been even better "not concentrating on the course, as well as some of the (other) greats. Letting birds, pretty girls, or just a little noise over there bother him."

DID YOU KNOW?

Even though Riviera is known as 'Hogan's Alley,' Sam Snead kept Ben Hogan from a fourth and final (and probably most famous) L.A. Open title by beating him in a playoff in 1950. That was also Hogan's miraculous return to competition just 11 months after his horrific head-on car crash with a Greyhound bus on a foggy night in Texas in February of 1949. As a result of the injuries from the crash, he was not expected to walk again...let alone play championship caliber golf. Incredibly, Hogan went on to win 12 more PGA tournaments (half of them majors) before hanging up his spikes for good.

❏ THE UNFORGETTABLE ROAR OF A ONE-LEGGED TIGER

It was June of 2008 and was I a crazy busy guy with the Lakers and Celtics fiercely battling for another NBA Title, while the golf world was focused on beautiful La Jolla for the 108th U.S. Open. I covered every minute of that tournament, while going back and forth from Staples Center to Torrey Pines, I wouldn't have had it any other way. In reality, I began writing this chapter on the 10th anniversary of Tiger Woods last major title (until 2019), when playing with a broken leg and a torn ACL, after most observers thought he was a very serious threat to break the Nicklaus record total of 18 majors—if not shatter it.

Torrey Pines was a tour stop that Tiger had owned, with six previous wins there. That week it produced the longest setup in major championship history at over 7600 yards. It also meant it was that much more walking and hacking it out of the rough for Woods on his two left-tibia stress fractures in his first tournament in two months (although we didn't learn of those exact injuries until a few days after the tournament).

After playing, while wearing a knee brace on the previous Sunday's practice round, which lasted only nine holes (he carded a pedestrian 53, with eight lost balls at Big Canyon CC in Newport Beach), Woods was then living on adrenaline, passion, and pure guts that entire tournament. We mere mortals were just trying to figure out how he could do it? He not only began the week with a double-bogey but then did the same two more times on No. 1 (including on Sunday). You DON'T win U.S. Opens that way, but he was Tiger.

Playing on media day at Torrey Pines in '08 was spectacular, yet physically grueling!

Not only did Woods make the cut, but he also made some improbable shots that anyone with two healthy legs would beg to clone, particularly under the most difficult U.S. Open conditions. How tough were they, you ask? I had played the course as a media-day invitee a few weeks prior, and USGA Exec and course setup guy Mike Davis told us with a smirk just before sending us out, the rough would be MUCH more rough for us hackers than the pros (which wasn't very friendly). It's one of the few times that my back was quite sore after constantly chopping any ball out of thick grass that was up to my knees and worse. It was more like doing chores as a farmer than a golfer that day, and my body paid for it!

Tiger had to battle the elements and his failing body (sometimes doubling over in pain, which was almost as painful to watch) on his Saturday charge, with one of the greatest rounds ever under the circumstances. Specifically, an amazing back nine, which included two impossible eagles and that unforgettable one-hop, chip-in birdie on 17 that got him laughing at himself in disbelief. Somehow, Woods was in the final group on Sunday, alongside Brit Lee Westwood with a one-shot lead and two ahead of the always personable 45-year old journeyman Rocco Mediate (who was actually wearing a 60s peace-sign belt buckle—welcome to SoCal), but could he actually pull this off?

That Sunday, Tiger needed a birdie from the thick rough on the 72nd hole to force a Monday 18-hole playoff with Rocco. First, he hit a wonderful shot about pin high to give himself a chance. Then, seemingly staring at his potential putting path forever, Tiger poured in a beautiful yet bumpy dramatic 12-footer that created his own personal time-stood-still roar, which has since become an iconic picture. Rocco immediately said, "I knew he would make it." Years later, Rocco repeated to me those exacts words to me, "I KNEW he would make it!, I just KNEW it!" He admired Woods so much, of course, who didn't at the time.

Tiger was simply different, with an aura that has never been seen before or since around any golfer or maybe even any athlete in general. Furthermore, the sound of him hitting a golf ball was like something I've only heard from one other golfer—Greg Norman. I describe it as the sound of wind then perfectly cracking a gigantic egg...the ultimate WHACK! But this week was different for the injured Woods, given that he couldn't torque or move around like usual.

At the time, the NBA Finals was a 2-3-2 series, with the middle three in L.A. (Tues-Thurs-Sunday). I wasn't about to miss any of those classic battles. So, it was off to the first round early on Thursday before hustling up the freeway to get to Staples for game four. After sending my postgame stuff, it was then back to San Diego for Friday's second round. Then on Sunday, I expected to cover the championship round and finish a very long day at the Lakers-Celtics Game 5 before finally getting a normal night's sleep...AU CONTRAIRE!

❏ PLAYOFFS!!

Driving back after the Lakers blew a 19-point lead only to barely (and temporarily) stave off elimination to the eventual NBA champs from Beantown, I dragged myself out of bed to leave my place at 3:30am to avoid traffic and get back to Torrey early enough to cover the 9am Monday playoff tee time. I first walked over to the practice green and there was Tiger and Rocco, but also the great teaching pro Eddie Merrins? I had no idea that the 'Lil' Pro was working with Mediate at the time. We stood and watched him putt for several minutes, while I got insight on Eddie's thoughts on his client, along with a recorded one-on-one, just minutes before the first tee shots.

Tiger on the practice green that Monday morning before making history

Merrins remarked, looking over at Tiger, "There's maybe the best clutch putter who ever lived!" On the other hand, he was also confident in his guy, "But Rocco can win this thing. He just needs to stay positive and trust his game, which is very good right now. Anything can happen in 18 holes. We'll see who pulls off the shots when they need them the most?"

History shows it took them 19 playoff holes to complete this historic U.S. Open. And those of us who were lucky to be on the grounds that day enjoyed every swing of the club.

Reminiscing with coach Merrins at Riviera CC about that great playoff round

I walked some with the surprisingly large Monday playoff gallery, while Rocco occasionally joked on the course with Tiger, who relished a 3-shot lead with eight holes to play. The veteran Mediate was obviously enjoying this rare journey in the international spotlight, as he fought all the way back and then fantastically found new life with three straight birdies for a one-shot lead through 15.

He was facing Tiger and major history, however. After Woods birdied 18 again for a tie, Rocco then bogeyed the 91st—and only sudden death hole while Woods made par to win the last 18-hole playoff in U.S. Open lore. Woods completed his amazing third career grand slam, won his 14th major, and passed Hogan in all-time wins at 65. Incredibly, Woods had not won a major since (until his Masterful comeback, which will be addressed shortly). This weekend goes down as one of the great ones in my career, for sure.

At the championship newser, Woods' coach at the time Hank Haney randomly walked towards the back of the room, where I was standing. I congratulated him, and while shaking his head in bewilderment, he responded with, "he COULDN'T EVEN WALK three weeks ago, AMAZING, simply amazing! He should be on crutches, NOT playing in the Open." Actually that was the look on most individuals in the room, who had watched something that few would believe if it had been made for the big screen.

I then got an opportunity to ask the following questions to Tiger (edited off the USGA transcripts) during that Monday newser:
- TS: "A two-parter, can you talk about being only four behind Jack (Nicklaus) now and getting the opportunity to check another one off your list, three years in advance of him? And also, any concerns at all, being an athlete, on the long-term ramifications of the knee thing?"
- WOODS: "Well, only being four back, it's hard to believe I'm in this situation, you know? It's hard to believe I've had this nice a run in my career. And hopefully, it will continue. I'm going to keep practicing, keep trying to grind and get better. As far as future ramifications, I'm not really good at listening to doctor's orders too well. So, I end up—hey, I won this week so, it is what it is."
- TS: "Did they tell you, though, that you could further injure it, Tiger? If you played?"
- WOODS: (Nods head affirmatively.)
- TS: "Yes?"
- WOODS: (Nods head affirmatively.)
- TS: "Did you?"
- WOODS: "MMM, Maybe?" (Giggled almost affirmatively)

You can be your own judge on Tiger's responses. I then wished him happy anniversary for his 500th straight week holding the number one ranking in the world. At that point, he then hobbled off into the sunset, with yet another trophy.

Walking some with the grimacing/limping Tiger the first few days, I truly wondered how he would ever be able to finish any rounds with his obvious leg injury—let alone contend and then get through an agonizing 91 holes? He just kept finding more, digging deeper than any golfer I'd ever witnessed. It's one of the most miraculous victories in the history of sports. As the great TV call by Dan Hicks from his 72nd hole putt suggested, "Expect anything different?" Not that year!

If Tiger called it "probably the greatest tournament I ever had," nothing more needs to be added...but I will anyway. I've been around great events with great feats accomplished by the greatest champions, but that 2008 U.S. Open was crazy good and totally one for the ages. Of course, I hadn't seen the 2019 Masters yet. WOW, what was about to come!

Tiger limped right past me, and I took this shot of him firmly and proudly grasping that trophy as he left the grounds.

❏ LUNCH WITH EARL

In its earlier years, a media day at Tiger's 'silly season' tournament at Sherwood Country Club meant that Woods and his father would be on hand to interview for marketing the event (before eventually doing them only via satellite). When I grabbed a table to eat lunch one time before getting to play this wonderful course, Earl Woods fortunately took a seat right next to me. It was my only opportunity to ever get some true alone time with him. For the next 15 minutes or so, we chatted. Between bites, I asked how he raised Tiger and was a bit surprised to hear that he "never pushed him hard when playing golf. "Tiger just always loved it from the first time he picked up a plastic club" he said.

I followed up with Earl that as a military dad, this just didn't seem quite possible. He stressed how much, however, that he had taught his only son more about self-discipline, without forcing him to do things and how he instilled in him to make a big difference for others—thus the TW Foundation. As disciplined a player that Tiger became, you have to wonder how his personal life may've gone differently had Earl lived on? We also talked about how the family was dealing with fame after growing up in the normal little town of Cypress, California? Of course, it helped when Tiger moved into his college phase at Stanford, and things evolved from there.

❑ MY THANKSGIVING LONGEST DRIVE

I was driving home to L.A. from my 2009 Thanksgiving family get together in Las Vegas, when I got a call from Olden. "Did you hear about Tiger?" No, I had just started heading out of town so what was he talking about? The early reports had Woods in a car accident and in the hospital. How serious was this? It seemed very, but we just didn't have enough details, and my mind was wandering into places that didn't feel comfortable.

Was Tiger Woods critically injured or what the hell was really going on? In the middle of the desert, I didn't have much of a signal to get many radio stations. What I'd heard, however, seemed very serious, so I would just have to deal with the wait and get a few more calls from Olden with his updates. Then he told me, it was Tiger's infamous domestic dispute, and we know the rest. Dealing with Woods since he was a teenager, I felt a different kind of kinship. Now, I was pissed that he could be so stupid. For his life, his legacy, and his adoring faithful fans.

That so-and-so strangely had me worried for him like he was a close friend (although really only getting to know him professionally). Then this incredible personal let down? It was all SO WRONG! But we're constantly disappointed by people whom we admire and must make decisions when to separate those feelings from their reality and flaws.

I had met Tiger's wife, Elin, once at Sherwood CC. She couldn't have been a more down to earth and genuinely friendly person. It was difficult to think of what she must've been going through, but such is life. What a waste and the embarrassing crap that was to follow. The PERFECT image came crashing to a halt. It took years for him to rebuild it. At the present time, all seems forgiven now, with hordes of people following him around like old times—if only that previous greatness could have remained through the down years?

❑ TORREY PINES, MY GLUTES!

In February of 2015, I was back at Torrey Pines for the umpteenth time during another of Tiger's attempted comebacks from his injured back, as well as other issues. I vividly recall watching on the big screen in the media room on Thursday and seeing him grimace with pain on a few early shots. The announcers, however, weren't saying anything. Were they watching the same shots that I was? I went on The Beast 980 with a live report and mentioned that I didn't like what I was seeing...and that Tiger was in some pain, AGAIN! This couldn't go on much longer.

Then it happened...after 11 holes Tiger simply said no more. He suddenly withdrew, taking a cart back to the parking lot, where his car awaited to whisk him away. Those of us in the media area were quickly notified that if we wanted to speak with Woods, it would have to be NOW! I had to hustle big time to the lot for his less than a two-minute presser, just before leaving Torrey in his getaway car, with more back issues along with a new ailment—deactivating glutes?

I stood directly behind Tiger, as he talked into my mic, along with the others in his face, "It's frustrating that I just can't stay activated!" Was this a new thing during this latest comeback? "Yeah, VERY!...It's just that my glutes are shutting off and they don't activate. Hence, it goes into my lower back so..I tried to activate my glutes the best I could in between, but they never stayed activated."

In the Torrey parking lot with Tiger, as he wraps up his very brief presser

As he turned to walk to his car, while stepping past me, I quickly said, "YOUR GLUTES?" Tiger even quicker replied, "YEP!", shrugging like a down-and-out frustrated duffer, as he headed for his car. That was a new one on me, and many questioned his explanation, describing it as ludicrous and simply an excuse. That was easy for others in their own bodies to say, while I had a more wait-and-see attitude.

For me, it was getting sadder by the day to watch one of the most dominant athletes ever show diminished skills in front of our eyes. If his aching back didn't greatly improve (and whose does as individuals age?), he'd simply fade away faster than you can say Jack Nicklaus' 18 major wins!

❏ LOOKING ANCIENT AT THE OLD COURSE

Only five months later, I once again went abroad to cover The Open Championship at St. Andrews. Guess who was going after his 4th Claret Jug? Tiger talked a confident game, but he wasn't his old self (although looking a bit older with thinning hair). This was his last shot there before turning 40. He finished a disappointing seven over par, missing the cut. I hustled into his post-round newser and tried to get him to open up about what was going on deep inside considering his incredible competitiveness? I pretty much only got the word "frustrating" out of him. But hey, I tried!

Then, we had a brief personal interaction, when Woods was walking off the grounds of St. Andrews and by chance heading right towards me. I stopped him and with my hands on hips flippantly said, "you know I came 6000 miles to see you play" (and he was going home early). Tiger then looked me straight in the eye with a half smile and said, "Thanks bud, and I'm a hell of a lot more disappointed than you are. See ya." He was then out of there in a flash!

Interviewing Woods after 2010 Sunday's round at St. Andrews

It was looking more and more like Tiger not only may have won his last major, but ANY tournament? As often as I was asked if Woods could ever win again, I would repeatedly say—ONLY if he can get fully healthy, otherwise it's over for him! Back, knees, glutes...? He wasn't getting any younger.

Then exactly 25 years after watching him hit his first tee shot as a teen at Riviera, Tiger underwent his fourth back surgery—this time a lumbar fusion, resulting in him missing out on playing in any majors during an 18-month period. Sounds extremely serious, right? Well he went from not being able to sit normally in a car or play with his kids to producing swing speeds that many much younger were jealous of. Woods described the results of the surgery as 'instant relief' that gave him a life again, which all of his fans hope is the case. Oh how he came alive AGAIN, like a phoenix rising, at Augusta in 2019, with a quiet confidence and fresh new friendly personality/attitude that I'd never seen before.

❏ THE COMEBACK OF ALL COMEBACKS

The doubters got louder as time passed, and Woods plunged to an unthinkable 1,199th in the world rankings. Few were still on his band wagon, which needed as much of an overhaul as his beat-up body. Even Tiger seemed to have as many unanswered questions as the rest of us, as I watched from the west coast. It took him 301 days to return to tournament play from that fused back in December of 2017. And now he seemed to have the yips in his short game, which often means the end of a competitive career is truly near.

I saw him at Torrey Pines and Riviera in early 2018, and there were some hopeful but inconsistent moments. My biggest question remained, could Tiger ever truly put together four championship caliber rounds again (while just staying healthy)? Maybe, Augusta could wake up the 'sleeping' Tiger? But he finished a very mediocre T-32 there. His comments into my microphone sounded like something from a rehabbing elder statesman, "to be able to just be out here competing again, if you had said that last year at this particular time, I would have said you're crazy!" Not exactly the fiery roar out of the 'you can NEVER beat me' younger Tiger.

I spoke with Rocco at the end of his March 2018 Champions Tour event in Newport Beach. His first question to me was, "What did Tiger do on 18?" (in a tournament that again had excited the golf nation, when finishing second by just one stroke). Mediate confided in me that he was watching Woods on his cellphone throughout the day on the course (which is a rules violation no-no). I swore to not use that comment or say anything to get him fined until using it in my book. Hopefully, there's a friendly statute of limitations on that?

Rocco on Tiger's comeback—which was far from complete at the time, "I'm so happy I can't stand it. I just wonder why it took so darn long? If anybody could do it, he's the one who could do it! I've said that if his back holds, these kids are in for a little surprise—and they're gonna get it!"

I followed up with "but doesn't his improved swing speed surprise you after his back fusion? Isn't THAT amazing?" Rocco emphatically replied, "NO, it doesn't amaze me. Because it's HIM! Nothing he does shocks me. I don't care (about his age)…I think he breaks Jack's record now. IF, he STAYS healthy? Just to the rest of the guys, BEST WISHES!"

Suddenly the 'old' Tiger was back prowling on the doorstep of victory. He tied for 6th in the Open and finished a fantastic 2nd at the PGA, with a Sunday 64. Look-out world. Finally, he ended his five-year drought with a win in the Tour Championship and career number 80 in front of a familiar (yet even greater) Pied Piper-like faithful group of followers. Time seemed to reverse itself. That doesn't happen in golf—not after all those major injuries!

❏ THE GPS-RX: MAGNOLIA LANE

2019 was the sixth straight year in which I was credentialed to the Masters (a few without Woods even on the grounds). It felt like the deepest field of contenders that I could ever recall. I began the week by interviewing seven previous Masters champs, including Gary Player, Ben Crenshaw, Fuzzy Zoeller, and fellow SoCal native Craig Stadler, along with network voices Jim Nantz and Scott Van Pelt, who all gave me one helluva golf podcast, which is still available to hear online.

It was 'Gentle Ben' who stressed to me on opening round Thursday morning, when I asked whose swing he currently loved to watch the most? "I'll tell you who's swing I've always loved to watch, swinging with a lot of grace and balance—Tiger Woods! I watched him warm up this morning, and he looks REALLY good! If he can make enough putts, and he's feeling like he can hole putts, he could be dangerous. I wouldn't put it past him." My response with a laugh was, "Wouldn't that be a LITTLE bit of a story?" Ben nodded, like he was his own bobblehead doll, "That would be INCREDIBLE. He'd be the second oldest, Jack was 46 when he won, and I was 43...he's (Tiger) 43."

Meeting up with Ben at the Walker Cup in L.A.

The proud Texan with his own pair of green jackets got those words stuck in my brain throughout the weekend, as Woods stayed in contention although he was four shots back of first-round leaders Brooks Koepka and Bryson DeChambeau. After his opening 18 holes, I asked Tiger about his score of 2-under 70, and if there was something to never shooting under par after his first round when he'd won the Masters? "No, it's not a bad start. We still have a LONG way to go, like tomorrow the wind's supposed to be up, so, I've got my work cut out for me the rest of the week. So does everyone else. I've shot this number and won four coats, and hopefully I can do it again!"

My biggest concern was still how Woods seemed to wear down on the weekends over the past several months. So, I asked if he did anything different to be ready for the long grind ahead? "No, the whole idea is trying to peak for four times a year. I feel like my body's good, and my game's good. It's sharp, so you just got to go out there and execute. I've got to do the proper things and that if I do miss, I miss in the proper spots. It's a matter of when to pick your spots and when to be aggressive."

Then, two rounds were in the books. Despite missing a few more putts from shorter distances, Tiger was aggressive when need be and sat just one shot off the lead after a 68. The buzz was building like an immense beehive, but we were only halfway there!

The rebuilt and redefined Tiger then found himself still two shots back of Italy's new GRANDE CAMPIONE Francesco Molinari after 54 holes with awful weather predicted on Sunday. So the powers that be at Augusta National did something they've never done before—schedule threesomes in the final round and move up the tee times to beat the expected thunderstorms, heavy winds, and even a tornado watch (which had me wanting to hide UNDER my beautiful solid wood radio booth). It was simply one of the deepest/tightest leaderboards in Masters history, and we couldn't wait for Sunday to get here.

As Tiger played with leader Molinari and the likeable and very talented Tony Finau, the fourth round saw a faltering DeChambeau conclusively get the first hole in one of his career. I dropped into our post-round chat that my dad 'supposedly' aced one in his first and only 18 holes of play. Bryson smiled and replied, 'WOW! That's the way it works, that's just the way golf is, anybody can strike gold at any moment. At the end of the day, however, it averages out. You're (my father) still going to be that 12 handicapper, and I'm going to be professional." Although, neither my non-playing Dad or myself ever got down to a 12, DeChambeau meant it well, and we'd take that!

Chatting with Bryson just months before bulking up when he stated, "I'm going to become MASSIVE!"

On DeChambeau doing it himself? "FINALLY! Back three years ago, I said to my caddy and everyone in my camp, I was going to make a hole in one here (on 16) one day and sure enough it was my first one three years later. A smooth 7-iron. I hit it perfectly, it came off, and I (thought) like this looks really good. I'd seen it a bunch of times on TV where that lands, it was like—that's REALLY GOOD. I heard the crowd and like, this is GOING IN! And sure enough it did, and I went nuts! It's a great moment that I'll never forget, and it's an honor to make it on 16." And a blast to chat with him about it.

Then there's that little par 3 at the 12th hole, the center piece of Amen Corner that always seems to be the difference on Sunday at the Masters. Oh how its famed Rae's Creek was hungry after lunchtime! Four of the final six players completely satisfied its appetite, gobbling up their tee shots (which had me smirking—to be explained shortly), resulting in key wet double-bogey 5's by Koepka and then leader Molinari, both of whose games began to unravel. Tiger then calmly two-putted the same hole from about 50 feet away for a par and went from two shots back to a share of the lead for the first time. It was like HOLY HOGAN, this thing is REALLY going to happen! Woods was suddenly in control of his fate, which usually means a green jacket at the end. That ancient almost mythical intimidating Tiger factor was back in business.

To say that Tiger doesn't move the needle, he IS the needle remains an understatement. And while speaking with DeChambeau well behind the first fairway, we heard an extremely loud roar. Was that for Woods? We questioned who and where that came from (although we knew). I asked Bryson how much did he notice those famous Tiger roars? "EVERY TIME! It's so obvious. At the second hole we were on the tee box and all of a sudden we hear THAT roar, and we're like (that's) TIGER, TIGER, TIGER. Hahaha Every time that happens, like (that's) TIGER" (more giggles).

The leaders were closing in on the back nine, and it was time for me to rejoin the huge herd of patrons on the course. I first headed to a quiet Amen Corner to enjoy that heavenly view one last time for the week. I then followed the top few groups, as they played a couple more holes. I even noticed a tall lanky familiar face in the sardine packed gallery, it was a beaming Michael Phelps. The most decorated Olympian of all-time was obviously freestyling his way through the woods while following Woods. Tiger, however, was chasing Jack's 18—not Phelps' 23 gold medals, as they marched on, hopefully, to history.

Then from behind me, came that sound again. A HUGE ROAR was a blast from 15—Tiger had just nailed a birdie putt to grab the lead. We've always heard that legendary stories are made on the back nine on Sunday at the Masters. NOW I was in the middle of it, literally feeling goose bumps—but more like the size of Tiger bumps. History is upon us, as I tried to take it all in. The throng, however, was too large to get close enough to see everything.

About to complete my daily exercise as a human windshield wiper, I hustled back to the media room again to grab my trusty recorder for any last remaining interviews. I then got back to watch Woods from afar par #17. If he didn't screw up his 72nd hole, everything was perfectly aligned for the comeback of comebacks. I could barely see Tiger on the 18th fairway. I couldn't get through the massive amount of humanity who were cheering him on like it was his farewell walk, all knowing they were witnessing ultimate greatness. So, I just stood well behind the green and awaited the sound after his final short putt, which will stick with me forever.

THE preeminent roar that maybe was only similarly heard in '86. YES SIR, Tiger's tap-in made him the 2019 Masters champ. To observe the happiness in that gigantic gallery was unmatched in anything I'd ever been around on a golf course. Yes, even including when he won with a broken leg. This was Augusta baby, where history appears even greater in its eternal funhouse mirror.

I then slithered my way down to the end of the path in front of the scoring area to which Woods would eventually walk. After observing his celebratory high-fives and hugs with a few ex-Masters champs and some future hopefuls before filling out his scorecard, I got closer to some of the dignitaries who were milling around in front. PGA Tour commissioner Jay Monahan suddenly stood next to me, and he laughed when I blurted out, "Nice headline maker for your sport, you couldn't have scripted it any better!"

All smiles was two-time champ Bubba Watson, as he proudly enjoyed this historic moment, while wearing his green jacket, when I joked, 'you're now ONLY three behind Tiger." His chuckling reply was, "at least we don't need to give up another locker up there, I'm just glad the (champions) locker room is staying the same size. He'll just have to fit his 5th jacket into his already full one."

Not being able to be two places at once, after having missed the very emotional 18th green family hugs and kisses, unexpectedly Tiger's mom Tida (and her grandkids) walked towards me. For the first time since 1992, we had a personal interaction, as I just congratulated her and all of the Woods gathering. She kindly smiled and said thanks. All I could think about was how amazing this was for Tiger to do this in front of his kids and his mother, who had the most prideful smile I could ever imagine.

As for how his late father Earl's reaction might have looked? Just maybe he was somewhere up there, keeping those ugly clouds from unloading its expected fury, long enough to allow his son to enjoy every drop of the moment. Somehow, the weather remained surprisingly dry, in contrast to so many of the patrons' eyes.

Realizing that Tiger had left from a different exit, I then rushed back to the media room, where the refreshingly candid co-runner up Koepka had begun his news conference. Smiling almost as if he had just won, he called what had just transpired, "probably the coolest back nine in a major championship I've ever been a part of, or just in golf in general." I then asked Brooks (who's also a proud multi-major champ) how much he heard that famous Tiger roar and did he pay much attention to it knowing that something special was obviously happening? "I've heard it. I heard it at the PGA. You hear it here...It's cool to see. If you take a step back while you're playing. IT'S FUN! You watch him walk down after he won on 18. I mean, it's just a monsoon of people. IT'S INCREDIBLE!"

Yeah, I knew that same feeling, luckily just experiencing it myself. Then, it was down to just having Tiger walk into the most crowded championship media gathering I'd ever witnessed, before he would head back to Butler Cabin. I got there ahead of the media herd for a great seat up close and was called on to ask the second question to the now five-time Masters champ, 14 long years since donning his last green jacket and 22 years after his legend was born there. "COMEBACK is going to be a word we're always going to think about here. So how would you describe that for you? Also, the doubts since some of us saw you at Torrey 11 years ago, and the doubts that you could EVER (realistically) do this again?"

Woods didn't hesitate with his answer, "I had SERIOUS doubts after what transpired a couple years ago. I could barely walk. I couldn't sit. Couldn't lay down. I really couldn't do much of anything. Luckily, I had the procedure on my back, which gave me a chance at a normal life. Then all of a sudden, I realized I could actually swing a golf club again. I felt if I could somehow piece this thing together that I still had the hands to do it. The next thing you know, if you look at it, my first 14 wins in majors were always—I had the lead in every one of them, or tied for the lead. To have the opportunity to come back like this, IT IS PROBABLY ONE OF THE BIGGEST WINS I'VE EVER HAD FOR SURE BECAUSE OF IT."

PROBABLY? That's how he felt in the moment when speaking the words that will forever be remembered as his official response to my question that described true greatness. Furthermore, he did it by playing so smart and gritty—totally earning another green jacket. Tiger's win was not only the most amazing sporting event I'd ever covered (considering the venue), but that Sunday April 14 made me (almost) forget about the following Tax Day—and that ain't easy! Even Uncle Sam winked with joy, when learning of the new Masters record-high first place check filled out for $2.07 million bucks. An Augusta tax bracket unlike any other!

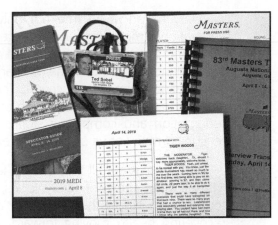

My 2019 Masters media medley to always remember this classic by

---

DID YOU KNOW?

Tiger's U.S. Open win at Torrey made him 14 of 14 when holding a 54-hole lead in major tournaments. He topped it off with his first come-from-behinder for major win #15 at Augusta.

❏ A MASTERFUL RECAP

Due to trying to get ahead of a bad weather forecast, wouldn't 36 holes in just over 24 hours, along with the mental and physical stress of competing against such an incredibly talented leaderboard on the grueling undulating hilly terrain of Augusta National, be a bit too much to ask of this aging Tiger Woods to overcome? And with his surgically repaired back and all that comes with it on a Masters Sunday?

Well, he did something that will always be recalled as THE COMEBACK story for any age or profession. Gary Player beautifully summed up his feelings for me on this most memorable moment:

Thank you Mr. Player for this wonderful personal footnote to such an historic day

> "Ted, quite frankly I had really mixed emotions. Over the last few years the few conversations I had with Tiger, he never thought he would ever play again. Then he said he would not return unless he believed he could win. At first it was a struggle, and I thought he had made a bad decision. Then, he wins last year and you start to hope all over again. But winning a major? Thrilling yes. Great for golf—no doubt. I actually cried tears of joy for him, when he embraced his mother and children. That was the moment. It just doesn't get any better."

Gary nailed it! For me not only getting to live it, but to cover his two generational moments (a one-legged Tiger winning the U.S. Open at Torrey Pines and then the Masters again at 43), have to be the two most inspirational performances by the same human in sports history and are an indelible exclamation point on my career. They are lessons that transcend sports and give any person a reason to push on to succeed at anything! Simply personal redemption and compelling stories for the ages, which is likely the biggest reason so many of us could get so emotional and appreciate witnessing each.

So the current all-time majors leaderboard has Jack Nicklaus on top with 18, still three ahead of Tiger Woods, who's still tied with Mr. Snead at 82 total tour wins. But now there's a huge cloud of uncertainty hovering over Tiger's recovering health moving forward, eerily similar to Ben Hogan's comeback from a life-threatening car accident. Woods suffered his own horrific solo car crash, two days after hosting that same event in 2021 (which he couldn't play in following a 5th back operation). Now we can just wish Tiger a return to a normal healthy family life, and take it slowly for any wishful return to greatness on the golf course.

But the absolute truth is, if anyone can pull it off, it is Eldrick Woods, who has never shied away from living up to his chosen name—Tiger.

With Tiger, after having lunch with his father Earl at Sherwood CC

Yes, Tiger is a flawed man, but then again who isn't? Anyone with a heart larger than a golf ball loves a comeback story, and this one's about possibly the most dominant athlete who ever lived and yet so transformational. Furthermore, maybe the most entitled superstar I had ever dealt with has now wonderfully evolved into a pleasant participant.

So, Where's Waldo? Well, I never saw him on the grounds at the National, certainly not wearing a Masters credential. I never saw Zelig either. I only recall an Eldrick who re-wrote his story (and thankfully mine) better than Shakespeare could've ever tried to, and it's simply incredible that I got to add this to a list of historic events which I've been a part of. Who knows what's to come? OMG, was it great to be there to cover as special a return to glory as there's ever been.

CHAPTER 15

RINKSIDE WITH THE GREAT ONES

❏ COLD AS ICE

Starting as a radio stringer in L.A. I covered a number of local sports since 1974, including Kings hockey. Although they were never a serious championship contender during most of their earlier years, they always seemed to have plenty of interesting story lines. Kings original owner and founder Jack Kent Cooke gave his team this name to bring forth an air of royalty. For too long, however, they only got to the level of paupers. The very demanding Mr. Cooke was all about marketing and giving EVERYONE a nickname for the fans to remember them by.

Some with the earliest nicknames became fan favorites, including Eddie 'The Jet' Joyal, Bill 'Cowboy' Flett, Real 'Frenchy' Lemieux, and Juha 'Whitey' Widing. I enjoyed my interactions with them all. It wasn't until 1977, however, that the Kings began receiving some national attention when they acquired Marcel Dionne (who never needed a nickname). This event was the catalyst in me getting a gig to 'string' for French-speaking Radio Canada. One minor problem existed—I didn't speak French, so now what?

It took awhile, but I eventually got it down to a science to let any and all French-speaking NHL players (specifically the stars) know that at any time, I might need a postgame comment from them. Fortunately, MOST knew at least enough English to communicate with me, although there were a few Francophones, for whom I needed to get one of their teammates to help out. My biggest concern was to not have any player mess with me and give some profane answer to a question, when I often didn't know what the hell they were truly telling me? Thank God, I had no nightmare examples of that occur.

So, it became like clockwork to have them give me their comments in French. Dionne (who facetiously called himself the #1 French-speaking player in Kings history), Rogie Vachon, and later Luc Robitaille, Steve Duchesne, and even Larry Robinson (who learned while playing for Montreal) would often respond to my questions (just as I had trained them), "In English or in French?"—To which, I would often reply, 'BOTH would be great!'

With Marcel at his 1990 Dionne Night after-party, with just a friendly bonne chance remark in French needed

Interviewing and messing with Luc the night before his statue unveiling in March 2015 at Staples Center

This also gave me a different type of access to some of the all-time greats, which had them feeling most comfortable to reply to my questions in their native language (most were from the province of Quebec). If you're into hockey, some of those names might seem quite familiar, like Guy Lafleur, Denis Savard, Ray Borque, Patrick Roy, Pierre Larouche, Pierre Turgeon, and Guy Carbonneau, as well as coaches Pat Burns, Jacques Lemaire, Jacques Demers, and even the winningest coach in NHL history Scotty Bowman (who knew enough French for his working knowledge, but still very kindly gave me what I needed when asked). Then there was a guy named Mario Lemieux.

❏ MR. 66 TRULY WAS 'LE MAGNIFIQUE'

'Super Mario' not only gave me dual language replies, but he was always a class act in his cooperation, going well beyond what would be expected given that I was really just another radio schmuck sticking a microphone near his mouth. After a few times seeing my mug in the locker room, he recognized me and knew what my needs were, which leads to my favorite Lemieux story by far (and one of my faves in any locker room).

In one of Mario's rare appearances in SoCal during the years when he either had some unfortunate health issues or Pittsburgh was simply not scheduled to play on the west coast much, his Penguins had just finished a game in Anaheim. Of course as the star of the team, I had to get some comments from Lemieux (in both languages). The problem was that I also needed to get Ducks sound, so I was bouncing back and forth to both locker rooms like a human windshield wiper.

I never did see Mario the first time I was in the Pens' room, and after returning, there he was standing all alone for a (rare) brief moment. I quickly hustled over and asked if he'd spoken with the media yet. He said yes, but in typical Mario fashion, said he would make time for me anyway (and it wasn't a rush job). He truly was giving me a one-on-one, not something we often get from the biggest stars. I had just begun to ask my first question, when a team P.R. person quickly interrupted and got between us (as if breaking up a fight) and sternly said, "Sorry, but Mario is done!", while staring at me like I was some fan begging for an autograph. DONE?

I was just about to tell this guy that Mario had said it was ok, when Lemieux's classy side took over shining like a perfect sunrise. He looked down at his 'media protector,' while forcefully stating. "I'm NOT done." He then threw his hand out like a fly swatter as if to say to this guy—go away, you're bothering us!

Folks, this just does not happen—and certainly not with arguably the greatest hockey talent who ever skated the earth. DAMN, If only I had video of that. It would be regularly shown for years on every sports channel imaginable, and it would be a great lesson to any athlete who has to deal with us media types, who also have a job to do. (Which in a few words—is to willingly or not, promote the athletes and their teams for free—on a nightly basis!)

I've thanked Mario a few times on being the gentleman he was on that occasion. We had some laughs about it when I reminded him of that story at the NHL 100 All-Star weekend in L.A. in January 2017. This event involved the greatest compilation of all-timers in the same room ever, which happened before our eyes for a once-in-any-lifetime hockey Touching Greatness opportunity.

Reminiscing with Mario

❏ "THE GREAT ONE" AND THE 'AVERAGE' ONE

My dealings with Wayne Gretzky over the years have been spectacular, given that he's one of the most down to earth real people who ever earned the title Superstar. I interviewed Wayne many times when he was a member of his Stanley Cup champion Edmonton Oilers. And there was one particularly interesting story regarding his team from the same 1982 playoff series, which featured the Kings' famed 'Miracle on Manchester' win at the Forum (a game which, unfortunately, I did not attend). I was there, however, trying to get in without a ticket, as my usher connections didn't come through that historic night. And just like then team owner Dr. Buss, I got to hear the comeback on the radio driving home.

It was the next home game in that series, when Oilers head coach Glen Sather got involved in an altercation with Kings P.R. guy Scott Carmichael in the hallway outside of the Edmonton locker room, where I was gathering my postgame sound. The Oilers had just gotten revenge in Game 4 to even the series, and I could hear an unpleasant Sather yelling out a few off-color remarks to the Kings front office guy. "I see you're not cheering tonight, you little BLEEP!" Then, after a little back and forth jawing, Sather took a swing at Carmichael for the 'unwritten' rule of no cheerleading by club officials (from after that previous Kings 'Miracle' win).

When I heard this loud commotion echoing off the walls maybe 30 feet away, I ran out to see what was happening. I noticed my longtime radio colleague and friend Joe McDonnell grabbing Sather, with Carmichael nearby obviously distraught after some minor fisticuffs with the coach who said afterwards, "He's (Carmichael) just like the fans in this building. No Class!" Big Joe fortunately intervened and stopped the charging Sather or else who knows what may've happened?

It looked like 'Slap Shot' was about to earn a sequel, when finally cooler heads prevailed. I thought Joe was going to send the coach flying into the Forum's hard brick walls. Let's just say that Big Joe easily weighed in at over three times what a usual Ted Sobel at 150 would have, so that was a total mismatch vs. Sather (nicknamed Slats) for sure. I later joked with the 'Big Nasty' that Slats vs. Fats was a draw. Joe then told me on several future occasions how he would've loved to have given the coach his best knuckle sandwich that day, after himself taking a stick in the shoulder from one of the protecting Oiler players. Sorry folks, No video of that either...but I'm sure that many would pay for front row seats to revisit that wild postgame show!

❏ L.A. BECOMES A WELL-OILED HOCKEY MACHINE

Six years later, Sather's Oilers suffered a different type of a 'Miracle on Manchester' loss. This time, it was their Superstar player Gretzky getting traded to the Kings. As a result, the city of L.A., always known as anything but, soon became a 'hockey town.' It was a Hollywood-like newsconference at a nice LAX hotel that was like none others any of us would ever attend. There must've been a dozen T.V cameras filling up the middle of a banquet room, as well as many more photographers whose cameras firing sounded more like machine guns going off when the Kings introduced their new team colors, with Wayne (not so surprisingly) coming out to be their first model.

A Kings game was suddenly the place to be seen, which amazed those of us who had followed this team from the beginning, while the entire country of Canada was truly in mourning. I went on a few Canadian radio shows and couldn't believe how the reaction was similar to when a great leader dies. This time it was "The Great One" who no longer was one of theirs, and the natives didn't know how to handle it. The *Edmonton Sun* newspaper's front page headlines read that day '99 Tears!'

Canadians were blaming Wayne's new American wife, Janet, like many Beatles fans had done towards Yoko Ono for breaking up their favorite group. Unfair and ridiculous of course—but welcome to FAN-DUMB!

President Reagan (still in the White House) got his seats right behind the glass alongside regulars and Hollywood power couple Goldie Hawn and Kurt Russell who were always very friendly. Even Lakers superstar 'Magic' Johnson became a season ticket holder. He then said something that I'd never heard before, "I talked to Wayne four or five years ago, and he was saying how he always wanted to be here (in L.A.)." It was Gretzky-Mania and we were loving it. So was Wayne's 16 year old brother Brent (whom I would later call some of his IHL games on the radio), "Los Angeles, that means I can fly to L.A. and check out the women!"

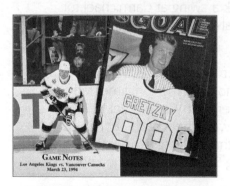

Wayne's debut program with the Kings when he scored on his first shot, and game notes from his record breaking 802 goal scoring night

I hope he had fun…the bottom line, however, is that the hockey world changed FOREVER when Wayne was sent to L.A. in definitely the biggest trade in North American sports history. The Babe Ruth of his sport was now entrenched in our neighborhood, and every game and practice was a happening.

Incredibly, the Kings finally had their first opening night sellout in history. I finally got to cover a hockey team with real championship expectations, who also just happened to have the greatest player in the world. Furthermore, Wayne was a great person to deal with, giving people like me many opportunities to get to know him and his family, including his father Walter, who would often be at practices while allowing us into his inner circle. We could easily see where Wayne got his down-to-earth manners from.

Although no Stanley Cups during the Gretzky years (and just an illegal curved stick away, that changed all momentum), I had some high quality moments with "The Great One." Among the most memorable was during the Gretzky watch in 1994, when each game would give him a chance to draw closer to Gordie Howe's all-time goal scoring record of 801. I traveled up to San Jose, with Wayne just two goals away from catching 'Mr. Hockey.' And when he stole the puck right in front of Sharks goalie Arturs Irbe and beat him five-hole for goal #800, we could taste it.

The Kings trailed 6-5 late in that game, when they pulled goalie Kelly Hrudey in the final minute. There was Wayne again, standing on the doorstep for his own rebound tap-in tying goal for his team and with Gordie at 801. The sold out 'Shark Tank' suddenly became Gretzky fans and gave him his much deserved loud standing ovation (as they loved being a part of history too). We left the Tank with Gretzky still needing one more goal to surpass Howe. I joked with Wayne afterwards that I couldn't afford to keep following him around outside of L.A., so to PLEASE get that record breaking goal ASAP—and preferably at home!

Yucking it up with "Mr. Hockey" during the Gretzky watch, with a fun note to say hello to Wayne for him—photo by Wen Roberts

Then, Gordie unexpectedly told me privately in the bowels of the arena, well after the game, that he was just too tired to continue this road show waiting for history to happen. As a result, he would be heading home and would have to enjoy the 'Gretzky Watch' from afar (and rejoin him soon after the record was broken).

The next game was at the Forum (without Howe in the building) on March 23 with the Vancouver Canucks in town. I did something I had never done before. Instead of sitting in my usual press box seat, I went down to the glass and watched from ice level, thanks to my usher friends who were nice enough to allow me to stand there. I parked myself in the Kings attacking zone to get a great view of hopeful history, and Gretzky rewarded my efforts by scoring his historic goal less than 50 feet away right in front of me (deep in the left faceoff circle) on a perfect return assist pass from his buddy Marty McSorley. #802 made Wayne Gretzky the greatest goal scorer in NHL history, and he looked as relieved as he was elated (then holding or sharing 83 National Hockey League records—numbers that would've even made Babe Ruth envious).

They stopped the game for about a 10 minute on-the-ice ceremony, during which Wayne addressed the crowd. We later had our normal postgame newsconference and then got my usual reactions from as many players possible in the jubilant locker room. You must know that since I was in radio, my sound would often not be played until the next morning. So, unlike the writers and most others, I had no tight deadlines and was able to milk my time in the joyous locker room on this very special night. Unintentionally staying until the very last person left the room, while waiting for the always last out of the shower (the very likeable McSorley) and just seconds away from leaving myself, suddenly the man of the night walked right up to me still grinning, and Gretzky said, "Ted, you're probably the only guy I didn't take a picture with tonight, so let's get one!"

Breaking media etiquette because of this most unusual celebrated circumstance, he held the 802 puck in front of us, and team photographer Wen Roberts kindly snapped a few shots. Wayne then placed that historic puck in my hands, and we both laughed about what had just occurred. Wen and I were at last both done for the night (past midnight), walking out together, as Gretzky could finally fully unwind—after a long grind that obviously left him completely spent.

What an incredibly nice gesture from not only the star player that he was, but to think of me assuring that I got a keepsake of the occasion after one of his most celebrated personal achievements was amazing to me. Furthermore, that's only half the story about this special picture.

A typical postgame chat in front of Wayne's locker, alongside my beat writer buddy Brian Golden (right)— photo by Wen Roberts

—— **DID YOU KNOW?** ——

Some of the greatest hockey enforcers, AKA 'goons,' have also been some of the best people. I was often fortunate to be around three of them, including McSorley AKA Gretzky's bodyguard, Stu 'The Grim Reaper' Grimson, and George Parros (the latter two both played for the Kings and Ducks). Parros and McSorley's names are each nicely etched on the Stanley Cup.

❏ THE CARD IS BORN

The next season Wayne only played in 48 games due to injuries, which turned out to be a strange blessing for me. I was designing my own personal business card at the time, which would have the four major sports championship trophies on it (not an easy task in those days before digital printing). I actually got ok's from the NFL, MLB, NBA, and NHL to do this, since it was not for profit. As I was about to get them printed, I had just received copies of the '802' photo with Gretzky and began imagining how it might look on the back of the card?

Of course, I would have to get Wayne's approval to make it happen, so during one of his too many games watching from the stands in a suit and not in his Kings uniform I asked him. Well, not only did he quickly say yes, we also talked about him personally endorsing me to give it an extra special touch (of course, this couldn't hurt my chances of getting a bigtime play-by-play gig either). So, we set it up to meet between periods at the next game, and he would help me out.

We met as planned, but where could we do this to have some privacy? After the 2nd-period intermission had just ended Gretzky said, 'follow me' into the Kings locker room. But wait! I can't be in the locker room during the game. I could have my pass revoked FOR ETERNITY, and I would never break the rules like that. Wayne looked at me funny and said, "You're with me—so no worries! Who's gonna bother us in here?" He had a good point!

Fortunately Gretz didn't write that I was his 99th choice during one of his GREATEST ASSISTS (at least to me!)—photo by Wen Roberts

Here we were, laying out the photos for him to sign as a personal endorsement that would fit on the card, and we quickly decided on "My #1 choice is Ted Sobel." That sounded just fine to me, and I thanked him for going totally out of his way to complete such a special favor. He was his usual gracious self, as we departed the room. I then had a business card that I still occasionally use to this day, as well as a priceless fun memory to forever recall.

❏ AT MELROSE PLACE

The following season was a tough one for the team and my last year at KMPC Sports Radio. I had fully established myself as not only an all-around sports reporter for the station, but definitely their 'hockey guy.' For months, I'd been bugging station management that we should have a hockey show and that I should be their host. Despite Gretzky-Mania, they still couldn't see that as an option (as a niche sport), but that didn't stop me from trying.

One day after a practice, I talked about it with then Kings coach Barry Melrose and he was very open to helping in any way he could to make it happen—of course, it would be more great local pub for his sport. So, we decided that maybe a personal letter from him to my bosses might work. Barry told me to get with him after a game, and we'd write it together.

Not long after, Barry caught my eye on his way into the locker room IMMEDIATELY after a game and waved me over, with almost a sense of urgency saying, "Lets do that letter now!" That was wonderful, BUT he hadn't held his postgame media chat yet. So of course, we would do it after that, right? Melrose with strong conviction, "No, let's get it done NOW!" OK!

He walked me into his office and closed the door, pulled out his personal stationary and began to hand write this letter with me. I kept saying that when team P.R. Director Rick Minch finds us doing this before his coach meets with the media, I'll be on his shit list forever! Barry said not to worry, insisting that the rest of the media could wait a few extra minutes. (Just what I needed, all of the beat writers and reporters pissed at me for doing something personal, as their deadlines approached. This wasn't how I'd envisioned any of this!)

As the guy who broke the story of Melrose being hired by the Kings, seeing him in town during the Cup Final, was even better when he wondered out loud, "When L.A. won the Cup the first time, it COULD'VE been us!"

Barry and I had just completed the letter when here comes Minch—with the intense look of a head hunter. He opens the door and says to me (and not to his coach), "Ted, what the fuck are you guys doing?" I, of course, looked at Melrose, who told him the truth, which didn't help matters. He was pissed at me for weeks after that, while Barry got some nice laughs out of it. The bottom line? The letter was excellent, and my bosses were impressed...but not enough to ever give me that show. Good try, although probably not worth the aggravation!

❑   NHL 100 WAS A PERFECT 10

It was an incredible event to cover for Sports USA, beginning with THE newsconference for the ages—Wayne Gretzky, Mario Lemieux, and Bobby Orr. To see probably the game's three greatest ever interact at a lunch table together, it can't get any better!

The media including moi was later invited to join the NHL 100 on-stage, immediately following their televised program two nights before the all-star game. What an honor to be around this living Hall of Fame group. I had to hustle just to speak with about 25 of the all-timers, many of whom were ready to leave as we walked out among them.

The first player I saw was Ex-Kings coach and player Larry Robinson, who greeted me by joking what was I doing standing alongside the greats of the game? He looked over my shoulder to make me realize that I had just walked between him and Bobby Orr, who was right next to me. I asked the best defenseman ever if I could get a few comments from him? Unfortunately, he was not in a talkative mood and turned down my interview offer faster than he skated around his opponents. It was fun, however, to hang with these guys before they dispersed from the building.

I did end up chatting with Mario Lemieux, Wayne Gretzky, Luc Robitaille, Marcel Dionne, Sydney Crosby, Teemu Selanne, and others, including 89 years young ex-Kings first coach 'Red' Kelly an eight-time Cup winner, who started this whole hockey in L.A. thing exactly 50 years earlier. All of the great's honest responses to my theme question "What's it like to wear that NHL 100 logo on your jacket?" were refreshingly sincere. You knew that they would be prideful of that honor for as long as they lived.

I later joyfully produced a 52-minute audio retrospective from the entire weekend and then got curious about how many of the NHL 100 I had any interactions with during my lifetime? Yes, I literally counted down the list and was truly amazed that the number was 84 of those top 100, which almost got me stupefied. All I could think about were the guys who could not be there as the league really made this a special event that was only missing those HOFers who just weren't around any longer.

We heard it over and over again and stressed by Bobby Orr, "Gordie (Howe) is in my mind the best that ever played the game," agreeing with Gretzky and Lemieux on what "Mr. Hockey" meant to the game. Gordie had passed away the previous June. It just couldn't be the same hockey party without him. Oh how I would've loved to have seen Howe, Jean Beliveau, Maurice Richard and others that weekend.

❏ ALL-TIME ALL-STARS ALL-ACCESS

This is a good time to bring up another all-star game from 2009 that put me face to face in a very exclusive way with hockey legends Howe and Beliveau. It was the centennial celebration for the Montreal Canadiens, and I braved the incredibly cold nights that week (down to 19 below zero), but it was worth every chill! After years of wondering if it might ever happen, I finally got to interview Jean Beliveau for the first time. He was as gracious as I remembered him, when wearing #4 and autographing my little book decades earlier at the other Forum in Inglewood. As classy an athlete as I'd ever dealt with, which is saying a lot! It was truly like speaking with royalty.

After making him blush when telling him, "I came all across the continent to hopefully speak with YOU!" He politely chuckled and replied in that perfect Maurice Chevalier-like french accent, "Well thank you very much, you're very kind." It was most unfortunate that his time was taken by some other reporter who saw me standing there, waiting for too many minutes, so I had to get this done pronto.

My aim was to ask Monsieur Beliveau what it was like playing in the early years at our Forum, since we'd always heard stories that it was a vacation for most teams when coming to sunny and mild L.A. Beliveau, who was up in years then, immediately put on his game face and said, "Not that I can recall! (but) look at how cold it is here today, so going to Los Angeles you don't mind for a few days to have this warm weather."

The result of a really nice gesture by Gordie and Wayne, who jokingly co-signed this to me 'the other Mr. Hockey'

Interviewing Penguins great Sidney Crosby after the All-Star game that weekend

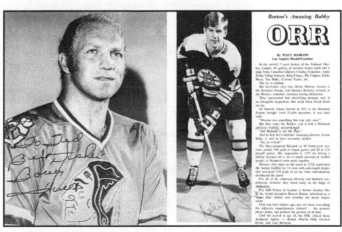

Hull and Orr signed these to me in front of the old Forum Club in L.A. when I was still a teen

(Top) Interviewing Mr. Beliveau and (bottom) he was between Habs' greats Henri Richard (left) and Guy Lafleur

Catching Beliveau and Lafleur turn heads when walking into the Canadiens dressing room together

I then asked 'Le Gros Bill' (his french nickname) how special was the entire week, celebrating a century of Canadiens' hockey in Montreal? "Oh, what memories it brings back to me. I played in 13 of those games (all-star games), and it's so nice to see the enthusiasm. Boy, I never see the enthusiasm of the fans as high as it is right now, and I've been 55 years here." I then asked Beliveau to sum up what it's been like being the ambassador and face of one of the greatest organizations in sports history? "It's a beautiful life…I'm a LUCKY person to spend my life in sport with this organization." I felt almost as lucky just to spend a few minutes chatting with this wonderful man, who graciously thanked me for waiting for him. I then watched him walk into the Canadiens' locker room for the last time.

❏   HOWE FANTASTIC!

Finally, there was my favorite Gordie story, when I was in the Montreal airport ready to fly home from that All-Star weekend. Walking towards my gate, I noticed "Mr Hockey" sitting nearby waiting for his flight back to Detroit, along with his grandson. I wandered over to say hello and reminded Gordie I was friends with his son Mark, which began when he'd come on my Long Beach Ice Dogs between periods radio segments while scouting somewhere on the road in the IHL. We first talked about family and almost anything but the game of hockey. When about 25 minutes had passed, there was suddenly an announcement coming from the loud speakers, "Mr. Howe, Mr. Gordon Howe, you must board the plane now as we are set for departure!"

Gordie jumped up and said "nice chatting with you, but I guess I better get the hell in there right now!" We got so into our conversation that it almost caused him to miss his flight home. Embarrassing? Yes. But Gordie Howe was as cool as he was on the ice—and even that much nicer as just a regular guy. I could've spoken with him for hours. He was enjoying sharing stories about his family that he loved so much. Another ultimate Touching Greatness moment for me for sure!

I did get several other personal moments over the years with Gordie, including at his son Mark's 2011 Hall of Fame induction weekend in Toronto. It was tremendous sharing some family stories with his brother, Marty, as well.

To see Gordie there after some very serious health issues was the icing on the cake. The family wasn't sure he'd be able to speak to the media that day, but "Mr. Hockey" came through as he always did for his teammates and gave us some outstanding inner thoughts about his son joining him in the Hall.

The funniest part of this day was getting to downtown Toronto just barely in time to make the media day ceremonies, still wearing my casual travel clothes, with no time to change. While we took some fun photos, nothing compares to when Gordie 'playfully' gave me one of his famous elbow shots for the picture (and I mean SHOTS!). He was starting to get tired, which affected his awareness. Subsequently, he got a bit over-zealous, not realizing just how hard his elbow had rammed into my jaw. This picture was taken a split second before feeling my teeth clench down on my tongue. I really did get a Gordie Howe elbow inside the Hall of Fame that I'll never forget! He was laughing, while I was recovering with a smile, yet checking to see if my face was still intact?

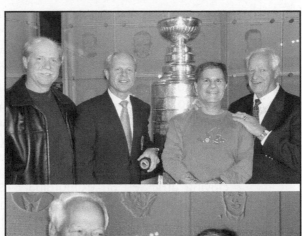

Sharing the moment with the Howes (L-R Marty, Mark and Gordie), and the ultimate elbow shot to the kisser that rung my bell!!

We then took a group shot, as Gordie suddenly pretended to choke me. I was beginning to feel like an opponent who could never avoid the rath of the commonly known as (pre-Gretzky) 'Greatest player ever'—and I loved every second of it! There was nothing better that weekend than watching Mark put on his father's #9 Red Wings jersey during his induction speech—the ultimate tribute to the man who meant everything to him and his family. It was tough to watch Gordie's health decline from there, but he dealt with life as he did as a player, refusing to lose until the final horn sounded.

ABOUT THE AUTHOR

Listed as one of seven distinguished Los Angeles City College Communications Department alumni, Ted Sobel has had an exemplary career in sports broadcasting covering more Super Bowls, college football and basketball national championship games, World Series, NBA & NHL finals, golf and tennis majors, and horse racing's Triple Crown & Breeders' Cups than any SoCal-based radio reporter. If the summer Olympics, World Cup soccer, MLS Cup Finals, and championship boxing are included, Ted has covered/attended more major events than Jack Nicklaus, Tiger Woods, and Roger Federer's combined major championship wins.

Having amassed an extraordinary list of notables interviewed (including greats in the music and entertainment industry), Ted has also enjoyed a lifetime of rubbing shoulders with over 750 Hall of Famers. He is a grateful rare U.S. radio reporter who had the opportunity to regularly cover world class events for a local station (e.g. The Masters, Wimbledon, Open Championship). During his almost 23 years at L.A.'s iconic KFWB radio, Ted broadcast over 40,000 sports updates and earned three 'Golden Mike' awards (for Best Sports Reporting/ Sports news segments), as an integral member of the station's unprecedented 10 straight SCSBA top L.A. sports anchor award winning teams.

A native Angeleno, Ted also worked for almost three decades (not consecutively) with L.A.'s KNX News Radio as a sports reporter/anchor. In addition, he has begun his 17th year as studio host/reporter for Sports USA Radio Network's NFL/NCAA football and NHL games of the week. Ted has also spent 10 years as a pro and college hockey play-by-play announcer. Internationally, he has been a regular American contributor to Japan's NHK-TV, doing seasonal analysis (in English) for their coverage of Super Bowls, World Series, and NBA Finals.